Success at Statistics

A Worktext With Humor

Sixth Edition

Fred Pyrczak

California State University, Los Angeles

Angela Kilb

Contributing Editor
Plymouth State University

 Pyrczak Publishing

P.O. Box 250430 • Glendale, CA 91225

Project Director: Monica Lopez.

Technical assistance provided by: Matthew Giblin.

Editorial assistance provided by Michael Baden-Campbell, Katy Norton Carrol, Jenifer Dill, Karen Sommerfeld, and Sharon Young.

Cover design by Roland Tran.

Cartoons by Randy Glasbergen. To view more of his cartoons, please visit www.glasbergen.com.

Printed in the United States of America by Bang Printing.

"Pyrczak Publishing" is an imprint of Fred Pyrczak, Publisher, A California Corporation.

ISBN 978-1-936523-46-7

SUSTAINABLE FORESTRY INITIATIVE — Certified Chain of Custody — Promoting Sustainable Forestry — www.sfiprogram.org — SFI-01268

SFI label applies to text stock

Contents

Continued →

Introduction

This book was written for students who need a solid grounding in basic statistical methods but who have anxiety about taking a math-related class. Some of the following features should help reduce students' anxiety:

- The humorous, self-checking, riddle-based worksheets bring a bit of levity to an important course that oftentimes seems dry. Much more important, however, is the instructional value of self-checking exercises that are based on riddles. If a student has incorrect answers on a worksheet, the answer to the riddle will not make sense. Thus, students get immediate feedback that one or more of their answers are wrong without being given the correct answers. Reviewing the material will usually lead to correct answers in short order, which gives students an opportunity to learn from their mistakes.

- The book is divided into short sections—each of which is much shorter than a typical chapter in a statistics textbook—which has benefits. First, a short section on technical material, often only two or three pages long, is less intimidating than a long chapter. Even if students have difficulty with a particular section, knowing that it is short and contains only a limited amount of material makes it easier to reread in order to achieve mastery. Second, anxiety about mastering difficult material should be reduced as students experience success in learning the material in short sections. Mastering a section, even if it is only two pages long, helps to reduce anxiety.

Few things in learning are more frustrating than struggling through a long chapter of technical material and then, while attempting end-of-chapter exercises, realizing that the whole chapter needs to be reread and reviewed. Frustration and intimidation often cause anxiety and failure. Frustration often leads to anxiety and feelings of intimidation, which decrease the likelihood of mastering the material. The short sections in this book should help students avoid this common problem.

Another advantage of short sections is that they allow instructors to customize their courses by (a) assigning only those sections needed to fulfill course objectives and (b) arranging the presentation of topics in a sequence best suited to their students' needs.

Where to Begin

Students whose basic math skills are rusty should begin with the Supplement in Part E of this book. It provides a review of skills that will be used throughout a basic statistics course.

About the Sixth Edition

This edition contains several new sections and other materials to help students gain a deeper understanding of and appreciation for the study of statistics. The additions include the following:

- **Section 1:** Explains the importance of statistical techniques in the advancement of scientific knowledge.
- **Section 11:** Provides practice with the summation operation before using it in multiple statistical tests.
- **Section 27:** This section on z-scores explains how to translate a percentile rank into a raw score.
- **Section 30:** Underlines the importance of figural representations of data, explains how to identify the most appropriate figure, and discusses how to label figures effectively.
- **Section 41:** Provides a deeper understanding of the relationship between p-values and critical values in a statistical test.
- **Appendix J:** A summary table of all statistical equations and guidelines for choosing a particular statistical test.
- **Table 1:** The format and discussion for the Table of the Normal Curve has been changed to a more conventional presentation of this statistical tool.

Contacting the Author

You can provide feedback on this book by writing to Info@Pyrczak.com or by mailing a letter to the address shown on the title page of this book. Comments and suggestions that will lead to improvements in the next edition are especially welcome.

Acknowledgments

The following individuals provided invaluable assistance in reviewing the current and previous editions of this book: Anne Hafner, Robert Morman, Deborah M. Oh, and Patricia Bates Simun, all of California State University, Los Angeles; Roger A. Stewart of the University of Wyoming; Richard Rasor of American River College; and George W. Burruss, Nicholas A. Corsaro, and Matthew Giblin, all of Southern Illinois University, Carbondale. Errors and omissions, of course, remain the author's responsibility.

A special thanks is extended to Contributing Editor Angela Kilb of Plymouth State University, who revised existing material and contributed the new material to this edition.

We at Pyrczak Publishing offer our condolences to the family of cartoonist Randy Glasbergen, who passed away while this edition was in production.

"If we learn from our mistakes, shouldn't
I try to make as many mistakes as possible?"

"It's the new keyboard for the statistics lab. Once you learn how
to use it, it will make computation of the standard deviation easier."

"Have you seen the latest longevity statistics
for frogs who live in biology labs?"

Notes

Section 1   Why is the Study of Statistics Important?

As humans, we are generally good at recognizing patterns using ***anecdotal information***. When we rely on anecdotal information, we are using our own observations about the world around us. Based on anecdotal information, I can predict that my grandmother is likely to fall asleep if I turn on a movie, my cat will hiss if a stranger reaches to pet her, and I will become very cranky if I do not eat by a certain time. While anecdotal information is useful in many situations, it becomes problematic when we try to draw general conclusions from it because anecdotal experience varies from person to person. Just because my cat hisses at strangers does not mean that all cats do!

Rather than drawing conclusions from anecdotal information, scientists use observations based on anecdotal information as a starting point for a set of procedures referred to as the scientific method. The ***scientific method*** is a system that scientists use to acquire new knowledge. Scientists who study psychology, meteorology, biotechnology, and so forth, use these additional steps to reduce the likelihood of drawing incorrect conclusions:

1. Make observations about a phenomenon.
2. Create a hypothesis that might explain the observations.
3. Collect data to challenge the hypothesis.
4. Interpret the data.
5. Draw conclusions that state whether the hypothesis held up under scrutiny.

Statistics is inextricably linked to science because of its crucial role in ***interpreting data*** (Step 4). Even when using the scientific method, drawing conclusions from the data can be risky if the scientist does not use the proper techniques for data interpretation. Patterns are sometimes misleading, as we can see in the example that follows.

Example 1
Alex conducted a memory experiment to see if monetary incentives increase performance. He presented students with a list of 20 words and told half of

them that they would receive $1 for each word correctly remembered. The other half were told they would earn no money for their memory responses. The results showed that the paid group correctly remembered an average of 9 items, and the unpaid group remembered an average of 6 items.

On the surface, 9 items is greater than 6, so Alex's conclusion might be that payment increases memory performance. However, additional information like variability must be considered before making a final conclusion. *Variability* describes how different the responses are from each other. For instance, if we gave everyone in the class the same exact set of instructions, should we expect everyone to remember the same number of items? Of course not. Factors other than payment, like amount of sleep, concentration level, and ability, can also affect the students' memory responses. Statistics help us determine whether the contribution of these other factors accounts for the differences observed between the two groups. The complete data set that follows tells a more detailed story.

	Paid group	Unpaid group
	16	4
	9	9
	2	2
	9	9
Average	**9**	**6**

The data set shows us that individuals in the paid group did not perform consistently better than the unpaid group. In fact, only the numbers in the top row (16 and 4) differ between the groups. If the payment manipulation were the true cause of the mean difference, we should see higher scores from more individuals in the paid than unpaid group. A likelier explanation is that the person who remembered 16 items has an exceptional memory and would have a high score regardless of the payment manipulation.

Rather than looking merely at averages like 9 and 6, we will learn how to examine variability, frequency distributions, and probabilities in order to determine whether data sets form *meaningful patterns* (e.g., paid students remember more than unpaid ones) or are simply due to ***random chance*** (e.g., the difference between the paid and unpaid groups is due to other factors, and the results are not likely to be replicated if the experiment were repeated with a different group of students). Using statistics allows us to determine whether we see a true pattern from which we can draw general conclusions or make rare observations that are unlikely to recur in future examinations.

Terms to Review Before Attempting Worksheet 1

anecdotal information, scientific method, interpreting data, variability, meaningful patterns, random chance

Worksheet 1   Why is the Study of Statistics Important?

> **Riddle: Why does Humpty Dumpty love autumn?**

DIRECTIONS: To find the answer to the riddle, write the answer to each question in the space immediately below it. In the solution section, the word in parentheses next to the answer to the first question is the first word in the answer to the riddle, the word beside the answer to the second question is the second word, and so on.

1. What process do scientists use to gain new knowledge?

2. Scientists rely on anecdotal information in the scientific method when making
   _____.

3. "My teacher will call on me if I make eye contact" is an example of what kind of information?

4. In the scientific method, what do scientists collect?

5. True or false: If everyone earns the same score on an exam, there is no variability.

6. If a certain result cannot be replicated, that result is said to illustrate _____.

7. What allows us to properly interpret data sets and identify patterns?

Worksheet 1 (continued)

Solution section:

a meaningful difference (long)   hypotheses (was)   observations (Humpty)

logical (he)   random chance (great)   data (had)   averages (the)

anecdotal (Dumpty)   conclusions (oval)   statistics (fall)   false (we)

variability (winter)   true (a)   scientific method (because)

Write the answer to the riddle here, putting one word on each line: _____   _____   _____   _____
_____   _____   _____

Notes

Section 2   Descriptive Versus Inferential Statistics

Descriptive statistics summarize *data*.[1] For instance, suppose you have the scores on a standardized test for 500 subjects.[2] Instead of presenting a list of the 500 scores in a research report, you might present an *average* score, which describes the performance of the typical subject. You will learn about three different averages in this book, all of which are examples of descriptive statistics.

Note that a set of data does not always consist of scores. For instance, you might have data on the political affiliations of the residents of a community. To summarize the data, you might count how many are Democrats, Republicans, Independents, and so on, then calculate the *percentage* of each. A percentage is a descriptive statistic that describes how many units per 100 have a certain characteristic. Thus, if 42% of a group of individuals are Democrats, 42 out of each 100 individuals in the group are Democrats.

The summaries provided by descriptive statistics are usually much more concise than the original data set (e.g., an average is much more concise than a list of 500 scores). In addition, descriptive statistics help us to interpret sets of data (e.g., an average helps us to understand what is typical of a group).

Inferential statistics are tools that indicate how much confidence we can have when generalizing from a *sample* to a *population*.[3] For instance, in national opinion polls, a carefully drawn sample of only about 1,500 adults is often used to estimate the opinions of the entire adult population of the United States. The pollster first calculates *descriptive statistics*, such as the percentage of respondents who are in favor of capital punishment and the percentage of respondents who are opposed to it. Having sampled, the pollster knows that the results may not be accurate because the sample may not be representative. In fact, the pollster knows that there is a high probability that the results are off by at least a small amount. This is why he or she often reports a *margin of error*, which is an inferential statistic. It is reported to

---

[1] Note that the word *data* is plural.

[2] In psychology, sociology, and many related disciplines, the *subjects* of a study are called *participants* if they voluntarily agree to participate. *Respondents* and *examinees* are other terms that are commonly used when referring to individuals who are being studied.

[3] The word *inferential* is derived from the word *infer*. When researchers generalize from a sample to a population, they are *inferring* that the sample is representative of the population.

warn that random sampling may produce errors, which should be considered when interpreting results.[4] For instance, a weekly news magazine recently reported that in a national poll, 58% of the respondents believed that the economy was improving. A footnote indicated that the margin of error was ±1.8%, which means that the pollster was confident that the true percentage for the whole population was within 1.8 percentage points of 58%.[5]

A **population** is any group in which a researcher is interested. It may be large, such as all adults age 18 and over who reside in the United States, or it may be small, such as all registered nurses employed by a specific hospital.[6] An investigator is free to choose a population of interest and should clearly identify it when writing a research report. This helps consumers of research determine to whom the results apply.

A study in which all members of a population are included is called a **census**. A census is often feasible and desirable when working with small populations (e.g., an algebra teacher may want to pretest all students at the beginning of a course to determine the most appropriate level at which to begin instruction). Inferential statistics are *not* needed when describing the results of a census because there is no sampling error.

When a population is large, it is more economical to use only a sample of the population. With modern sampling techniques, highly accurate information can be obtained through the use of relatively small samples. Various methods of sampling are described later in this book.

Descriptive tools, such as averages and percentages for census data, should be called **parameters**, not **statistics**. For instance, an average score based on a study of a population (i.e., a census) should be referred to as a *parameter*, but an average for a sample should be referred to as a *statistic*. Following is a visual aid for remembering the difference.[7]

---

[4] The measurement techniques, especially the wording of the question(s), may also produce errors. That is why consumers of research usually want to know the exact wording of a survey question, especially if important decisions are to be made based on the results.

[5] Margins of error are described in detail in several sections in Part B of this book.

[6] Notice that all members of a population have at least one characteristic in common, such as being registered nurses employed by a specific hospital.

[7] Reports in the mass media often refer to parameters as statistics.

Statistics come from **S**amples

Parameters come from **P**opulations

Terms to Review Before Attempting Worksheet 2

**descriptive statistics, data, average, percentage, inferential statistics,
sample, population, margin of error,
census, parameters**

**"My presentation is called *How to Overcome
Your Fear of Statistics*. You can't. The end."**

Worksheet 2 Descriptive Versus Inferential Statistics

> ## Riddle: What does the warning sign at the lake say?

DIRECTIONS: To find the answer to the riddle, write the answer to each question in the space immediately below it. In the solution section, the word in parentheses next to the answer to the first question is the first word in the answer to the riddle, the word beside the answer to the second question is the second word, and so on.

1. Is an average a descriptive *or* an inferential statistic?

   descriptive

2. Do descriptive *or* inferential statistics help researchers to generalize from a sample to a population?

   inferential

3. What is the term for the entire group in which a researcher is interested?

   census

4. Which statistic mentioned in Section 2 is an example of an inferential statistic?

   samples

5. When all members of a population in which a researcher is interested are included in a study, the study is called a _____.

   census

6. "National opinion polls often use a sample of about 20,000 respondents." Is this statement true *or* false?

   false, 1,500

7. "Some populations are small." Is this statement true *or* false?

   yes, can be small or large

Worksheet 2 (continued)

8. Is the term *data* singular *or* plural?

   plural

9. Should a percentage obtained from a census be referred to as a *statistic or* as a *parameter*?

   statistic

10. Should an average for a sample be referred to as a statistic?

   NO, it should be referred to as a parameter.

Solution section:

scores (swim)   subjects (boat)   descriptive (never)   parameter (both)

inferential (test)   information (and)   population (the)   census (of)

economical (bait)   singular (because)   pollster (fish)   plural (with)   true (water)

false (the)   margin of error (depth)   investigator (warn)   yes (feet)   no (the)

Write the answer to the riddle here, putting one word on each line: _____ _____ _____ _____

_____ _____ _____ _____ _____

_____

Notes

Section 3   Scales of Measurement

Scales of measurement (also known as *levels of measurement*) help research-ers determine what types of statistical analyses are appropriate for a given set of data. It is important to master this section because it is referred to in a number of other sections that follow.

The lowest level of measurement is **nominal** (also known as *categorical*). It is helpful to think of this level as the *naming* level. Here are three examples:

- Individuals name the political parties with which they are affiliated.

- Trees are categorized according to their type.

- Different regions of the United States are described by their location.

Notice that the categories in the above examples do *not* put the information in any particular order. There is no basis on which we could all agree for saying that Republicans are logically higher or lower than Democrats. The same is true for tree types and regions of the U.S.

The next level of measurement is **ordinal**. While ordinal measurement puts data in *order* from high to low, it does *not* specifically indicate how much higher or lower one value is in relation to another. It is helpful to think of this level as the *ranking* level. To understand this level, consider these examples:

- Individuals are ranked according to their height, with a rank of 1 for the tallest, a rank of 2 for the next tallest, and so on.

- Three brands of hand lotion are ranked according to consumers' preferences for them, with a rank of 1 for the most preferred, a rank of 2 for the next favorite, and so on.

- Individuals rank the situation comedy programs on network television, giving a rank of 1 to their favorite, a rank of 2 to their second favorite, and so on.

In the preceding examples of ordinal measurement, the measurements indicate the relative standings of individuals but not the amount of the differences among the individuals. For instance, we know that an individual with a rank of 1 is taller than an individual with a rank of 2, but we do not know by how much. The first individual may be only one quarter of an inch taller *or* two feet taller than the second.

The next two levels, ***interval*** and ***ratio***, both indicate *how much* the values differ from each other. It is helpful to think of these as the *equal distance* levels.

For instance:

- The height of each individual measured to the nearest inch.

- The number of times each pigeon presses a button in the first minute after receiving a reward.

- The number of days each student is late arriving at school during the school year.

Notice that if one individual is 5'6" tall and another is 5'8" tall, we not only know the height order of the individuals, but we also know by how many inches the individuals differ from each other. Both *interval* and *ratio* scales have equal intervals. For instance, the difference between 5'6" and 5'7" is the same as the difference between 5'7" and 5'8".

In most statistical analyses, *interval* and *ratio* measurements are analyzed in the same way. There is a mathematical difference, however. An *interval* scale does *not* have an absolute zero. For instance, when measuring intelligence, researchers do not know exactly what constitutes zero intelligence and, thus, cannot measure it.[1] In contrast, a *ratio* scale has an absolute zero. For instance, we know where the zero point is on a tape measure when measuring height.

If you are having trouble mastering levels of measurement, first memorize the following environmentally friendly phrase. The first letters of the words (NOIR) are the first letters in the names of the four levels of measurement in order from lowest to highest (**N**ominal, **O**rdinal, **I**nterval, and **R**atio).

No **O**il **I**n **R**ivers

---

[1] Most applied researchers treat most sets of scores obtained through the use of standardized tests as being at the *interval* level, even though there is some controversy as to whether, for instance, the difference between an IQ of 100 and one of 110 is the same as the difference between an IQ of 110 and one of 120.

Understanding scales of measurement is important in statistics because knowing them helps in the selection of appropriate statistics for a given set of data. For instance, you will learn about three averages in Sections 12 and 13. For a given set of data, typically only one average is selected to be included in a research report. The selection of the most appropriate average hinges, in large part, on the scale of measurement used to collect the data. In Section 13, you will learn how knowledge of scales of measurement is used when selecting an average.

Terms to Review Before Attempting Worksheet 3

nominal, ordinal, interval, ratio

"Remember the old days when we used to eat his statistics homework?"

Worksheet 3 Scales of Measurement

Riddle: How do you know when you are making too many errors?

DIRECTIONS: For each example of measurement, circle the scale of measurement that it exemplifies. The word in parentheses to the right of the correct answer to the first question is the first word in the answer to the riddle, the word in parentheses to the right of the second correct answer is the second word, and so on.

1. Gender measured by asking each subject whether he or she is male or female.
   nominal (when)   ordinal (make)   interval (some)   ratio (only)

2. Weight measured in pounds and ounces using an accurate scale.
   nominal (only)   ordinal (if)   interval (of)   ratio (the)

3. Verbal aptitude measured by the College Board's Scholastic Aptitude Test: Verbal (assuming each point from 200 to 800 represents an equal amount of aptitude).
   nominal (calculate)   ordinal (stumble)   interval (eraser)   ratio (become)

4. Cheerfulness measured by having a teacher give a rank of 1 to the student judged to be the most cheerful, a rank of 2 to the student judged to be the next-most cheerful, and so on.
   nominal (too)   ordinal (wears)   interval (for)   ratio (out)

Worksheet 3 (continued)

5. The amount of juice in a bottle measured in fluid ounces.

    nominal (big)   ordinal (weak)   interval (inside)   (ratio)(out)

6. Length of a telephone conversation measured by recording the number of seconds from the beginning to the end of the conversation.

    nominal (count)   ordinal (person)   (interval)(mistakes)   ratio (ahead)

7. Height measured by having 10 individuals take off their shoes and line up according to height, with the tallest person at the front of the line, and giving that person a rank of 1, giving the next person a rank of 2, and so on.

    nominal (are)   (ordinal)(of)   interval (the)   ratio (made)

8. Birthplace measured by having each subject write the name of the country in which she or he was born.

    (nominal)(the)   ordinal (seeing)   interval (caught)   ratio (also)

9. Writing skills measured by having all subjects write for 15 minutes about the same topic and having an English teacher put the essays in order from best to worst.

    nominal (when)   ordinal (pencil)   (interval)(person)   ratio (wrongly)

Solution section:

Write the answer to the riddle here, putting one word on each line: _when_ _the_ _eraser_ _wears_ _out_ _mistakes_ _of_ _the_ _person_

17

Notes

Section 4   Frequencies, Percentages, and Proportions

A *frequency* is the number of individuals or cases. Its symbol is *f*. Note that *f* is lowercase and italicized. In general, almost all statistical symbols are italicized. Throughout this book, pay attention to the case of the symbols. For instance, a lowercase *f* stands for *frequency*, while an uppercase *F* stands for another important statistic, described later in this book.

If it is reported that *f* = 23 for a score of 99, you know that 23 subjects had a score of 99. Another symbol, *N*, meaning *number of cases*, is also used to stand for frequency.[1] Thus, the same result could be reported as *N* = 23 for a score of 99.

A *percentage* has a symbol of % or an uppercase *P*. It indicates the number per hundred who have a certain characteristic. Thus, if 44% of the individuals in a town are registered as Democrats, you know that for each 100 registered voters, 44 are Democrats. To determine how many (*frequency*) are Democrats, multiply the total number of registered voters by .44. For instance, if there are 2,313 registered voters, .44 × 2,313 = 1,017.72, which rounds to 1,018.

To calculate a percentage, use division. Consider this example: If 22 of 84 children in a sample say they are afraid of the dark, determine the percentage by dividing the number who are afraid by the total number of children and then multiplying by 100—thus, 22 ÷ 84 = .2619 × 100 = 26.19%. This result indicates that, based on the sample, if you questioned 100 *individuals* from the same population, you would expect about 26 of them to report being afraid of the dark. Notice that only 84 individuals were actually studied, yet the resulting percentage is still based on 100.

A *proportion* is a fraction of one (1). In the previous paragraph, the proportion of the sample of children who are afraid of the dark is .2619 or .26, which is the value obtained before multiplying by 100. This indicates that *twenty-six hundredths of the sample* are afraid of the dark. Clearly, proportions are harder to interpret than percentages. Thus, percentages are usually preferred to proportions in statistical reporting. However, proportions are occasionally reported in scientific writing.

---

[1] An uppercase *N* should be used when describing a population. A lowercase *n* should be used when describing a sample.

When reporting percentages, it is a good idea to also report the underlying frequencies because percentages alone can sometimes be misleading or fail to provide sufficient information. For instance, if you read that 8% of the foreign language students at a university were majoring in Russian, you would not have enough information to make informed decisions on how to staff the foreign language department and how many classes in Russian to offer. If you read that $f = 12$ (8%), based on a total of 150 foreign language students, you would know that 12 students need to be accommodated.

Percentages are especially helpful when comparing two or more groups of different sizes. Consider these data

	College A	College B
Total number of foreign language students	$f = 150$	$f = 350$
Russian majors	$f = 12$ (8%)	$f = 14$ (4%)

Notice that the frequencies indicate that College B has more Russian majors (14 versus 12), while the percentages indicate that *per 100 students*, College A has more Russian majors (8% versus 4%).

Terms to Review Before Attempting Worksheet 4
frequency, percentage, proportion

Worksheet 4   Frequencies, Percentages, and Proportions

> **Riddle**: How are famous surgeons similar to pelicans?

DIRECTIONS: To find the answer to the riddle, write the answer to each question in the space immediately below it. In the solution section, the word in parentheses next to the answer to the first question is the first word in the answer to the riddle, the word beside the answer to the second question is the second word, and so on.

1. What is the symbol for frequency?

f

2. N is a symbol for what words?

#F of cases

3. If 24% of the 1,511 students in a school qualify for a school lunch program, to two decimal places, how many qualify?

302.04

4. If 368 teenagers in a population of 4,310 report that they have smoked at least one cigarette during the past year, to one decimal place, what percentage reported this?

8.5%

5. If 3,100 individuals in a population of 46,785 complain of chronic headaches, to one decimal place, what percentage complain of this?

6.6%

6. If 340 adults in a community of 6,532 report getting sufficient aerobic exercise, to three decimal places, what proportion of adults get this exercise?

0.052

Worksheet 4 (continued)

7. To one decimal place, what is the percentage that corresponds to the proportion in the answer to Question 6?

5.2%

8. According to the text, are percentages *or* proportions usually easier for readers to comprehend?

percentages

9. According to the text, it is a good idea to report what statistic when reporting percentages?

yes

10. If 6% of the students in School A and 6% of the students in School B are classified as gifted, do the two schools necessarily have the same number of students classified as gifted?

no

Solution section:

> no (bills)   frequencies (their)   .066% (medicine)   percentages (of)
>
> 5.2% (size)   9.5% (operate)   .052 (the)   36.26 (hospital)   6.6% (by)
>
> 8.5% (recognized)   362.64 (be)   yes (fly)   number of cases (can)
>
> *f* (both)   x (ocean)   .85% (blood)   7.2% (fleeting)   .66% (resting)

Write the answer to the riddle here, putting one word on each line: *both* *can* *be* *recognized* *by* *the* *size* *of* *fly* *bills*

22

Section 5 Introduction to Frequency Distributions

A *frequency distribution* shows how many cases had each score. Its purpose is to display scores so that they can be scanned by readers for an overview of the data. Table 1 shows the distribution of scores for a class of college students who took a 40-item basic math test. As you would expect, most students did quite well on this test. The frequency distribution makes it clear that most of the students marked 34 or more items correctly.

The distribution in Table 1 is *skewed*. In a skewed distribution, most of the scores are either near the top or the bottom, with a scattering of scores toward the other end. Skewed distributions are discussed in more detail in later sections of this book.

Table 1
Distribution of Basic Math Scores
for College Students

X	f
37	8
36	4
35	3
34	6
33	1
32	3
31	1
30	1
29	2
28	2
27	0
26	0
25	1
24	1
	$N = 33$

As you can see, a frequency distribution is an effective way to present data. There are, however, a number of conventions that are followed when constructing them. The most important are listed on the next page.

1. Each table should be given a number. Usually, tables are numbered sequentially in a research report, starting with the number 1. In the example on the previous page, "Table 1" indicates that it is the first table in this section of the book.

2. Each table is given a brief descriptive **caption** (or title). Captions often name the population and the variable measured. Thus, the caption for Table 1 is *Distribution of Basic Math Scores for College Students*.

3. The number and caption are placed at the top of the table.[1]

4. A horizontal line sets off the table number and caption from the body of the table. This line is called a **rule**. There is also a rule at the bottom of the table to indicate where it ends.

5. The symbol X stands for the scores. Be sure to use an uppercase, italicized X because a lowercase, italicized x has another meaning, which is discussed later in this book.

6. The scores are listed in order with the highest score placed at the top, and the lowest score placed at the bottom.

7. The symbol f stands for frequency. The symbol N may be used instead of f at the top of the table. N stands for number of cases.

8. When no cases exist for a given score—such as scores 26 and 27—a frequency of zero is entered.

9. The sum of the frequencies is shown at the bottom of the table. Instead of an N, it is also acceptable to use ΣN, which means *sum of the number of cases,* or Σf, which means *sum of the frequencies*.

Terms to Review Before Attempting Worksheet 5

frequency distribution, skewed, caption, rule, X, f, N, Σ, ΣN, Σf

---

[1] For statistical figures, the figure number and caption are usually placed below the figure.

Worksheet 5   Introduction to Frequency Distributions

Riddle: Arthur Godfrey said that he was proud to be paying taxes. What else did he say?

DIRECTIONS: To find the answer to the riddle, write the answer to each question in the space immediately below it. In the solution section, the word in parentheses next to the answer to the first question is the first word in the answer to the riddle, the word beside the answer to the second question is the second word, and so on.

1. According to Table 1 in Section 5, how many students had a score of 32?

3

2. What type of distribution has most of the scores near either the top or bottom, with a scattering of scores toward the other end?

skewed

3. What is another name for the title of a table?

caption

4. What are the horizontal lines that identify the top and bottom of a table called?

rule

5. For what does *X* stand?

scores

6. Should the highest *or* the lowest score be at the bottom of a frequency distribution?

lowest

Worksheet 5 (continued)

7. Should the sum of the frequencies be shown in a frequency distribution?

yes

8. What symbol may be substituted for *f* in a frequency distribution?

N

9. What is the symbol for the *sum of the frequencies*?

ΣN

10. In Table 1 in Section 5, did any of the students have a score of 26?

NO

Solution section:

no (money)   ~~N (half)~~   X (politics)   normal (president)   headline (going)   free (it)

~~Σf (the)~~   2 (party)   0 (helpful)   ~~3 (he)~~   skewed (could)   ~~rules (just)~~

~~caption (be)~~   ~~score (as)~~   ~~yes (for)~~   highest (courts)   double lines (it)

~~lowest (proud)~~   XF (views)   Σx (audit)   omit (IRS)   unbalanced (was)

Write the answer to the riddle here, putting one word on each line: *he*   *could*   *be*   *just* *as*   *proud*   *for*   *half*   *the* *money*

Section 6 Frequency Distribution for Grouped Data

Because the purpose of a frequency distribution is to organize data so that they can be presented concisely, do not list more than about 20 scores. If there are more than 20, group the scores as shown in Table 1. For instance, the scores 39, 40, and 41 are in the group labeled "39–41" in the table.

Table 1
Frequency Distribution of Scores on the AIDS Knowledge Test

X	tally marks	f
39–41	/	1
36–38	/	1
33–35		0
30–32	///	3
27–29	/////	5
24–26	/////	5
21–23	///// /	6
18–20	///// //	7
15–17	////	4
12–14		0
9–11	/	1
6–8	/	1
		$\Sigma f = 34$

Table 1 presents the scores shown in Table 2. Notice that Table 1 is much more effective than Table 2 for communicating the performance of the subjects on the test. It is clear from Table 1 that most subjects have scores between 15 and 32. This is not immediately obvious in Table 2.

Table 2
Unarranged Scores on the AIDS Knowledge Test

30	10	15	17	41	37	23	29	18	6
16	17	21	21	23	29	29	21	22	31
32	27	27	24	18	18	25	26	18	25
26	19	20	19						

Following are guidelines for constructing frequency distributions for grouped scores:

1. There should be about 10 to 20 groups of scores. These groups are called *score intervals*. The bottom interval in Table 1 is for scores 6 through 8. This covers 3 points—thus, the *interval size* is 3 points.

2. All score intervals must have the same interval size. Note: Start by listing the bottom interval first, build up until you have included the highest score, and make the top interval the same size as the others, even if the top interval extends beyond the highest score earned.

3. To estimate the interval size, subtract the lowest score from the highest score (i.e., $41 - 6 = 35$) and divide the answer by 15 ($35/15 = 2.33$).[1] Thus, each interval should be *about* 2 points wide in order to yield 10 to 20 intervals. In this case, 3 was used.

4. Use an odd interval size because this makes it easier to plot a distribution on graph paper, which is described in later sections. Thus, in Table 1, an interval size of 3 was used instead of 2, which was obtained in the previous step.

5. When you tally, work from the unarranged scores to the distribution. For instance, put your finger on the first score (30) in Table 2. Make a tally to the right of 30–32 in Table 1. Then cross off the 30 in Table 2. Repeat the process for each of the remaining scores. Some students use the reverse procedure: They take the top score interval in the distribution (39–41) and then search through all the unarranged scores looking for scores of 39, 40, and 41. This is a slow method and is likely to lead to errors.

6. As a partial check on your work, make sure that the sum of the frequencies is the same as the total number of scores with which you started.

7. Erase the tally marks before submitting your distribution.

It is often desirable to include percentages. In Table 3, a column showing percentages has been added. To obtain the percentages, divide each frequency (f) by the total number of cases (Σf), and then multiply by 100. Here are two examples:

---

[1] The constant 15 is used because it is halfway between 10 and 20. By using 15, you will get the approximate interval size that will yield between 10 and 20 intervals.

The frequency of 1 divided by 34 = 0.0294 × 100 = 2.94 = 2.9% (the percentage for the bottom interval).

The frequency of 4 divided by 34 = 0.1176 × 100 = 11.76 = 11.8% (the percentage for the interval fourth from the bottom).

Note that the percentages are calculated to two decimal places and rounded to one, and it is customary to report them to one or two places in scientific reports. Also note that the percentages will not always sum to exactly 100% because of rounding.

Table 3
Frequency Distribution of Scores on the
AIDS Knowledge Test

X	tally marks	f	P
39–41	/	1	2.9
36–38	/	1	2.9
33–35		0	0.0
30–32	///	3	8.8
27–29	/////	5	14.7
24–26	/////	5	14.7
21–23	///// /	6	17.6
18–20	///// //	7	20.6
15–17	////	4	11.8
12–14		0	0.0
9–11	/	1	2.9
6–8	/	1	2.9
	Σf =	34	99.8

Terms to Review Before Attempting Worksheet 6

score intervals, interval size

"According to a recent survey, 51% is a majority."

Worksheet 6   Frequency Distribution for Grouped Data

Riddle: According to the cynic, what will happen when the meek inherit the earth?

DIRECTIONS: To find the answer to the riddle, construct a frequency distribution for the scores in the box below. Follow all of the guidelines in Section 6 and include a column with percentages rounded to one decimal place.

Answer each question in the space immediately below it. In the solution section, the word in parentheses next to the answer to the first question is the first word in the answer to the riddle, the word beside the answer to the second question is the second word, and so on.

> 15, 12, 18, 14, 36, 37, 42, 45, 48, 19, 32,
> 29, 18, 21, 36, 40, 41, 54, 33, 35, 34, 42,
> 40, 36, 33, 19, 15, 39

33-35

1. What value did you obtain when you subtracted the lowest score from the highest score?

   interval size

2. Based on a divisor of 15, what odd number is an appropriate interval size?

   3

3. What scores are shown in the first column for the bottom (lowest) score interval?

   12-14

4. What scores are shown in the first column for the top (highest) score interval?

   52-54

5. What is the frequency for the highest score interval?

   1

Worksheet 6 (continued)

6. What is the frequency for the 33–35 score interval?

7.1%

7. What is the sum of the frequencies?

28

8. What is the percentage for the 51–53 score interval?

0

9. What is the percentage for the 42–44 score interval?

7.1%

10. What is the sum of the percentages?

Solution section:

43 (religion)	2 (angels)	10–12 (only)	52–54 (civilization)	71% (all)
100.1% (details)	100.0% (crook)	0.0% (out)	99.9% (he)	7.1% (the)
42 (the)	3 (lawyers)	54–56 (be)	10.0% (being)	12–14 (will)	28 (work)
1 (there)	24–26 (fruitful)	4 (to)	55 (bible)	98.9% (Eden)

Write the answer to the riddle here, putting one word on each line: _____ _____ _____ _____

_____ _____ _____ _____ _____

_____

Section 7   Cumulative Frequencies, Cumulative Percentages, and Percentile Ranks

A *cumulative frequency* (*cf*) indicates how many cases are *in and below* a given score interval. For instance, the *cf* column in Table 1 contains cumulative frequencies.

Table 1
Frequency Distribution of Scores on the Political Knowledge Test With Cumulative Frequencies

X	f	cf
39–41	1	34
36–38	1	33
33–35	0	32
30–32	3	32
27–29	5	29
24–26	5	24
21–23	6	19
18–20	7	13
15–17	4	6
12–14	0	2
9–11	1	2
6–8	1	1
	34	

- In the bottom interval, 6–8, there is one case in the interval (where *f* = 1) and there are zero cases below the interval. Therefore, the *cf* for this interval is $1 + 0 = 1$. (Remember that the frequency column, *f*, indicates the number of cases in each score interval.)

- In the next interval, 9–11, there is one case in the interval and one case below the interval. Therefore, the *cf* for this interval is $1 + 1 = 2$.

- In the next interval, 12–14, there are zero cases in the interval and a total of two cases in all the intervals below it. Therefore, $0 + 2 = 2$.

In Table 2, the percentages for each score interval and the ***cumulative per-centages* (cumulative %)** are shown. Cumulative percentages have a meaning similar to cumulative frequencies. Specifically, each cumulative percentage indicates the percentage *in and below* a given score interval.

Table 2
Frequency Distribution of Scores on the Political Knowledge Test With Cumulative Frequencies and Cumulative Percentages

X	f	cf	%	cumulative %
39–41	1	34	2.9	99.8
36–38	1	33	2.9	96.9
33–35	0	32	0.0	94.0
30–32	3	32	8.8	94.0
27–29	5	29	14.7	85.2
24–26	5	24	14.7	70.5
21–23	6	19	17.6	55.8
18–20	7	13	20.6	38.2
15–17	4	6	11.8	17.6
12–14	0	2	0.0	5.8
9–11	1	2	2.9	5.8
6–8	1	1	2.9	2.9
	34		99.8	

- For the 39–41 score interval, 99.8% scored in and below that interval. (Note that it is not 100.0% because of errors created by rounding to one decimal place.)

- For the 36–38 score interval, 96.9% scored in and below that interval.

The cumulative percentages are approximate ***percentile ranks***, which indicate the percentage who scored at or below a given score level.[1] For instance, we could report to students with scores of 27, 28, and 29 that their percentile rank is 85 (based on the cumulative percentage of 85.2)—indicating that, relative to the group, their

---

[1] More precise methods are usually covered in measurement courses. This method is sufficient for most applied applications.

scores are high because they scored as high as or higher than 85% of the total students. Reporting percentile ranks is usually more informative than reporting *raw scores* (i.e., the number of points earned).

Terms to Review Before Attempting Worksheet 7

**cumulative frequency, cumulative percentages,
percentile ranks, raw scores**

Worksheet 7   Cumulative Frequencies, Cumulative Percentages, and Percentile Ranks

Riddle: What proves that many gas station owners think toilet paper is worth more than money?

DIRECTIONS: To find the answer to the riddle, construct columns for the cumulative frequencies, percentages, and cumulative percentages in Table 3 below.

Write the answer to each question in the space immediately below it. In the solution section, the word in parentheses next to the answer to the first question is the first word in the answer to the riddle, the word beside the answer to the second question is the second word, and so on.

Table 3
Distribution for Worksheet 7

X	f	cf	%	cumulative %
67–71	2			
62–66	1			
57–61	2			
52–56	4			
47–51	6			
42–46	7			
37–41	8			
32–36	5			
27–31	2			
22–26	0			
17–21	2			
12–16	1			
	N = 40			

Worksheet 7 (continued)

1. What is the cumulative frequency for the 67–71 score interval?

2. What is the cumulative frequency for the 22–26 score interval?

3. How many subjects scored in and below the 12–16 score interval?

4. How many subjects scored in and below the 32–36 score interval?

5. What percentage of the subjects scored in the 22–26 score interval?

6. What is the cumulative percentage for the 22–26 score interval?

7. What is the cumulative percentage for the 57–61 score interval?

8. What is the cumulative percentage for the 67–71 score interval?

9. What is the approximate percentile rank for a score of 39?

10. What is the approximate percentile rank for a score of 64?

Worksheet 7 (continued)

Solution section:

95 (unlocked) 45 (registers) 43 (press) 100.0 (cash) 2 (between) 4 (need)

10 (toilets) 0.0 (locked) 39 (wishes) 8.5 (only) 9.5 (tires) 7.5 (but)

40 (they) 1 (their) 99.9 (pump) 92.5 (their) 90.0 (being) 11 (gasoline)

10.5 (dollars) 15.5 (cars) 3 (keep) 69.5 (policy) 46 (windshield)

Write the answer to the riddle here, putting one word on each line: _____ _____ _____ _____

_____ _____ _____ _____ _____

_____

GLASBERGEN

"I'm learning how to relax, doctor—but I want to relax better and faster! I WANT TO BE IN THE TOP PERCENTILE RANK OF RELAXATION!"

Section 8   Histograms

A distribution of scores may be displayed in a ***histogram***, which is a type of statistical ***figure*** (i.e., a drawing or graph). Figure 1 shows a histogram for the distribution in Table 3 on page 36 (see Worksheet 7). As you can see, the histogram is a graphic alternative to a frequency distribution.[1]

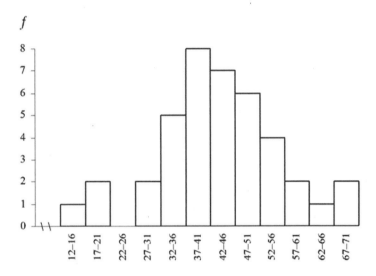

Figure 1. Histogram for data in Table 3 in Worksheet 7.

In Figure 1, frequencies are shown on the vertical axis (formal name: the ***ordinate***). Note that the symbol f at the top of the vertical axis stands for *frequency*. The scores (or score intervals) are shown on the horizontal axis (formal name: the ***abscissa***). You may also prepare a histogram for percentages by placing percentages instead of frequencies on the vertical axis.

The following are guidelines for preparing histograms:

1. Draw the histogram on graph paper.

2. Make sure the vertical axis is somewhat shorter than the horizontal axis. A ratio of 3 to 5 is about right. That is, if the vertical axis is about 3 inches, the horizontal axis should be about 5. To accomplish this, you may need to let each line on the

---

[1] The choice between a frequency distribution and a histogram depends on three factors: (1) Some audiences might find a histogram more comprehensible, (2) a histogram may be more visually appealing and more likely to draw readers' attention, and (3) histograms should be professionally drawn whenever possible, which makes them more difficult and expensive to produce.

graph paper represent more than one frequency on the vertical axis. For instance, if the highest frequency in a distribution is 100, you might need to let each line represent 10 cases in order to keep the figure reasonable in size.

3. Place the scores on the horizontal axis, with the lowest score interval on the left and the highest on the right.[2]

4. Label the histogram with a number and a brief title (i.e., caption). Note that because the histogram is a statistical figure (i.e., a drawing or graph), it is called a *figure* and not a *table*.

5. Note that in many fields of study, figure numbers and titles are placed *below* the figure, and table numbers and titles are placed *above* the table.

6. All bars must be equal in width so that a misleading figure is not produced.

7. If there is a score interval within a distribution with a frequency of zero, a space should appear there. Notice the space for the interval 22–26 in the histogram on the previous page, which has a frequency of zero.

Terms to Review Before Attempting Worksheet 8

histogram, figure, ordinate, abscissa

---

[2] Notice in Figure 1 that the scores between zero and 12 are not shown because no one had those scores. The horizontal line is broken just to the right of zero with a double slash to indicate that some scores are not shown.

Worksheet 8   Histograms

Riddle: According to Benjamin Franklin, what should you do with your eyes to have a successful marriage?

DIRECTIONS: To find the answer to the riddle, write the answer to each question in the space immediately below it. In the solution section, the word in parentheses next to the answer to the first question is the first word in the answer to the riddle, the word beside the answer to the second question is the second word, and so on.

1. "A histogram is an example of a statistical table." Is this statement true *or* false?

2. "A histogram is an example of a statistical figure." Is this statement true *or* false?

3. What is the formal name of the vertical axis in a graph?

4. What is the formal name of the horizontal axis in a graph?

5. In a histogram, which axis (vertical *or* horizontal) should be longer?

6. What should be listed along the horizontal axis of a histogram?

Worksheet 8 (continued)

7. What is the symbol for frequency?

8. Should the lowest score shown in a histogram be on the left *or* the right side of the figure?

9. Should the bars in a histogram be of equal width?

10. In Figure 1 on page 39, which score interval has the highest frequency?

11. In Figure 1 on page 39, which score interval has the lowest frequency?

Solution section:

f (marriage)	no (running)	false (keep)	37–41 (shut)	one (vows)
true (your)	27–31 (ring)	right (someone)	left (and)	yes (half)
abscissa (wide)	caption (feel)	horizontal (open)		
scores or score intervals (before)	ordinate (eyes)	vertical (love)		
frequencies (begin)	22–26 (afterwards)	42–46 (he)		

Write the answer to the riddle here, putting one word on each line: _____ _____ _____ _____
_____ _____ _____ _____ _____
_____ _____

Section 9 Frequency Polygons

A *frequency polygon* represents a frequency distribution in graphic form. It is an alternative to a histogram for presenting a distribution. The polygon shown in Figure 1 is based on the distribution in Table 1. Notice that the highest frequency in Table 1 is 8, for a score of 19. Likewise, the highest point in the polygon in Figure 1 is for a score of 19.

Table 1
Distribution of Depression Scores

X	f
22	1
21	3
20	4
19	8
18	5
17	2
16	0
15	1
	N = 24

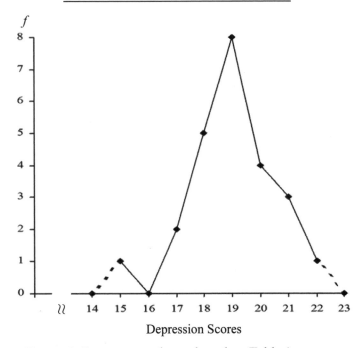

Figure 1. Frequency polygon based on Table 1.

Following are guidelines for constructing frequency polygons:

1. If possible, draw the figure on graph paper.

2. List the frequencies (f) on the vertical axis (i.e., the ordinate or y-axis) and label the axis with an f.

3. List the scores on the horizontal axis (i.e., the abscissa or x-axis) and label the axis (in this case, "Depression Scores"). Begin with one score lower than any obtained by a subject and end with one score higher than any obtained. This will make the polygon rest, or anchor, on the horizontal axis. For instance, in Table 1, the lowest score is 15, but the polygon begins with an anchor score of 14—at which point the line rests on the horizontal axis at a frequency of zero. At the upper end of the distribution, the polygon is anchored at a score of 23. Dashed lines have been used to indicate that the anchor scores of 14 and 23 were not obtained by any of the examinees.

4. Make the horizontal axis somewhat longer than the vertical axis. A ratio of about 3 to 5 is about right (i.e., if the vertical axis is about 3 inches, the horizontal axis should be about 5). To accomplish this, you may need to allow more than one space on your graph paper among the frequencies or the scores that you list.

5. Put a dot on the graph paper at the point at which each score intersects each frequency. (For instance, in Figure 1, a dot was placed where a score of 15 intersects a frequency of 1). Then connect the dots with a ruler.

6. Be sure to connect dots that are on the horizontal axis. For instance, in Figure 1, there is a frequency of 0 (zero) at a score of 16. At that point, the line drops to the horizontal axis.

7. Label the polygon with a number and a brief title (i.e., caption).

If the scores have been grouped into score intervals (as in Table 2 on the next page) you must first determine the ***midpoint*** of each interval, which are shown in Table 2. For instance, 40 is the midpoint (i.e., middle score) of the 39–41 score interval.[1] List the midpoints on the horizontal axis in the polygon (as shown in Figure 2 on the next page).

---

[1] If an odd number is used as the size of the score interval, the midpoint will be a whole number.

Table 2
*Frequency Distribution of Number of Days
Served in Prison*

X	midpoints	f
39–41	40	1
36–38	37	1
33–35	34	0
30–32	31	4
27–29	28	4
24–26	25	4
21–23	22	6
18–20	19	6
15–17	16	4
12–14	13	0
9–11	10	1
6–8	7	1
		$N = 32$

Figure 2. Frequency polygon based on Table 2.

With large samples, the lines on a frequency distribution usually will be fairly smooth—unlike the above examples, in which the polygons are jagged. When a smooth polygon emerges, it is usually referred to as a ***curve***. Types of curves are described in the next section.

Terms to Review Before Attempting Worksheet 9

frequency polygon, midpoint, curve

"Professors are fighting back against students who cut class. Today I was the victim of a drive-by statistics quiz!"

Worksheet 9   Frequency Polygons

DIRECTIONS: Construct a frequency polygon for the distribution shown below. Follow all the guidelines described in Section 9. Refer to your work while answering the questions.

To find the answer to the riddle, write the answer to each question in the space immediately below it. In the solution section, the word in parentheses next to the answer to the first question is the first word in the answer to the riddle, the word beside the answer to the second question is the second word, and so on.

Table 1
Frequency Distribution for Worksheet 9

X	f
95–99	3
90–94	4
85–89	6
80–84	8
75–79	11
70–74	12
65–69	15
60–64	10
55–59	5
50–54	4
45–49	0
40–44	2
	N = 80

Worksheet 9 (continued)

1. What is the midpoint for the 95–99 score interval?

2. At how many points does the polygon touch the horizontal axis (at a frequency of zero)?

3. How many midpoints are listed along the horizontal axis?

4. The highest point of the polygon is at which midpoint?

5. What is shown on the vertical axis?

6. What is the midpoint at the far-right end of the horizontal axis?

7. Is the vertical axis somewhat longer than the horizontal axis?

8. At what frequency is the highest dot placed?

9. Does the figure have a number and a caption (title)?

Worksheet 9 (continued)

Solution section:

8 (farm)   1 (tune)   midpoints (song)   yes (pig)   10 (same)

99 (success)   19 (a)   3 (wastes)   97 (it)   37 (being)   8 (small)   23 (in)

frequencies (and)   2 (belief)   figure (helpless)   no (annoys)   table (seeing)

14 (your)   67 (time)   102 (it)   15 (the)   0.00 (barn)   99 (farmer)

Write the answer to the riddle here, putting one word on each line: _____ _____ _____ _____ _____ _____ _____ _____ _____

Notes

Section 10   Shapes of Distributions

After a set of scores has been organized from lowest to highest, it is referred to as a ***distribution***. One of the best ways to see a distribution's shape is to create a frequency polygon (see Section 9). When the number of cases is large, the polygon usually has a smooth shape, often referred to as a ***curve***.

The most important shape is that of the ***normal curve***—often called the bell-shaped curve—which is illustrated in Figure 1. It is important for two reasons. First, it is a shape often found in nature. For instance, the heights of women in a large population are normally distributed. There are small numbers of very short women (which is why the curve is low on the left), there are many women of about average height (which is why the curve is high in the middle), and there are small numbers of very tall women (which is why the curve is low on the right). Another example: The distribution of average annual rainfall in Los Angeles over the past 110 years is approximately normal. There are a very small number of years in which there was extremely little rainfall, many years with about average rainfall, and a very small number of years with a great deal of rainfall. The second reason the normal curve is important is because it is used in inferential statistics, a topic that is covered in Part B of this book.

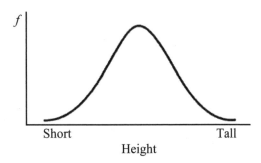

Figure 1. A normal distribution.

Some distributions are ***skewed***. A skewed distribution is unbalanced because of either some very high or very low scores. For instance, when the distribution of income for a large population is plotted on a polygon, it has a ***positive skew*** (i.e., is skewed to the right). Examine Figure 2 on the next page, which indicates that there are large numbers of individuals with relatively low incomes. Thus, the curve is high on the left. The curve drops off dramatically to the right, forming a tail on the right. This tail is created by the small number of individuals with very high incomes. Note that skewed distributions are named for their tails. On a number line, positive numbers are to the right, hence the term *positive skew.*

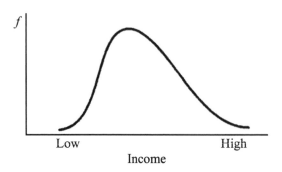

f

Low   High

Income

Figure 2. A distribution skewed to the right (positive skew).

When the tail is to the left, a distribution is said to have a ***negative skew*** (i.e., is skewed to the left), which is illustrated in Figure 3. A negative skew would be formed, for instance, if a large population of individuals were tested on skills in which the individuals had been thoroughly trained. If you tested a very large population of recent nursing school graduates on basic nursing skills, a distribution with a negative skew should emerge. There should be a large number of nurses with high scores, but there should also be a tail to the left created by a small number of nurses who, for one reason or another (such as being ill the day the test was administered), did not perform well on the test.

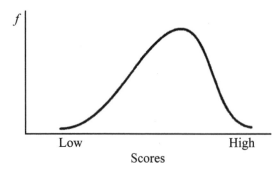

f

Low   High

Scores

Figure 3. A distribution skewed to the left (negative skew).

Bimodal distributions have two high points. A curve such as that in Figure 4 on the next page is called bimodal even though the two high points are not equal in height. Such a curve is most likely to emerge when human intervention or some rare event has changed the composition of a population. An example of human intervention is the decision of a school board to establish a school to which only high achievers and low achievers are admitted because the school is to be a model of peer tutoring in which the high achievers tutor the low achievers. The distribution of scores on an achievement test for students admitted to the school should be bimodal. Another example: When a war costs the lives of many young adults, the distribution of age after the war might be bimodal, with a dip in the middle.

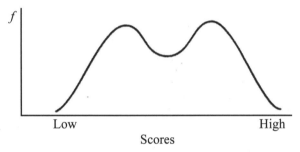

Figure 4. A bimodal distribution.

Bimodal distributions are much less common than normal distributions or skewed distributions.

The shape of a distribution should always be examined before proceeding with additional statistical analyses. The shape has important implications for determining which average to compute—a topic that will be taken up later in this book—and for determining which other statistics are appropriate to compute.

Terms to Review Before Attempting Worksheet 10

distribution, curve, normal curve, skewed, positive skew, negative skew, bimodal distributions

Worksheet 10   Shapes of Distributions

> *Riddle*: Woody Allen said, "It's not that I'm afraid to die, it's just that..."

DIRECTIONS: To find the answer to the riddle, write the answer to each question in the space immediately below it. In the solution section, the word in parentheses next to the answer to the first question is the first word in the answer to the riddle, the word beside the answer to the second question is the second word, and so on.

1. What should be placed on the horizontal axis of a frequency polygon?

   scores

2. What is the most important type of curve?

   normal curve

3. A curve with a tail to the left is said to have what type of skew?

   negative

4. A curve with a tail to the right is said to have what type of skew?

   positive

5. "Income in a large population is usually normally distributed." Is this statement true *or* false?

   false

6. In a normal curve, is the highest point to the left, to the right, *or* in the middle of the distribution?

   middle

Worksheet 10 (continued)

7. "A distribution that is skewed to the right has a positive skew." Is this statement true *or* false?

    True

8. How many high points does a bimodal distribution have?

    two

9. From left to right in a frequency polygon, are the scores arranged from high to low *or* from low to high?

    low to high

Solution section:

~~two (it)~~ left (evil) right (coffin) three (pure) false (be)			
middle (there) ~~true (when)~~ high to low (flowers) one (selfish) frequencies (in)			
scores (I) ~~positive (to)~~ ~~normal (don't)~~ shape (everything)			
lines (funeral) ~~negative (want)~~ low to high (happens)			

Write the answer to the riddle here, putting one word on each line: __I__ __don't__ __want__ __to__ __be__ __there__ __when__ __it__ __happens__

Notes

Section 11   Introduction to Summation

In statistics, we often sum series of scores when making intermediate calculations. While adding numbers is a straightforward operation, you may be less familiar with the statistical notation involved. The Greek letter sigma, $\sum$, stands for *sum of* in statistics and indicates that we need to sum a set of numbers represented by algebraic terms. Suppose that we are told that X represents a sequence of four numbers: 1, 2, 3, 5. If we are asked to find $\sum X$, then we need to find the sum of all of the X values, as follows:

$$\sum X = 1 + 2 + 3 + 5 = 11$$

The **summation** must be considered when following the **order of operations** rules. We have three rules from Section A of the Basic Math Review (located in Part E near at the end of this book):

✓ **Rule 1**: When there are parentheses, perform the operations inside the parentheses first.

✓ **Rule 2**: Unless parentheses indicate otherwise, multiply and divide before adding and subtracting.

✓ **Rule 3**: If there are both parentheses and brackets, solve first within the parentheses, then within the brackets, then perform any remaining operations.

To include a summation, we must add two additional rules:

✓ **Rule 4**: Unless parentheses indicate otherwise, summation is done before other addition or subtraction, but after all other operations.

Note that the following expressions all produce different results:

A. $\sum X + 10 = 1 + 2 + 3 + 5 + 10 = 21$

B. $\sum (X + 10) = (1 + 10) + (2 + 10) + (3 + 10) + (5 + 10) = 61$

C. $\sum (X)(10) = (1)(10) + (2)(10) + (3)(10) + (5)(10) = 110$

D. $\dfrac{\sum X}{10} = \dfrac{1+2+3+5}{10} = 1.1$

E. $\Sigma X^2 = 1^2 + 2^2 + 3^2 + 5^2 = 39$

F. $(\Sigma X)^2 = (1 + 2 + 3 + 5)^2 = 121$

In A above, we sum all of the values of X before adding the 10 because other addition comes after summation. In B, we first follow the parentheses, adding 10 to each value of X before summing everything. Multiplication precedes the summation in C, and we treat the numerator and denominator separately before obtaining the final answer in D. Because squaring is a form of multiplication, we square the numbers first before adding them together in E. However, the parentheses in F tell us to sum the values of X before squaring the final answer.

Following is an example in which more rules are combined. Assume that Y represents a sequence of four new numbers: 2, 3, 4, 6.

$$\sqrt{\Sigma XY^2 + 10}$$

✓ **Rule 5**: After adhering to parentheses and brackets, exponents should be followed, then multiplication and division.

Step 1: There are no parentheses, so we begin by squaring each of the Y-values.

$$2^2 = 4$$
$$3^2 = 9$$
$$4^2 = 16$$
$$6^2 = 36$$

Step 2: Our next step is to multiply each set of the X- and squared Y-values (in order).

$$(1)(4) = 4$$
$$(2)(9) = 18$$
$$(3)(16) = 48$$
$$(5)(36) = 180$$

Step 3: Next, we follow the summation sign and sum the products from Step 2.

$$4 + 18 + 48 + 180 = 250$$

Step 4: The next step is to add 10 to our sum.

$$250 + 10 = 260$$

Step 5: Finally, we take the square root to obtain the final answer.

$$\sqrt{260} = 16.2$$

Terms to Review Before Attempting Worksheet 11

$\sum$, summation, order of operations

Worksheet 11   Introduction to Summation

Riddle: According to Terry Pratchett, what is the trouble with having an open mind?

DIRECTIONS: To find the answer to the riddle, write the answer to each question in the space immediately below it. In the solution section, the word in parentheses next to the answer to the first question is the first word in the answer to the riddle, the word beside the answer to the second question is the second word, and so on.

$X = 3, 4, 5, 6$

$Y = 7, 8, 9, 10$

1. $\sum X = ?$

2. $\sum XY = ?$

3. $\sum X^2 = ?$

4. $(\sum X)^2 = ?$

5. $\sum (XY)^2 = ?$

6. $\sum (X + Y) = ?$

Worksheet 11 (continued)

7. $\sum XY^2 = ?$

8. $100 - \sum X = ?$

9. $\dfrac{\sum X^2}{\sum Y} = ?$

10. $\sqrt{\Sigma(X-Y)^2} = ?$

11. $\dfrac{300}{\sqrt{\Sigma(XY)^2}} = ?$

12. $13 + \sqrt{\Sigma X(3)} = ?$

13. $2(\Sigma Y^2 - 10) = ?$

Worksheet 11 (continued)

Solution section:

11.64 (mind)   324 (on)   3 (want)   18 (people)   17 (whatever)   0.04 (leaving)

776 (quit)   86 (insist)   508 (it)   612 (rely)   82 (trying)   22 (every)   8 (put)

52 (along)   1408 (and)   23 (creative)   42 (won't)   14 (none)   20.35 (in)

7090 (coming)   34 (out)   2.53 (to)   16 (they)   3.56 (things)   158 (will)

Write the answer to the riddle here, putting one word on each line: _____ _____ _____ _____
_____ _____ _____ _____ _____
_____ _____ _____ _____

Section 12 The Mean: An Average

The most popular average is the **mean**.[1] It is so popular that it is sometimes simply called *the average*. However, the term *average* is ambiguous because there are several types of averages used in statistics.

Computation of the mean is quite simple: Just sum (i.e., add up) the scores and then divide by the number of scores. Here is an example:

Scores: 5, 6, 7, 10, 12, 15

Sum of scores: 55

Number of scores: 6

Computation of mean: $55/6 = 9.166 = 9.17$

Notice that in the above example, the answer was computed to three decimal places and rounded to two. In scientific work, the mean is usually reported to two decimal places.

There are several symbols for the mean. In professional journals, the most commonly used symbols are **M** and **m**. (Strictly speaking, the uppercase *M* should be used when describing an entire population, and the lowercase *m* should be used when describing a sample drawn from a population.) In addition, mathematical statisticians often use this symbol when referring to the sample mean

$$\overline{X}$$

It is pronounced *X-bar*. (Remember that *X* without the bar stands for a score or a set of scores.) Mathematical statisticians also use the following symbol when referring to the population mean:

$$\mu$$

It is pronounced *mu*. Throughout this book, the symbols *M, m,* and μ will be used to stand for the mean.

---

[1] Its full, formal name is the *arithmetic mean*. Other averages are described in Section 13.

Although calculating the mean is simple, it is important to become familiar with the symbols in the formula because they will be used later in this book in other formulas. The formula for the mean is

$$M = \frac{\Sigma X}{N}$$

As we saw in Section 11, the symbol Σ stands for *sum of* in statistics. The X stands for *score* or *scores*. N is the number of cases or participants. Thus, the formula says: *The mean equals the sum of the scores divided by the number of cases.*

An important characteristic of the mean is that it is the balance point of the distribution. In other words, it is the *point around which the deviations sum to zero.*[2] The scores in Table 1 illustrate this characteristic. The sum of the scores is 60. Dividing this by 5 yields a mean of 12.00. Subtracting the mean from each score produces the deviations from the mean. These deviations sum to zero.[3] (Notice that the negatives cancel out the positives when summing.)

Table 1
Scores and Their Deviations From Their Mean

Score	Mean	Deviation
7	12.00	−5
11	12.00	−1
11	12.00	−1
14	12.00	2
17	12.00	5
	Sum of deviations = 0	

A major drawback of the mean is that it is drawn in the direction of extreme scores. This is a problem if there are either some extremely high scores that pull it up or some extremely low scores that pull it down (i.e., when a distribution is highly skewed [see Section 10]). Below is an example that shows, in cents, the contributions that two groups of children made to a charity.

[2] This is a defining characteristic of the mean. There is only one value that has this characteristic for a given distribution. Any value that does *not* have this characteristic is *not* the mean.
[3] If the mean is not a whole number, the sum of the deviations may vary slightly from zero because of rounding when determining the mean. A rounded mean is not *precisely* accurate.

Group A: 1, 1, 2, 3, 3, 4, 4, 4, 5, 5, 5, 5, 6, 6, 6, 7, 8, 10, 10, 10, 11
 Mean for Group A = 5.52

Group B: 1, 2, 2, 3, 3, 3, 4, 4, 5, 5, 5, 6, 6, 6, 6, 6, 9, 10, 10, 150, 200
 Mean for Group B = 21.24

Notice that, overall, the two distributions are quite similar. Yet the mean for Group B is much higher than the mean for Group A because of two students who gave extremely high contributions of 150 cents and 200 cents. If only the mean for Group B is reported, and not all of the individual contributions, it suggests that the average student in Group B gave about 21 cents when, in fact, none of the students made a contribution of about this amount. Thus, the mean is misleading in describing the average contribution in Group B. An average that would provide a more accurate indication of the center for this type of distribution is described in the next section.

Another limitation of the mean is that it is appropriate for use only with interval and ratio scales of measurement (see Section 3) because its value is dependent upon the magnitude of the scores, which creates the size of their deviations from the mean. This is not true of the averages described in Section 13.

Note that another term for *average* is ***measure of central tendency***. Although the latter term is seldom used in reports of research in professional journals, you may encounter it if you refer to other statistics texts.

Terms to Review Before Attempting Worksheet 12

mean, *M*, *m*, *X*, *N*, measure of central tendency

Worksheet 12   The Mean: An Average

> ## Riddle: What type of magic can auto mechanics do?

DIRECTIONS: To find the answer to the riddle, write the answer to each question in the space immediately below it. In the solution section, the word in parentheses next to the answer to the first question is the first word in the answer to the riddle, the word beside the answer to the second question is the second word, and so on.

1. To two decimal places, what is the mean of these scores: 10, 15, 17, 17, 20, 22?

    10.83

2. To two decimal places, what is the mean of these scores: 0, 0, 2, 5, 8, 9, 12?

    5.14

3. In professional journals, what is the most common symbol for the mean?

    M or m

4. In statistics, what does Σ stand for?

    Sum of

5. What does N stand for?

    number of cases

6. Assume that the mean for a group is 15.00. Sylvia, who is a member of the group, obtained a score of 14. What is the value of the deviation score associated with Sylvia's score?

    -1

7. If the mean is subtracted from each of the scores underlying it and the deviations are summed, what value is obtained?

    zero

Worksheet 12 (continued)

8. "For a skewed distribution, the mean is pulled in the direction of the extreme scores." Is this statement true *or* false?

True

9. Suppose that 2 homes at the top of a hillside community were sold for very high prices, and 20 homes farther down the hill were sold for modest prices. Would the mean be likely to give an accurate indication of the average home price in the community?

NO

10. What is another term for the word *average*?

Measures of central tendencies

Solution section:

X-bar (fix)   false (transmission)   true (underneath)   no (their)

measures of central tendency (car)   X (hat)   1 (hand)   16.83 (they)

zero (from)   number of cases (person's)   sum of (a)   sigma (seeing)

7.20 (lift)   5.14 (can)   14.43 (never)   M or m (pick)   −1 (pocket)

Write the answer to the riddle here, putting one word on each line: *They   can   pick   a   person's   pocket   from   underneath   their   car*

Notes

Section 13   Mean, Median, and Mode

The *mean*, which was described in the previous section, is the *balance point* in a distribution. It is the most frequently used average.[1]

An alternative average is the *median*. It is the value in a distribution that has 50% of the cases above it and 50% of the cases below it. Thus, it is the *middle point* in a distribution. In Example 1, there are 11 scores, ordered from low to high. The middle score, with 50% on each side, is 81, which is the median. Note that there are five scores above 81 and five scores below 81.[2]

Example 1
Scores (arranged in order from low to high)
    61, 61, 72, 77, 80, 81, 82, 85, 89, 90, 92

In Example 2, there are six scores. Because there is an even number of scores, the median is halfway between the middle two scores. To find this value, sum the two middle scores (7 + 10 = 17) and divide by 2 (17/2 = 8.5). Thus, 8.5 is the median of this set of scores.

Example 2
Scores
    3, 3, 7, 10, 12, 15

An advantage of the median is that it is insensitive to extreme scores.[3] This is illustrated by Example 3, in which the extremely high score of 229 has no effect on the value of the median. The median is 8.5, the same value as in Example 2, despite the extremely high score of 229.

Example 3
Scores
    3, 3, 7, 10, 12, 229

---

[1] Another term for *average* is *measure of central tendency*.

[2] When there are tie scores in the middle—that is, when the middle score is earned by more than one subject—this method for determining the median is only approximate and the result should be referred to as an *approximate median*.

[3] As noted in Section 12, the mean is pulled in the direction of extreme scores, which may make it a misleading average for skewed distributions. This is not true of the median.

Example 3 is skewed because of the single high score of 229. The example illustrates an important difference between the median and the mean when a distribution is skewed. The mean for the scores is 44 (obtained by summing the scores and dividing by the number of scores). Note that the mean has been pulled up from the center of the distribution by the score of 229. The median, however, is 8.5, which is a better representation than the mean of the typical case in this skewed distribution because most participants have scores closer to 8.5 than 44.

The *mode* is another average. It is defined as the *most frequently occurring score*. In Example 4, the mode is 7 because it occurs more often than any other score.

Example 4

Scores

2, 2, 4, 6, 7, 7, 7, 9, 10, 12

A disadvantage of the mode is that there may be more than one mode for a given distribution. This is the case in Example 5, in which both 20 and 23 are the mode.

Example 5

Scores

17, 19, 20, 20, 22, 23, 23, 28

Here are three guidelines to use when choosing an average:

- Other things being equal, choose the mean because more powerful statistical tests (described later in this book) can be applied to it than to the other averages. However, (1) the mean is appropriate only for approximately symmetrical distributions and is inappropriate for describing the average of a highly skewed distribution (i.e., a distribution with some extreme scores on one side of the distribution), and (2) the mean is appropriate only for describing interval and ratio data. (See Section 3 to review scales of measurement.)

- Choose the median when the mean is inappropriate. The exception to this guideline applies when describing nominal data. Nominal data (see Section 3) are naming data such as political affiliation, ethnicity, and so on. Natural order is not inherent in nominal data. Therefore, they cannot be put in an ordered sequence, which must be done for the median to be determined. Remember that scores or ranks must be ordered from low to high in order for the median to be calculated.

● Choose the mode when an average is needed to describe nominal data. Note that when describing nominal data, it is often not necessary to use an average. For instance, if there are more Democrats than Republicans in a community, the best way to describe this is to give the percentage of people registered in each party. To simply state that the modal political affiliation is Democratic (which is the average in this case) is much less informative than reporting percentages.

Note that in a perfectly symmetrical distribution (such as the normal distribution), the mean, median, and mode all have the same value. In skewed distributions, their values are different, as illustrated in Figure 1. In a distribution with a *positive skew*, the mean has the highest value because it is pulled in the direction of the extremely high scores. In a distribution with a *negative skew*, the mean has the lowest value because it is pulled in the direction of the extremely low scores. As noted earlier, do not use the mean when a distribution is highly skewed. See Table 1 on the next page for a review of these concepts.

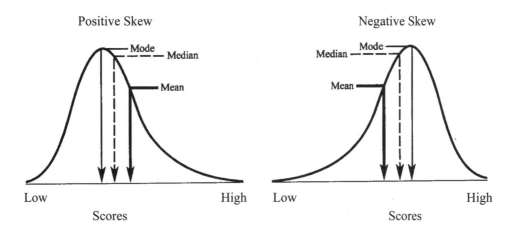

Figure 1. Positions of three averages in distributions with positive and negative skews.

Table 1
Comparison of Three Averages

	Mean (*M*)	**Median (*Mdn*)**	**Mode (*Mo*)**
Definition	Balance point	Middle point	Most frequent score
When to use	Symmetrical distributions of interval/ratio data	When mean is inappropriate (except for nominal data)	Nominal data
Frequency of use in scientific reporting	Very frequent	Somewhat frequent	Very infrequent[1]
Relative values for positive skew[2]	Higher than *Mdn* or *Mo*	Between *M* and *Mo*	Lower than *M* or *Mdn*
Relative values for negative skew	Lower than *Mdn* or *Mo*	Between *M* and *Mo*	Higher than *M* or *Mdn*

[1]Although nominal data (for which the mode is appropriate) are frequently reported in scientific writing, most researchers report percentages for each category rather than reporting the modal category. Thus, the mode is seldom used.

[2]See Section 10 to review skewed distributions.

Terms to Review Before Attempting Worksheet 13

mean, median, mode, positive skew, negative skew

Worksheet 13   Mean, Median, and Mode

Riddle: How are political speeches similar to food?

DIRECTIONS: To find the answer to the riddle, write the answer to each question in the space immediately below it. In the solution section, the word in parentheses next to the answer to the first question is the first word in the answer to the riddle, the word beside the answer to the second question is the second word, and so on.

1. Which average is defined as the value that has 50% of the cases below it?

    median

2. What is the median of these scores: 0, 5, 7, 9, 9?

    7

3. What is the median of these scores: 10, 12, 14, 17?

    13

4. What is the median of these scores: 50, 40, 29, 52, 54?

    29 40, 50, 52, 54

5. What is the mode of these scores: 11, 12, 12, 15, 18, 20?

    12

6. Which average is appropriate only for describing interval and ratio data?

    mean

7. Should the mean be used to describe highly skewed distributions?

    NO

8. Which average is most appropriate for describing nominal data?

    mode

Worksheet 13 (continued)

9. Do the mean, median, and mode all have the same value in a normal distribution?

yes

10. "In a distribution with a positive skew, the mean has a higher value than the median." Is this statement true *or* false?

True

11. "In a distribution with a negative skew, the median has a lower value than the mean." Is this statement true *or* false?

false

Solution section:

8 (win)   9 (election)   12.5 (hungry)   median (very)   13 (they)
7 (often)   mean (baloney)   false (thought)   39 (being)   12 (just)   50 (are)
true (for)   yes (food)   no (disguised)   51 (kitchen)   14 (weakness)
7.5 (milk)   averages (windfall)   9.5 (sensitivity)   mode (as)

Write the answer to the riddle here, putting one word on each line: *very*   *often*   *they*   *are*   *just*   *baloney*   *disguised*   *as*   *food*   *for*   *thought*

Section 14   Variability: The Range and Interquartile Range

Variability refers to the differences among scores (i.e., how much the scores *vary* from each other). Synonyms for *variability* are *spread* and *dispersion*, and the statistics used to describe variability are referred to as *measures of variability*.

How much individuals in a group vary is important for statistical and practical reasons. Suppose, for instance, you were going to teach fourth grade next year and were offered a choice between two classes—both of which were very similar in terms of average scores obtained in those classes' standardized tests. Before making a choice, you would be wise to ask about variability. Suppose you learned that one class had very little variability—its standardized test scores were all very close to the average score—and that the other class had tremendous variability—its standardized test scores varied greatly from the highest to the lowest score possible, with a great deal of spread in between. Which class would you choose to teach? Clearly, information on variability would be important in helping you to make this decision.

A simple statistic that describes variability is the ***range***. It is computed by subtracting the lowest score from the highest score.[1] For the scores in Example 1, the range is 18 (20 – 2). A researcher could report 18 as the range or simply state that the scores range from 2 to 20.

Example 1
Scores
>   2, 5, 7, 7, 8, 8, 10, 12, 12, 15, 17, 20

Note that if you count on your fingers from 2 to 20, you will count to 19—not 18. Thus, some statisticians add 1 to the difference between the highest and lowest scores when computing the range.

A weakness of the range is that it is based on only two scores, which may not reflect the true variability of all the scores. Consider Example 2 on the next page,

---

[1] Some statisticians add the constant 1 to the difference when computing the range.

in which the range is also 18. Note, however, that there is actually very little variability among the scores in Example 2. The individual with a score very different from the others (the score of 20) had an undue influence on the range.

Example 2

Scores

2, 2, 2, 3, 4, 4, 5, 5, 5, 6, 7, 20

Scores such as the 20 in Example 2 are known as **outliers**. They lie outside the range of the vast majority of the scores and can greatly increase the size of the range. Thus, the range is usually inappropriate for describing a distribution with outliers.

A better measure of variability is the **interquartile range** (IQR). It is defined as the range of the middle 50% of the cases. To find the interquartile range, do the following:

1. Put the scores in order from low to high. Then, determine how many scores constitute one-quarter of the scores. In Example 3 on the next page, there are 12 scores, so one-quarter of them ($12 \div 4$) equals 3.

2. Count up from the lowest score the number of scores you calculated in Step 1. In Example 3, when you count up 3 scores, you come to the arrow on the left, which is between the scores of 2 and 3. Halfway between them is a value of 2.5.

3. Count down from the highest score the number of scores you calculated in Step 1. In Example 3, when you count down three scores, you come to the arrow on the right, which is between the scores of 5 and 6. Halfway between them is a value of 5.5.

4. Subtract the answer to Step 2 from the answer to Step 3 ($5.5 - 2.5 = 3.0$). Thus, 3.0 is the value of the *interquartile range* for this set of scores.[2] When you report 3.0 to your audience, they will know that the range of the middle 50% of the participants is only 3 points. Note that the undue influence of the outlier of 20 has been overcome by using the *interquartile range* instead of the *range*.

---

[2] This procedure is approximate when there are tie scores at the points at which you are working. When this is the case, the answer should be reported as the *approximate interquartile range*.

Example 3

Scores

2, 2, 2, 3, 4, 4, 5, 5, 5, 6, 7, 20
⇧   ⇧

The interquartile range may be thought of as a first cousin of the median. (Remember that to calculate the median, you count to the middle of the distribution.) Thus, when the median is reported as the average for a set of scores, it is customary to report the interquartile range as the measure of variability.[3]

Terms to Review Before Attempting Worksheet 14

variability, range, outliers, interquartile range

"You've been working awfully hard on your statistics homework. If you need a little fresh air and sunshine, you can go to www.fresh-air-and-sunshine.com."

---

[3] The measure of variability that is associated with the mean is introduced in Section 15. See Section 13 for guidelines on when to report the median and the mean.

Worksheet 14   Variability: The Range and
Interquartile Range

> ## Riddle: Who are your real friends?

DIRECTIONS: To find the answer to the riddle, write the answer to each question in the space immediately below it. In the solution section, the word in parentheses next to the answer to the first question is the first word in the answer to the riddle, the word beside the answer to the second question is the second word, and so on.

1. *Spread* and *dispersion* are synonyms for what term?

   variability

2. If two groups are equal on average, will they necessarily be equal in their variability?

   NO

3. What is the range of these scores: 6, 8, 8, 10, 12, 13?

   7

4. What is the outlier in this set of scores: 2, 18, 18, 20, 20, 21, 22?

   2

5. What percentage of the participants is encompassed by the interquartile range?

   50%

6. Is the interquartile range *or* the range a better measure of variability?

   interquartile range

7. What is the interquartile range of these scores: 10, 10, 11, 12, 13, 13, 14, 14, 15, 17, 18, 18?

   4.5   11.5

                                                          we

Worksheet 14 (continued)

8. What is the interquartile range of these scores: 5, 5, 0, 1, 2, 11, 11, 11, 10, 9, 7, 6, 5, 5, 0, 4?

0, 0, 1, 2, 4, 5, 5, 5, 5, 6, 7, 9, 10, 11, 11, 11
↑
3

↑
9.5

6.5

9. The interquartile range is associated with which average?

median

Solution section:

```
median (back)   6.5 (your)   15 (young)   6 (smile)   mean (fell)

      interquartile range (you)   4.5 (behind)   5 (friendly)

   mode (being)   68% (figure)   yes (loving)   variability (those)

2 (well)   7 (speak)   no (who)   50% (of)   99% (brilliant)   95% (calling)
```

Write the answer to the riddle here, putting one word on each line: Those   who   speak   well   of   you   behind   your   back

79

Notes

Section 15   Variability: Introduction to the Standard Deviation

The ***standard deviation*** is a measure of how much scores differ (or *vary*) from the mean of the scores. The mean is the average that was introduced in Section 12.

Statisticians use the symbol S or σ (the lowercase Greek letter sigma) for the standard deviation of the scores of a population.[1] Authors of applied research in journals may use the symbol ***S.D.***—sometimes with and sometimes without the period marks.

The formula that defines the standard deviation is

$$S = \sqrt{\frac{\Sigma(X-M)^2}{N}}$$

$$\frac{\text{sum of (scores - mean of scores)}^2}{\text{\# of cases}}$$

To obtain the deviations $(X - M)$ for Example 1, first calculate the mean (in this case, $78/6 = 13.00$) and subtract the mean from each score, as shown below. Then square the deviations and sum the squares, as indicated by the symbol Σ. Enter this value in the formula along with the number of cases (N) and perform the calculations as illustrated at the top of the next page.

Example 1

Scores (X)	Deviations $(X - M)$	Deviations squared $(X - M)^2$
10	$10 - 13.00 = -3$	9.00
11	$11 - 13.00 = -2$	4.00
11	$11 - 13.00 = -2$	4.00
13	$13 - 13.00 = 0$	0.00
14	$14 - 13.00 = 1$	1.00
19	$19 - 13.00 = 6$	36.00
		$\Sigma x^2 = 54.00$

$M = 13$

$78/6$

---

[1] The formula for the standard deviation of a population is given in this section. The formula for estimating the standard deviation of a population from a sample is given in the second example in Appendix A.

Thus,

$$S = \sqrt{\frac{54.00}{6}} = \sqrt{9} = 3.00$$

An algebraically equivalent formula, known as the *computational formula*, which is slightly easier to use, is presented in Appendix A.[2] It is advantageous to use this formula when analyzing a large number of scores using a calculator. Of course, a computer is recommended for calculating a very large number of scores.

A closer examination of the way in which the standard deviation is calculated reveals the definition of the standard deviation. As the formula on the previous page indicates, the standard deviation is *the square root of the average squared deviation from the mean.* Thus, the larger the deviations from the mean, the larger the standard deviation. Conversely, the smaller the deviations from the mean, the smaller the standard deviation.

At the extreme, when all the scores are the same, the standard deviation equals zero. For instance, if each individual in a population has a score of 20, then the mean of the scores is 20.00. When the mean of 20.00 is subtracted from each score of 20, the resulting deviations will all be zero. When they are squared, they will still equal zero. When they are summed, the sum will equal zero. When zero is entered into the numerator of the formula, the solution for S will be zero, which is as it should be. When there is no variation, S equals zero—indicating there is no variation.

The standard deviation takes on a special meaning when considered in relation to the normal curve (see Section 10) because it was designed expressly to describe this distribution. Here is a simple rule to remember: *About two-thirds of the cases lie within one standard deviation unit of the mean in a normal distribution.* (Note that "within one standard deviation unit" means one unit on both sides of the mean.) For instance, suppose that the mean of a set of normally distributed scores equals 70.00 and the standard deviation equals 10.00. About two-thirds of the cases lie within 10 points of the mean. More precisely, 68% of the cases lie within 10 points of the mean, as illustrated in Figure 1 on the next page.

---

[2]The *definition* formula is presented in this section because it is the one that most readily conveys an understanding of what influences the size of the standard deviation for a set of scores.

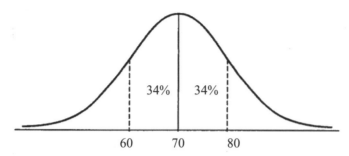

Figure 1. Normal curve with a standard deviation of 10.00.

Suppose that for another group, the mean of its normal distribution also equals 70.00, but its standard deviation equals 5.00. Then, 68% of the cases lie within 5 points of the mean, as illustrated in Figure 2.

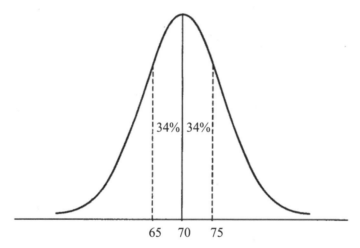

Figure 2. Normal curve with a standard deviation of 5.00.

At first, this seems like magic—regardless of the value of the standard deviation, 68% of the cases lie within one standard deviation unit in a normal curve. Actually, it is not magic but a property of the normal curve. When calculating the standard deviation, you are actually calculating the number of points that one must go out from the mean to capture the middle 68% of the cases.[3] This two-thirds rule does not strictly apply if the distribution is not normal. The less normal it is, the less accurate the rule is. Other rules are described in Section 16.

---

[3]When you go out one standard deviation on both sides of the mean, you reach the *points of inflection*— the points where the curve changes direction and begins to go out more quickly than it goes down.

Remember that the standard deviation is a first cousin of the mean. Thus, when researchers report the mean (the most popular average), they usually also report the standard deviation.

Terms to Review Before Attempting Worksheet 15

standard deviation, *S, S.D.*

Worksheet 15 Variability: Introduction to the Standard Deviation

---

Riddle: According to Abraham Lincoln, how are vices and virtues related?

DIRECTIONS: To find the answer to the riddle, write the answer to each question in the space immediately below it. In the solution section, the word in parentheses next to the answer to the first question is the first word in the answer to the riddle, the word beside the answer to the second question is the second word, and so on.

1. What symbol do statisticians use for the standard deviation?

    S σ

2. What is the symbol for the deviation of a score from its mean?

    x

3. To two decimal places, what is the standard deviation of these scores: 3, 5, 6, 7, 8?

    1.72 $\sqrt{\dfrac{14.8}{5}}$

    3   3 - 5.8 = -2.8²   7.84
    5   5 - 5.8 = -0.8²   0.64
    6   6 - 5.8 = 0.2²   0.04
    7   7 - 5.8 = 1.2²   1.44
    8   8 - 5.8 = 2.2²   4.84
                                    14.8

4. To two decimal places, what is the standard deviation of these scores: 0, 2, 5, 9, 12?

    4.41 $\sqrt{\dfrac{97.2}{5}}$

    0   0 - 5.6 = -5.6   31.36
    2   2 - 5.6 = -3.6   12.96
    5   5 - 5.6 = -0.6   0.36
    9   9 - 5.6 = 3.4   11.56
    12   12 - 5.6 = 6.4   40.96
    28   97.2

5. According to the standard deviations, are the scores in Question 3 *or* Question 4 more variable?

    question 4

6. If everyone in a population has the same score, what is the value of the standard deviation for those scores?

    zero

Worksheet 15 (continued)

7. The standard deviation was designed expressly to describe what type of distribution?

normal

8. If the mean for a group equals 40.00 and the standard deviation equals 5.00, what percentage of the cases in a normal distribution lies between 40 and 45?

34%

9. If the mean for a group equals 27.00 and the standard deviation equals 3.00, what percentage of the cases in a normal distribution lies between 24 and 30?

68%

Solution section:

34% (few) X (evil)   68% (virtues)   2.93 (weary)   4.70 (slavery)

99% (shift)   ~~zero (have)~~   normal (very)   ~~S (folks)~~   ~~1.72 (have)~~

x (who)   4.41 (no)   scores in Question 3 (sleepless)   50% (helpful)

~~scores in Question 4 (vices)~~   skewed (being) Σ (goodness)

Write the answer to the riddle here, putting one word on each line: folks   who   have   no   vices   have   very   few   virtues

Section 16   A Closer Look at the Standard Deviation

The *standard deviation*—which is a measure of how much scores vary from their mean—was introduced in the previous section, where you learned that about 68% of the scores in a normal distribution lie within one standard deviation unit of the mean, which is known as the **68% rule**. This section presents some additional rules for interpreting the standard deviation.[1]

The **approximate 95% rule** says that approximately 95% of the cases lie within two standard deviation units of the mean in a normal distribution. Following is an example of the application of the approximate 95% rule:

Example 1

The mean for a group equals 35.00 and the standard deviation equals 6.00. Two standard deviation units equal 12.00 points ($2 \times 6.00 = 12.00$). Thus, if you (a) go up 12 points from the mean ($35.00 + 12.00 = 47.00$) and (b) go down 12 points from the mean ($35.00 - 12.00 = 23.00$), you have identified the scores (47.00 and 23.00) between which approximately 95% of the cases lie. This example is illustrated in Figure 1.

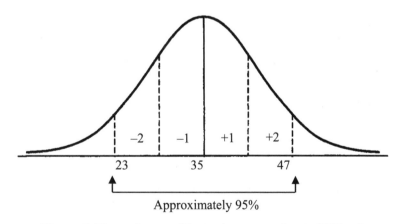

Figure 1. Normal curve illustrating approximate 95% rule.

---

[1]The rules are derived from the table of the normal curve, which is introduced in Section 20.

The **99.7% rule** says that going up and down three standard deviation units from the mean identifies where 99.7% of the cases lie. For the information in Example 1 on the previous page, multiply the standard deviation by 3 (6.00 × 3 = 18.00). Going up and down 18 points from the mean yields these scores: 53.00 and 17.00, as illustrated in Figure 2.

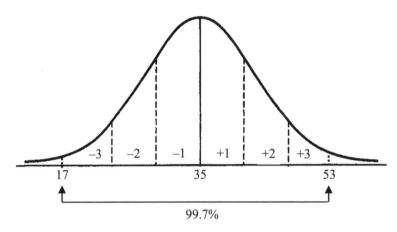

Figure 2. Normal curve illustrating 99.7% rule.

In review,

If M = 35.00 and S = 6.00, then
(1) 68% of the cases lie between 29.00 and 41.00,
(2) 95% of the cases lie between 23.00 and 47.00, and
(3) 99.7% of the cases lie between 17.00 and 53.00.

Figure 2 illustrates that almost all the cases (99.7%) in a normal distribution lie within 3 standard deviation units of the mean. Thus, for practical purposes, a normal distribution has only 6 standard deviation units—3 above the mean and 3 below the mean.

Keep in mind that the standard deviation is computed to determine the variability in a set of scores. Consider Example 2 on the next page, which illustrates this. The mean is the same as in Example 1, but the standard deviation is only half its size. Results of applying the three rules are shown. When the two examples are compared, it becomes obvious that the smaller the standard deviation, the less far out you need to go to capture a given percentage of cases. In fact, with a standard deviation of only 3.00, going out to only 26.00 and 44.00 captures 99.7% of the cases.

Example 2
When $M = 35.00$ and $S = 3.00$, then approximately
(1) 68% of the cases lie between 32.00 and 38.00,
(2) 95% of the cases lie between 29.00 and 41.00, and
(3) 99.7% of the cases lie between 26.00 and 44.00.

In a research report in which the groups in Example 1 and Example 2 are being compared, a researcher could say that the two groups are equal on average (as determined by the mean) but that the first group has twice the variability (as determined by the standard deviation) of the second group. This information could be very important for readers of the research.

When completing Worksheet 16, keep the multipliers below in mind. Multiply the standard deviation for a set of scores by the appropriate multiplier before adding and subtracting (i.e., adding to the mean and subtracting from the mean).

Rule	Multiplier
68%	1
95%	2
99.7%	3

Additional rules are discussed in the next section. Remember, all of these rules strictly apply only in the case of a normal distribution.

Terms to Review Before Attempting Worksheet 16

68% rule, approximate 95% rule, 99.7% rule

Worksheet 16   A Closer Look at the Standard Deviation

Riddle: When do most people stop believing in
         heredity?

DIRECTIONS: To find the answer to the riddle, write the answer to each question in the space immediately below it. In the solution section, the word in parentheses next to the answer to the first question is the first word in the answer to the riddle, the word beside the answer to the second question is the second word, and so on.

1. If you go out 1 standard deviation unit on both sides of the mean in a normal distribution, what percentage of the cases will be captured?

   68%

2. If you go out 3 standard deviation units on both sides of the mean in a normal distribution, what percentage of the cases will be captured?

   99.7%

3. For $M = 100.00$ and $S = 10.00$, approximately what percentage of the cases lie between 80.00 and 120.00?

   95%

4. For $M = 55.00$ and $S = 7.00$, between what two values do approximately 95% of the cases lie in a normal distribution?

   41- 69

5. For $M = 90.00$ and $S = 15.00$, between what two values do 99.7% of the cases lie in a normal distribution?

   45-135

6. What is the multiplier for the approximate 95% rule?

Worksheet 16 (continued)

7. What is the multiplier for the 99.7% rule?

3

8. For all practical purposes, the normal curve has how many standard deviation units?

6

Solution section:

1 (birth)   4 (grandparents)   51.30–128.70 (years)   2 (act)

6 (delinquents)   68% (when)   99% (becoming)   99.7% (their)

95% (children)   48.00–62.00 (useful)   3 (like)   41.00–69.00 (start)

50% (happening)   14.00–28.00 (wild)   34% (heaven)   45.00–135.00 (to)

Write the answer to the riddle here, putting one word on each line: when   their   children   start   to   act   like   delinquents

Notes

Section 17   Another Look at the Standard Deviation

The standard deviation indicates the amount of variability in the distribution. For instance, suppose you read the following statement in a report:

> For the population of Martians, the mean score on the Human Awareness Scale is 44.00, and the standard deviation is 4.00. The distribution is normal.

Based on this information, you would know that about 68% of the Martians had scores between 40.00 and 48.00.[1] Put another way, the vast majority of the Martians had scores within 4 points of the mean. This indicates the amount of variability because it indicates the number of points within which the vast majority (68%) of the cases lie. The remaining 32% had scores lower than 40.00 and higher than 48.00.

As indicated in Section 16, approximately 95% of the cases lie within 2 standard deviation units of the mean. To be more precise, use the ***precise 95% rule***, which says that if you go out 1.96 standard deviation units from the mean in a normal distribution, you will find 95% of the cases.[2]

The following is the application of the precise 95% rule to the Martian example shown above:

1. Multiply 1.96 by S ($1.96 \times 4.00 = 7.84$).

2. Subtract the result of Step 1 from the mean ($44.00 - 7.84 = 36.16$).

3. Add the result of Step 1 to the mean ($44.00 + 7.84 = 51.84$).

The results of Steps 2 and 3 yield the points between which 95% of the cases lie. Thus, 95% of the cases in this normal distribution lie between 36.16 and 51.84.

---

[1] To review the 68% rule, see Sections 15 and 16.

[2] Note that 1.96 is very close to 2, which led to the approximate rule. The constant 1.96 is derived from the definition of the normal curve. The table of the normal curve is introduced in Section 20. When you examine it, you will again encounter the constant 1.96.

The **99% rule** says that if you go out 2.58 standard deviation units from the mean, you will identify the values between which 99% of the cases lie.[3] Let us apply the 99% rule to the Martian example:

1. Multiply 2.58 by S ($2.58 \times 4.00 = 10.32$).

2. Subtract the result of Step 1 from the mean ($44.00 - 10.32 = 33.68$).

3. Add the result of Step 1 to the mean ($44.00 + 10.32 = 54.32$).

The results of Steps 2 and 3 yield the points between which 99% of the cases lie. Thus, 99% of the cases in this normal distribution lie between 33.68 and 54.32.

Keep in mind that these rules are accurate only when interpreting normal distributions. The less normal a distribution is, the less accurate the rules will be.

The standard deviation has been examined in detail not only because it is useful in describing the variability in a group but also because it is used in a variety of other statistical procedures, described later in this book.

Terms to Review Before Attempting Worksheet 17

precise 95% rule, 99% rule

---

[3]In the previous section, you learned that if you go out 3 standard deviation units from the mean, you identify the values between which 99.7% of the cases lie. As you will see later in this book, 99% is of more interest than 99.7% for advanced statistical work.

Worksheet 17   Another Look at the Standard Deviation

Riddle: What happens if a wealthy person dies
without a will?

DIRECTIONS: To find the answer to the riddle, write the answer to each question in the space immediately below it. In the solution section, the word in parentheses next to the answer to the first question is the first word in the answer to the riddle, the word beside the answer to the second question is the second word, and so on.

1. If $M = 500.00$ and $S = 100.00$ in a normal distribution, what percentage of the participants have scores between 400.00 and 600.00?

2. According to the precise 95% rule, how many standard deviation units should you go out from the mean in order to capture 95% of a population in a normal distribution?

3. "The multiplier for the precise 99% rule is 2.58." Is this a correct statement?

4. In a normal distribution with $M = 78.56$ and $S = 12.92$, between what two values does the middle 95% of a population lie according to the precise rule?

5. In a normal distribution with $M = 50.00$ and $S = 8.00$, what percentage of the population lies between 29.36 and 70.64?

95

Worksheet 17 (continued)

6. In a normal distribution with $M = 150.00$ and $S = 20.00$, what percentage of the population lies between 110.80 and 189.20?

7. In a normal distribution with $M = 11.52$ and $S = 1.40$, between what two values does 99% of the population lie?

8. If Group A has $M = 52.39$ ($S = 3.44$) and Group B has $M = 41.55$ ($S = 4.19$), which group has greater variability?

Solution section:

Group B (heirs)   7.91–15.13 (his or her)   no (visible)   2.58 (death)

99% (sides)   95% (become)   Group A (estate)   10.12–12.92 (feeling)

68% (the)   yes (on)   99.7% (funeral)   34% (jumping)   65.64–91.48 (wealth)

1.96 (lawyers)   34.00–66.00 (wishing)   53.24–103.88 (both)   average (dispute)

Write the answer to the riddle here, putting one word on each line: _____ _____ _____ _____ _____ _____ _____ _____

Section 18   Standard Scores

Up to this point, the emphasis has been on describing a distribution in order to get an overview of the data for a group as a whole—by using either a table (such as a frequency distribution) or a figure (such as a histogram) or by reporting an average and a measure of variability. In this section and the next, some methods for describing where an individual stands in a group are considered.

Raw scores (i.e., the number of points earned) are often reported to individuals. Raw scores are obtained from many kinds of measures: multiple-choice tests, instruments that measure blood pressure, point systems for creativity in an artistic endeavor, essay examinations, and so on.

Sometimes raw scores are easily interpreted because we have a frame of reference for them. For instance, a person who has to monitor her blood pressure over time probably already knows what the normal range is and what values might be dangerous. Such a person is engaging in a *norm-referenced interpretation*. That is, the norms for normal, below average, and above average, based on what has been commonly observed among large numbers of patients, provide reference points for interpreting raw scores.

Frequently, however, raw scores have little meaning to the recipient. Suppose you were administered a new paper-and-pencil depression scale and were told that your raw score was 56. What does this mean? Obviously, it means very little without additional information.

Standard scores (also called *z-scores*) help interpret raw scores by indicating where an individual stands in a group. Specifically, a standard score indicates *how many standard deviation units a person's score is from the mean and whether his or her score is above or below the mean.* For instance, suppose a person is told that she has a z-score of 1.00. This indicates that she is exactly one standard deviation unit from the mean. Furthermore, because a positive z-score indicates that a person is above the mean and a negative z-score indicates that a person is below the mean, we also know that she is above the mean. Drawing on our knowledge of the normal curve, we also know that a z-score of 1.00 puts her above about 84% of the participants in a normal distribution, which is how we know this: First, 50% of the participants lie below the mean in a normal distribution.[1] Second, about 34% of the cases lie between the mean and 1 standard deviation unit above the mean, which is illustrated in Figure 1.

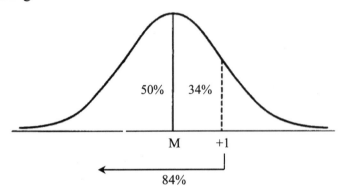

Figure 1. Normal curve illustrating percentage below a *z*-score of 1.00.

Suppose that another individual has a *z*-score of 0.00. This indicates that the person has a score with a value the same as the value of the mean (i.e., zero standard deviation units above or below the mean).

Finally, suppose that someone has a *z*-score of –2.00. This indicates that the person is 2 standard deviation units below the mean.

Because 3 standard deviation units on both sides of the mean encompass 99.7% of the cases in a normal curve, *z*-scores are seldom higher than 3.00 or lower than –3.00. Figure 2 illustrates the effective range of *z*-scores:

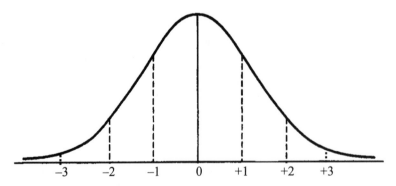

Figure 2. The effective range of *z*-scores (based on the 99.7% rule).

---

[1]Remember that the normal distribution is perfectly symmetrical and the mean is in the middle. Therefore, 50% of the cases are above the mean and 50% are below the mean.

To determine an individual's z-score, apply this formula:

$$z = \frac{X - M}{S}$$

Before using the formula, consider what it indicates. The numerator says to subtract the mean from a person's score. This indicates how many raw score points an individual's score is from the mean. By dividing this difference by the standard deviation, we are determining *how many standard deviation units* a person is from the mean.

Suppose that a child weighs 55.00 pounds and that, for her age, height, and gender, the mean is 60.00 pounds and the standard deviation is 5.00. Entering this information in the formula, we find that she is one standard deviation unit below the mean, which is much more meaningful than knowing just her weight expressed in pounds. Note that pounds are raw scores.

$$z = \frac{55.00 - 60.00}{5.00} = \frac{-5.00}{5.00} = -1.00$$

Consider Example 1:

Example 1

$M = 75.00$, $S = 5.00$ for a group on the Weirdness Scale.

Here are some of the scores:

Participant	Raw score	z-score
Jean	80	1.00
Tom	75	0.00
Sam	65	–2.00
Alice	62	–2.60

In Example 1, notice that Jean is 5 raw score points above the mean. Because 5 is the value of the standard deviation, she is 1 standard deviation unit above the mean, which gives her a z-score of 1.00. Tom is right at the mean and therefore has a z-score of 0.00. Sam is 10 raw score points below the mean. Because this is 2 standard deviation units below the mean ($2 \times 5.00 = 10.00$), he has a z-score of

−2.00. The z-score for Alice illustrates that not everyone has a whole number for a z-score and that z-scores should be computed to one or two decimal places.

It is quite possible that you cannot recall ever being given a z-score for your performance on a task. If they are so useful, why have they not been reported to you? Actually, they probably have, but only after being transformed to another scale. The transformation of z-scores into other scales is described in Section 19.

Terms to Review Before Attempting Worksheet 18

raw scores, standard scores, z-scores

"I'm the consultant they brought in to create some new statistical buzzwords."

Worksheet 18 Standard Scores

> *Riddle*: What will the ultimate luxury car of the future do?

DIRECTIONS: To find the answer to the riddle, write the answer to each question in the space immediately below it. In the solution section, the word in parentheses next to the answer to the first question is the first word in the answer to the riddle, the word beside the answer to the second question is the second word, and so on.

1. What term is used to refer to the number of points earned by an individual?

raw scores

2. What is another term for *z*-scores?

Standard scores

3. If a person has a *z*-score of 1.50, is that person's score above *or* below the mean of the group?

above

4. A person with a *z*-score of 1.00 has a score that is higher than what percentage of the group in a normal distribution?

84%

5. A person with a *z*-score of 0.00 has a score that is higher than what percentage of the group in a normal distribution?

50%

6. According to this topic, *z*-scores are seldom lower than what value?

−3

Worksheet 18 (continued)

7. What is the highest value in the effective range of z-scores?

3

8. If $M = 42.35$ and $S = 2.87$ and June has a raw score of 45, what is the value of her z-score?

0.92

9. If $M = 95.00$ and $S = 5.00$ and Jake has a raw score of 90, what is the value of his z-score?

-1

10. If $M = 511.12$ and $S = 20.28$ and Sarah has a raw score of 460, what is the value of her z-score?

-2.52

11. Examine Questions 8, 9, and 10. Notice that Sarah has the highest raw score. Who has the highest z-score?

June

Solution section:

490.84 (less)   39.48 (jump)   90.00 (dealer)   Sarah (being)   ~~above (just)~~

84% (sit)   ~~raw score (it)~~   Jake (cost) z-score (gasoline)   15 (useful)

64% (start)   ~~June (neighbors)~~   ~~-3.00 (the)~~   ~~0.92 (and)~~   34% (oil)

~~standard scores (will)~~   ~~50% (in)~~   0.00 (garage)   ~~-1.00 (impress)~~

3.00 (driveway)   ~~-2.52 (the)~~   below (speedy)   99.7% (Detroit)   95% (list)

Worksheet 18 (continued)

Write the answer to the riddle here, putting one word on each line: It will just sit in the driveway and impress the neighbors

"He's determined to be above the
mean, the median, *and* the mode!"

Notes

Section 19 Transformed Standard Scores

As indicated in the previous section, *standard scores* (i.e., *z*-scores) describe how many standard deviations a participant is from the mean of his or her group. Figure 2 in Section 18 indicates that, for all practical purposes, standard scores range from –3.00 to 3.00. A *z*-score of 0.00 indicates that a participant is at the mean—that is, exactly average.

Although *z*-scores are quite understandable to individuals who have studied statistics, they are likely to confuse those who have not received such training. Consider an individual who knows she is about average and has worked hard on a test. If she is told that her score is 0.00, she is likely to be confused. Likewise, another individual who is about average and obtains a *z*-score of –.10 (a tenth of a standard deviation below the mean) would probably be confused by his negative score. To get around this problem, *z*-scores are usually transformed to another scale that does not have zero as the average and does not have negatives. These scores will be referred to here as ***transformed standard scores (TSS)***.[1]

A statistician named McCall suggested the following transformation, which he called a ***T score***:

$$T = (z)(10) + 50$$

As you can see, the transformation is quite simple. To calculate a set of *T* scores, simply multiply each person's *z*-score by 10 and add 50. Consider what happens to a *z*-score of 0.00 when the transformation is applied:[2]

$$T = (0.00)(10) + 50 = 0.00 + 50 = 50.00 = 50$$

Notice that the constant that is added (50) becomes the new mean of the set of scores. Keep in mind that the person who had a *z*-score of 0.00 was exactly at the mean. This individual now has a *T* score of 50, yet the individual is still exactly at the mean after all of the scores have been transformed. Because all of the scores in

---

[1]There is no standard symbol for transformed standard scores. For the sake of brevity, the acronym *TSS* is used here.

[2]Note that *TSS* are usually reported as whole numbers.

a set are transformed, participants do not change positions in the group. Only their scores change to a new scale.

Let us transform a z-score of -1.00 to a T score:

$$T = (-1.00)(10) + 50 = -10.00 + 50 = 40.00 = 40$$

Remember that a z-score of -1.00 indicates that the person is one standard deviation unit below the mean. The person remains at this position but now has a T score of 40. Thus, 40 is one standard deviation unit below the mean.

Because 50 is the mean of a set of T scores and 40 is one standard deviation unit below the mean, 10 (the difference between 50 and 40) must be the value of the *new standard deviation*. In Figure 1, this is illustrated with a normal curve, although the distribution does *not* have to be normal for the transformation to apply.

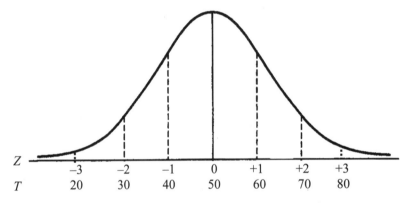

Figure 1. Normal curve with z-scores and equivalent T-scores.

A variety of other transformations have been developed. Following is a common one. To obtain a set of **IQ scores**, use this formula:[3]

$$IQ = (z)(15) + 100$$

You should be able to see that a person with a z-score of 0.00 will have an IQ of 100, and a person with a z-score of 1.00 will have an IQ of 115. Thus, the mean of a set of IQ scores for the norm group is transformed to 100, and the standard deviation is transformed to 15, as illustrated in Figure 2 on the next page.

---

[3]On some IQ tests, a multiplier of 16 is used.

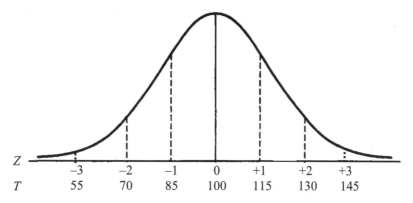

Figure 2. Normal curve with *z*-scores and equivalent IQ scores.

Another widely known transformation is the one originally used by the College Entrance Examination Board (CEEB) for its Scholastic Aptitude Test (SAT). Originally, it was applied separately for the verbal and quantitative tests as shown below, which made the mean equal to 500 and the standard deviation equal to 100. The ***CEEB scores*** were derived as follows:

$$CEEB = (z)(100) + 500$$

For a person with a *z*-score of 1.50, the CEEB score was derived as follows:

$$CEEB = (1.50)(100) + 500 = 150 + 500 = 650$$

Figure 3 illustrates the effective range of CEEB scores:

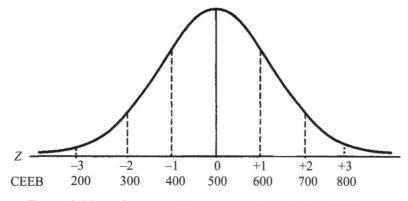

Figure 3. Normal curve with *z*-scores and equivalent CEEB scores.

A test maker may, of course, select any two constants to use in the formula for transformed standard scores. The generalized formula for obtaining them is

$$TSS = (z)(\text{new standard deviation}) + (\text{new mean})$$

Keep in mind that whatever constant is multiplied by all of the z-scores will become the new standard deviation, and whatever constant is added to the product will become the new mean.

Terms to Review Before Attempting Worksheet 19

transformed standard scores (TSS), T score, IQ scores, CEEB scores

**"Statistics class will be important to you
later in life because there's going to
be a test six weeks from now."**

Worksheet 19 Transformed Standard Scores

Riddle: According to Napoleon, what is the problem
        with the credit assigned for winning battles?

DIRECTIONS: To find the answer to the riddle, write the answer to each question in the space immediately below it. In the solution section, the word in parentheses next to the answer to the first question is the first word in the answer to the riddle, the word beside the answer to the second question is the second word, and so on.

   To answer some of the questions, you will first need to use the formula for converting raw scores to z-scores, which is presented in Section 18.

1. What is the mean of a set of T scores?

2. If $M = 35.00$ and $S = 5.00$ for a set of raw scores, what is Stan's T score if he has a raw score of 30?

3. In Question 2, how many standard deviation units is Stan from the mean?

4. If $M = 95.32$ and $S = 8.88$ for a set of raw scores, what is June's T score if she has a raw score of 112?

5. What is the mean of a set of IQ scores?

6. If $M = 49.55$ and $S = 5.11$ for a set of raw scores, what is Lyle's IQ score if he has a raw score of 45?

Worksheet 19 (continued)

7. If $M = 66.47$ and $S = 9.68$ for a set of raw scores, what is Jennifer's CEEB score if she has a raw score of 85?

8. In terms of standard deviation units, which of these is the highest score: $T = 70$, $IQ = 105$, $CEEB = 466$?

9. If $M = 22.00$ and $S = 4.00$ and Fernando has a z-score of 1.00, what is his TSS on a scale with a new mean of 300 and a new standard deviation of 50?

Solution section:

40 (win)	691 (get)	10 (keeping)	$IQ = 105$ (war)	350 (credit)
69 (but)	$CEEB = 466$ (famous)	113 (wishing)	$T = 70$ (the)	
5 (bloody)	50 (soldiers)	1 (battles)	87 (generals)	100 (the) 115 (fight)

Write the answer to the riddle here, putting one word on each line: _____ _____ _____ _____

_____ _____ _____ _____ _____

110

Section 20   Standard Scores and the Normal Curve

For any given standard score (z-score), we can determine the percentage of cases above and below it by using the ***table of the normal curve*** in Table 1 near the end of this book. In the left-most column, you will find a list of z-values that increase by 0.1. In the top row, you will see another list of z-values that increase by 0.01. To locate a z-value of 1.00, we look in the row labeled "1.00," then choose the column with the appropriate hundredths place. Our z-value has a 0 in the hundredths place, so we look under the heading for ".00" to find a value of .8413 (if our z-value were 1.01, we would look under the ".01" label to find a value of .8438). Our value of .8413 is the probability of scores at or below a z-value of 1.00. The probability of a score at or higher than a z-value of 1.00 is 1 minus .8413, or .1587. Figure 1 illustrates these numbers as percentages, which sum to 100%.

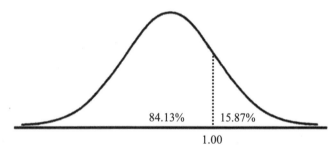

Figure 1. Percentage of cases above and below a z-score of 1.00.

It is important to note that Table 1 has two separate pages: one for negative z-values and one for positive z-values.

As indicated in the discussion of the standard deviation in Section 17, going out 1.96 standard deviation units in both directions from the mean captures 95% of the cases. This can be confirmed by looking up z-scores of -1.96 and 1.96 in Table 1 near the end of this book. For a z-value of -1.96, you will find a probability of .0250 (or 2.5%) to the left of z. For a z-value of 1.96, you will find a probability of .9750 (or 97.5%) to the left of z. To identify the percentage of scores above 1.96, we subtract 97.5% from 100% to get 2.5%. We know now that 5% of the scores are beyond 1.96 standard units from the mean and that 95% (100 – 5.00 = 95.00) of the cases lie within this interval, as illustrated in Figure 2.

In Section 17, you learned you need to go out 1.96 standard deviations on both sides of the mean to capture precisely 95% of the cases. Table 1 confirms that this is true, and Figure 2 illustrates this finding. Later in this book, 1.96 will be used for other statistical purposes.

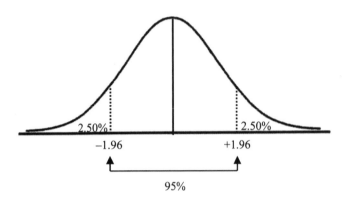

Figure 2. Percentage of cases between –1.96 and 1.96.

Table 1 applies to all normal curves. The table is abbreviated, showing only selected values of *z* because only certain values will be needed in later sections of this book.

Term to Review Before Attempting Worksheet 20

table of the normal curve

Worksheet 20 Standard Scores and the Normal Curve

Riddle: How do many economics professors stay fit?

DIRECTIONS: To find the answer to the riddle, write the answer to each question in the space immediately below it. In the solution section, the word in parentheses next to the answer to the first question is the first word in the answer to the riddle, the word beside the answer to the second question is the second word, and so on.

1. To two decimal places, what percentage of the cases in a normal distribution lie above a z-score of -1.00?

   ~~15.87%~~   84.13%

2. To two decimal places, what percentage of the cases in a normal distribution lie below a z-score of 1.96?

   97.50%

3. To two decimal places, what percentage of the cases in a normal distribution lie above a z-score of 1.00?

   ~~84.13%~~   15.87%

4. To two decimal places, what percentage of the cases in a normal distribution lie below a z-score of 3.00?

   99.87%

5. To two decimal places, what percentage of the cases in a normal distribution lie below a z-score of -2.00?

   2.28%

6. To two decimal places, what percentage of the cases in a normal distribution lie between a z-score of 1.00 and a z-score of -1.00?

   15.87   84.15

Worksheet 20 (continued)

7. To two decimal places, what percentage of the cases in a normal distribution lie between a *z*-score of 1.96 and a *z*-score of −1.96?

95.00% 97.5 / 2.5   0.0150 / 0.9150

8. To two decimal places, what percentage of the cases in a normal distribution lie between a *z*-score of 2.58 and a *z*-score of −2.58?

99.51 / 0.49   0.9951 / 0.0049

Solution section:

50.00% (money) 68.26% (a) 99.02% (cycle) 100.00% (exercise)	

50.00% (money) 68.26% (a) 99.02% (cycle) 100.00% (exercise)

95.00% (business) 84.13% (they) 44.00% (jumping) 97.50% (ride)

15.87% (to) 0.13 (numbers) 99.87% (school) 2.28% (on)

49.51% (tenure) 86.13% (having) 99.51% (everything)

Write the answer to the riddle here, putting one word on each line: *they   ride   to   school   on   a   business   cycle*

Section 21   Conceptual Introduction to Correlation

Correlation refers to the extent to which two sets of scores are related. Consider scores on the College Entrance Examination Board's *Scholastic Aptitude Test* (SAT) and first-year GPA in college. Because the SAT is widely used as a predictor in college student selection, there should be a correlation between these scores and GPA. Consider Example 1, in which SAT-V refers to the verbal portion of the SAT. Is there a relationship?

Example 1

Student	SAT-V	GPA
John	333	1.0
Janet	756	3.8
Thomas	444	1.9
Scotty	629	3.2
Diana	501	2.3
Hillary	245	0.4

Indeed, there is a relationship. Notice that students who scored high on the SAT-V (such as Janet and Scotty) had the highest GPAs. Also, those who scored low on the SAT-V (such as Hillary and John) had the lowest GPAs. This type of relationship is called *direct* or *positive*. In a direct relationship, those who score high on one variable tend to score high on the other, and those who score low on one variable tend to score low on the other.

Example 2 shows the relationship between a personality scale that measures willingness to take orders (on a scale from 0 to 20, where 20 represents eagerness to take orders) and the number of days served in county prison for a misdemeanor. Is there a relationship? If you consider the scores carefully, you will see that there is. Notice that those who have a high willingness to take orders (such as Jake and Dean) served the fewest days in prison, while prisoners who have a low willingness (such as Jason and Joan) served the most days in prison. Such a relationship is called *inverse* or *negative*. In an inverse relationship, those who score high on one variable tend to score low on the other.

Example 2

Prisoner	Willingness	Days served
Jake	20	3
Jason	1	65
Sarah	10	20
Dick	11	24
Dean	18	7
Joan	3	40

It is important to note that just because a correlation has been established, it does not necessarily indicate that a *causal relationship* exists. In a causal relationship, one variable causes changes in the other—that is, one variable affects the other. Consider the hypothetical relationship between willingness to take orders and days served in prison. Although a relationship was found, there could be many causal explanations. For instance, those who have better attorneys may have had better instruction on how to be compliant (and thus are willing to take orders), and those same prisoners' attorneys (because they are better) may have had greater success in getting them released from prison early. Many other causal explanations also may be possible for such a relationship.

In order to determine *cause and effect*, a controlled *experiment* in which one or more treatments are administered to participants is needed. If a treatment that is given to an experimental group leads to a change not found in a comparable control group, this would provide evidence regarding causality.

Even though we generally should not infer causality from a correlational study, correlation is still of interest to researchers for several reasons. First, correlations can provide hints about causality, which can later be explored in experiments. Second, correlations are helpful in understanding how well tests work. For instance, the College Board and the colleges that use its test are interested in how well the test works in predicting success in college, so it is not necessary to show what causes high GPAs in college in order to make the test useful as a predictor. Third, correlations are of interest in developing theories. For instance, a theory may predict that X should be correlated with Y. If a correlation is found, it helps to support the theory.

Up to this point, we have examined the scores of only small numbers of participants in clear-cut cases. However, in practice, large numbers of participants are usually studied, and there are almost always exceptions to an inverse or direct trend. Consider Example 3, which has the same students as Example 1 but with the addition of two others—Joe and Patricia.

Example 3

Student	SAT-V	GPA
John	333	1.0
Janet	756	3.8
Thomas	444	1.9
Scotty	629	3.2
Diana	501	2.3
Hillary	245	0.4
Joe	630	0.9
Patricia	404	3.1

Joe has a high SAT-V score but a very low GPA. He is an exception to the rule that high values on one variable are associated with high values on the other. There may be a variety of explanations for this exception: Joe may have had a family crisis during his first year in college, or he may have abandoned his good work habits in favor of late-night parties when he moved away from home to attend college. Patricia is another exception. Perhaps she made an extra effort to apply herself to college work, which could not be predicted by the SAT. When studying hundreds of participants, there will be many exceptions—some large and some small. To make sense of such data, some statistical techniques will be required, which will be explored in the next few sections of this book.

Terms to Review Before Attempting Worksheet 21

**correlation, direct *or* positive relationship,
inverse *or* negative relationship, causal relationship,
cause and effect, experiment**

**"I don't like to give a lot of homework over
the weekend, so just read every other word."**

Worksheet 21   Conceptual Introduction to Correlation

> *Riddle*: What happens just when you think you have hit bottom?

DIRECTIONS: To find the answer to the riddle, write the answer to each question in the space immediately below it. In the solution section, the word in parentheses next to the answer to the first question is the first word in the answer to the riddle, the word beside the answer to the second question is the second word, and so on.

1. In the examples in this section, how many scores did each individual have?

2

2. What is another term for a direct relationship?

positive

3. What is another term for an inverse relationship?

negative

4. Do the scores in the box immediately below indicate a direct *or* an inverse relationship?

direct

Student	Test A	Test B
Paula	9	3
Lucy	30	20
Mike	15	10
Christine	2	0
Rick	28	17

Worksheet 21 (continued)

5. "Establishing a correlation establishes a causal relationship." Is this statement true *or* false?

6. "A controlled experiment is desirable in order to establish a cause-and-effect relationship." Is this statement true *or* false?

7. Do the scores in the box immediately below indicate a direct relationship?

Participant	Depression scale	Cheerfulness scale
Edward	80	50
John	90	40
Barbara	100	30
Cynthia	110	20
William	120	10

8. When working with hundreds of participants, should an investigator expect many *or* few exceptions to an overall trend?

many

Solution section:

many (shovel)   few (low)   true (a)   false (you)   yes (illness)   2 (someone)

negative (above)   1 (loss)   inverse (weakness)   direct (tosses)   3 (sick)

positive (up)   no (bigger)   mixed (bourbon)   numerical (sickness)   4 (joining)

Worksheet 21 (continued)

Write the answer to the riddle here, putting one word on each line: Someone ___ up ___ above ___ tosses ___ you ___ a ___ bigger ___ shovel

Notes

Section 22   Scattergrams

A *scattergram* (also known as a *scatter diagram* or *scatterplot*) is a graphic representation of the relationship between two variables. Figure 1 shows the scattergram for the scores of the six participants who took the Scholastic Aptitude Test-Verbal (SAT-V) and their GPAs earned during their freshman year in college. (See Example 1 in Section 21 for a listing of the scores.)

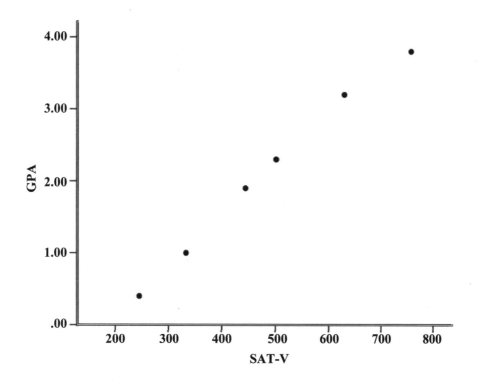

Figure 1. Scattergram for SAT-V scores and GPA.

There is one dot for each subject, and each dot is placed where the two scores for that subject intersect. Thus, the dot in the upper-right corner is for Janet, who had an SAT-V score of 756 and a GPA of 3.8. The dot in the lower-left corner is for Hillary, who had an SAT-V score of 245 and a GPA of 0.4.

The overall pattern in Figure 1 is from the lower-left corner to the upper-right corner. This indicates that there is a direct (i.e., positive) relationship. Because the pattern is very clear, this relationship is characterized as *very strong*.

Following are guidelines for constructing scattergrams:

1. Draw two axes of equal length. Notice that, though GPAs can vary from 0.00 to only 4.00 whereas SAT-V scores can vary from 200 to 800, the two axes in Figure 1 are equal. This was done by planning the spacing for each in advance.

2. Use graph paper.

3. Label each axis with the name of a variable. If one variable was measured before the other (e.g., the College Board's SAT was administered before college GPAs were earned), it is customary to place the one measured first on the *x*-axis (i.e., the horizontal axis).

4. Place one dot where the two scores for each individual intersect.

5. Label the scattergram as a *figure* and give it a number and a brief title.

Very strong relationships such as the one in Figure 1 are relatively rare in the social and behavioral sciences. Usually, there are a number of exceptions to the rule, and these exceptions create what is referred to as *scatter* on a scattergram. Figure 2 illustrates about the best that can be expected when using multiple-choice tests to predict subsequent academic achievement.

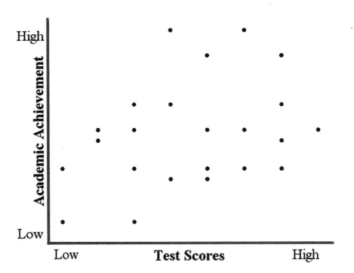

Figure 2. A direct relationship with many exceptions.

Notice that in Figure 2, the relationship is direct because the pattern of the dots is from lower left to upper right. There are, however, many exceptions to the overall pattern. Because of these exceptions, the relationship is characterized as direct and only moderately strong.

When a relationship is inverse, the pattern is from the upper-left corner to the lower-right corner, as illustrated in Figure 3. Notice that those subjects in the upper-left corner have low scores on Variable *X* but high scores on Variable *Y*. Those in the lower-right corner have high scores on Variable *X* but low scores on Variable *Y*.

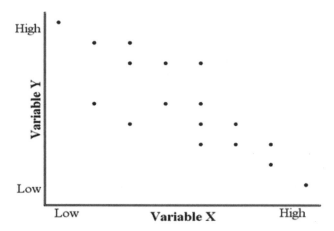

Figure 3. An inverse relationship.

Compare Figures 2 and 3. Not only are they different in direction (i.e., direct vs. inverse), they are also different in strength. The dots in Figure 3 cluster more tightly together than those in Figure 2. Therefore, Figure 3 represents a stronger relationship than that in Figure 2.

The three figures examined so far all have a common feature: They illustrate what are known as ***linear relationships***. In a linear relationship, the dots form a pattern that follows a single straight line (even though there may be scatter around the line). Such relationships are frequently found in nature as well as in the social and behavioral sciences.

Occasionally, investigators find ***curvilinear relationships***—one of which is illustrated in Figure 4 on the next page. The dots in this figure form a curve that, starting from the left, goes up for a while (indicating a direct relationship) and then turns downward (indicating an inverse relationship). Thus, the overall relationship is neither direct nor inverse. Instead, it is described as curvilinear.

Although curvilinear relationships are rare in the behavioral and social sciences, they can be very interesting. The variables for the hypothetical data in Figure 4 are anxiety and performance on a test of manual dexterity. The figure indicates that those who are extremely anxious about their performance and those who have very little anxiety both perform poorly on the test of dexterity. Those who are only moderately anxious perform best.

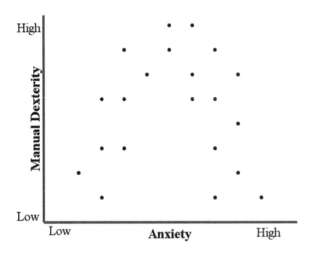

Figure 4. A curvilinear relationship.

Sometimes, there is no pattern in a scattergram, and the dots are scattered throughout, as in Figure 5. In this case, there is no discernible relationship.

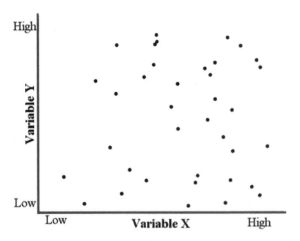

Figure 5. No relationship.

Constructing a scattergram should be the first step in analyzing the relationship between two variables. It gives a researcher an overview of the relationship and indicates whether it is linear. In the next several sections, statistics that concisely describe relationships are discussed.

Terms to Review Before Attempting Worksheet 22

scattergram (scatter diagram, scatterplot), linear relationships, curvilinear relationships

**"The reason I'm successful in statistics class
is because I'm lucky. But I didn't get lucky
until I started studying 90 hours a week!"**

Worksheet 22 Scattergrams

Riddle: What is the main problem with refusing to conform to the values of your peers?

DIRECTIONS: To find the answer to the riddle, write the answer to each question in the space immediately below it. In the solution section, the word in parentheses next to the answer to the first question is the first word in the answer to the riddle, the word beside the answer to the second question is the second word, and so on.

1. How many scores for each individual are required for a scattergram to be drawn?

    one

2. If the dots on a scattergram tend to go from the lower-left corner to the upper-right corner, is the relationship direct *or* inverse?

    direct

3. If the dots on a scattergram tend to go from the upper-left corner to the lower-right corner, is the relationship direct *or* inverse?

    inverse

4. If there is no pattern formed by the dots on a scattergram (with dots scattered throughout), is there a relationship?

    NO

5. What is the name for the type of relationship in which the dots follow a curve instead of a straight line?

    Curvilinear

128

Worksheet 22 (continued)

6. What is the name for the type of relationship in which the dots follow a straight line?   *linear*

7. Which one of the following scattergrams (A, B, or C) indicates the strongest relationship?   *C*

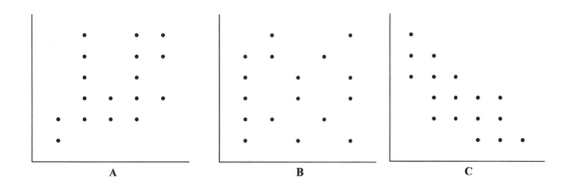

A   B   C

8. Which one of the scattergrams (A, B, or C) indicates the weakest relationship?   *B*

Solution section:

+(talking)   3 (self)   B (night)   C (every)   curved (back)

linear (alone)   none (lies)   2 (it)   <u>direct (gets)</u>   no (sitting)

A (fun)   <u>inverse (boring)</u>   lined (becoming)   curvilinear (home)   4 (friends)

Write the answer to the riddle here, putting one word on each line: *Talking gets boring Sitting home alone every night*

Notes

Section 23   Introduction to Sampling

Inferential statistics help researchers to make inferences (i.e., generalizations) from samples to populations. For instance, we might be interested in the attitudes of all registered nurses in Maryland toward individuals with AIDS. The nurses would constitute the population. If we administered an AIDS attitude scale to all these nurses, we would be studying the population, and the summarized results (such as means and standard deviations) would be referred to as *parameters*. If we studied only a sample of the nurses, the summarized results would be referred to as *statistics*.

No matter how researchers sample, it is always possible that the statistics obtained do not accurately reflect the population parameters that would have been obtained if researchers had studied the entire population. In fact, researchers always expect some amount of error when they have sampled.

If sampling creates errors, why do researchers sample? First, it is not always possible, for economic and physical reasons, to examine an entire population. Second, with proper sampling, researchers can obtain highly reliable results and can estimate the amount of error to allow for in the interpretations of the data.

The most important characteristic of a good sample is that it be free from *bias*. A bias exists whenever some members of a population have a greater chance of being selected for inclusion in the sample than others. Following are some examples that would produce biased samples:

- A professor wants to study the attitudes of all sophomores at a college (the population) but asks only those enrolled in her introductory psychology class (the sample) to participate in the study. Note that only those who are in the class have a chance of being selected. All other sophomores have no chance.

- A politician wants to predict the results of a citywide election (the population) but queries the intentions of only voters whom he encounters in a large shopping mall (the sample). Note that only those in the mall whom he decides to approach have a chance of being selected. All other voters have no chance.

- A magazine editor wants to determine the opinions of all rifle owners in the United States (the population) on gun-control measure but mails questionnaires only to those who subscribe to her magazine (the sample). Note that only subscribers have a chance to respond and that all other rifle owners have no chance.

In the previous examples, *samples of convenience* (also called *accidental samples*) were used, which increased the odds that some would be selected and reduced the odds that others would—but there is an additional problem. Even those who have a chance of being included may refuse to participate. This problem is often referred to as *volunteerism*. Volunteerism is presumed to create a bias because those who decide not to participate have no chance of being included in the data. Furthermore, many studies comparing participants with nonparticipants suggest that participants tend to be more highly educated and from higher socioeconomic-status (SES) groups than their counterparts. Efforts to reduce the effects of volunteerism include offering rewards, stressing to potential participants the importance of the study, and making it easy for people to respond, such as by providing them with a self-addressed, stamped envelope.

To eliminate bias, some form of *random sampling* is needed. A classic form of random sampling is *simple random sampling*.[1] In this technique, each member of the population is given an equal chance to be selected. A simple way to accomplish this with a small population is to put the name of each member of a population on a slip of paper, thoroughly mix the slips, and have a blindfolded assistant select the number desired for the sample. After the names have been selected, efforts must be made to encourage all of those selected to participate. If some members refuse, as often happens, we have a biased sample even though we started by creating an equal chance that any one person's name would be selected.

Suppose that we are fortunate. We have selected names using simple random sampling, and we have obtained the cooperation of everyone selected. In this case, we have an *unbiased sample*. Can we be certain that the results we obtain from the

---

[1]Another method for selecting a *simple random sample* and other types of random samples is described in Section 24.

sample accurately reflect those we would have obtained by studying the population? Certainly not! There is now the possibility of random errors, which statisticians call *sampling errors*. At random (i.e., by chance), we may have selected a disproportionately large number of Democrats, males, low-SES-group members, and so on. Such errors may affect the results.

If both biased and unbiased sampling is subject to error, why do researchers prefer unbiased sampling? They prefer it for two related reasons: (1) Inferential statistics allow researchers to estimate the amount of error to allow for when they are interpreting the results from unbiased samples, and (2) the amount of error obtained from unbiased samples is small when large samples are used.

It is important to note that selecting a very large biased sample does not reduce potential errors. For instance, if the politician (mentioned earlier) who is trying to predict the results of a citywide election is very persistent and spends weeks at the shopping mall asking all registered voters he encounters how they intend to vote, he will obtain a very large sample of people who may differ from the population of voters in various ways—such as by being more affluent, having more time to spend shopping, and so on. Increasing the sample size in this case will not reduce the amount of error due to bias.

Suppose that we have wisely decided to use random sampling. How large should the sample be? This depends on a variety of factors, but here are three generalizations that guide researchers:

1. The larger the sample, the better—but increasing sample size produces diminishing returns. For instance, using a sample of 200 instead of 100 has a much greater effect on reducing sampling errors than using a sample of 3,100 instead of 3,000. In concrete terms, this means that an extra 100 participants added to a small sample has a much greater effect on precision than adding 100 participants to a large sample. In fact, in many national surveys, samples of only 1,500 to 2,000 carefully selected participants yield highly accurate results.

2. When there is little variability in a population, even a small sample may yield highly accurate results. For instance, if you take a random sample of eggs that have been graded as "extra large" and weigh them, you will probably find only a small amount of variation among them. For this population, a small random

sample should yield an accurate estimate of the average weight of extra-large eggs.

3. When there is much variability in a population, small samples may produce data with much error. Suppose you wanted to estimate the math achievement of sixth graders in a very large metropolitan school district and drew a random sample of only 100 students. Because there is likely to be tremendous variation in math ability across a large school district, a sample of 100, even though it is random, could be very inaccurate. By chance, for instance, you may obtain a disproportionately large number of high achievers. Using a much larger sample would greatly reduce this possibility.

Often, it is impractical or impossible to use a random sample, yet information is needed from a sample in order for a decision to be made. For instance, a soft-drink manufacturer wishes to test-market a new soda but knows it is impractical to obtain a random sample of all potential customers in the United States. In this case, the manufacturer might resort to some form of *quota sampling*. Using previously collected national statistics on what the typical soda drinker is like in terms of gender, ethnicity, and income, the manufacturer might test the new product with a sample that has the same gender, ethnic, and income characteristics. The manufacturer could obtain the sample by screening people in public places or by going door-to-door until enough men and enough women are found, enough people from each ethnic group are found, and so on. Notice that this technique is *not* random and is subject to bias. Even if the manufacturer has the correct proportion of males, for instance, the males selected might tend to be from a particular region of the United States that has different tastes than the national population of male soda drinkers. Thus, the results of quota sampling should be viewed with skepticism.[2]

Strictly speaking, the inferential statistics in the rest of this book should be applied only to data obtained from random samples. In practice, however, they are

---

[2]Another approach in this situation is to test-market the product in selected areas of the country, focusing on areas that are believed to be *typical* of the country at large. This is called *purposive sampling* because the collection of areas is believed to have residents with characteristics similar to those of the national population.

often misapplied. When inferential statistics applied to results based on biased samples are encountered in journals and other sources, they should be viewed with caution.

Note that research in which biased samples are used does not always produce worthless results. There are many situations in which researchers have no choice but to use biased samples. For instance, for ethical and legal reasons, much medical research is conducted on volunteers who are willing to risk using a new medication or undergo a new procedure. If promising results are obtained in initial studies, larger studies with better (but usually still biased) samples are undertaken. At some point, despite the possible role of bias, decisions—such as Food and Drug Administration approval of a new drug—need to be made on the basis of biased samples. Little progress would be made in most fields if the results of all studies with biased samples were summarily dismissed.

Terms to Review Before Attempting Worksheet 23

parameters, statistics, bias, samples of convenience (accidental samples), volunteerism, random sampling, simple random sampling, unbiased sample, sampling errors, quota sampling

"My answers aren't wrong.
They just have random features."

Worksheet 23 Introduction to Sampling

Riddle: Why are people who can laugh at themselves
fortunate?

DIRECTIONS: To find the answer to the riddle, write the answer to each question in the space immediately below it. In the solution section, the word in parentheses next to the answer to the first question is the first word in the answer to the riddle, the word beside the answer to the second question is the second word, and so on.

1. Suppose the population of first-grade teachers in a school district was surveyed on their attitudes toward a curriculum change, and all of the teachers in the population participated. Then percentages were computed. Are the percentages statistics *or* parameters?

   parameters

2. A researcher wishes to generalize to all sociology students and uses volunteers in a sociology class as subjects. Is the sample biased *or* unbiased?

   biased

3. Suppose the names of all members of a population are put on slips of paper, the slips are thoroughly mixed, and 10% of the names are drawn for a sample. Is the group selected for the sample biased *or* unbiased?

   unbiased

4. What is the name of the type of sampling described in Question 3?

   random

5. Can a researcher be certain that there are no sampling errors if he or she uses random sampling?

   NO

Worksheet 23 (continued)

6. "Using a very large sample is an effective way to reduce the errors created by a bias in sampling." Is this statement true *or* false?

false

7. Assume that Population A has very little variability and that Population B has much variability. For which population would a larger sample be needed for precise results to be achieved?

population B

8. "Adding individuals produces diminishing returns in terms of reducing sampling errors." Is this statement true *or* false?

True

Solution section:

> parameters (because)   statistics (happy)   quota (are)   biased (they)
>
> yes (becoming)   unbiased (will)   Population A (thoughtful)
>
> simple random sampling (never)   sample size (joke)   no (cease)   false (to)
>
> true (amused)   Population B (be)   sample size (speed)   volunteerism (laughter)

Write the answer to the riddle here, putting one word on each line: *because   they   will   never   cease   to   be   amused*

Section 24   A Closer Look at Sampling

As noted in the previous section, an unbiased sample may be obtained by using **simple random sampling**. Putting names on slips of paper and drawing the number needed for the sample is a classic method for obtaining such a sample. For larger populations, it is more efficient to use a **table of random numbers**, a portion of which is shown in Table 2 near the end of this book.[1] In this table, there is no sequence to the numbers, and in a large table, each number appears about the same amount of times. To use the table, first assign each individual in the population a *number name*. For instance, if there are 90 people in the population, name the first person 01, the second person 02, the third person 03, and so on, until you reach the last person, whose number is 90.[2]

To use the table, go to any page in a book of random numbers and put your finger on the page without looking to determine your starting point. Suppose your finger landed on the upper-left corner of Table 2. Because each person has a two-digit number name, the first two digits identify the first subject. In this case, the number is 21, so Individual Number 21 is selected. The next two digits to the right (ignoring the spaces between the columns, which are provided only as a visual aid while reading the table) are 0 and 4. Thus, Person 04 is also selected for the sample. The next two-digit number is 98. Because the population only has 90 individuals, this number does not select anyone. To the right, the next number is 08, which is the number of the next person drawn. Continue moving across the rows to select the sample.

Stratified random sampling is usually superior to *simple random sampling*. In this technique, the population is first divided into strata (i.e., subgroups) that are believed to be relevant to the variable(s) being studied. Suppose, for instance, that you wanted to conduct a survey of opinions on women serving in political leadership roles. If you suspected that men and women might differ in their opinions on

---

[1]Books of random numbers can be located online and in academic libraries. Statistical computer programs can also generate them.

[2]The number of digits in the number names must equal the number of digits in the population total. For instance, if there are 500 people in a population, there are three digits in the total, and there must be three digits in each name. Thus, the first case in this population would be named 001.

this issue, it would be desirable to first stratify the population according to gender and then draw separately from each stratum at random. Specifically, you would draw a random sample of men and separately draw a random sample of women.

When drawing a stratified random sample, the same percentage should be drawn from each stratum (i.e., each subgroup). For instance, if you wanted to sample 10% of a population consisting of 1,600 men and 2,000 women, you would draw 160 men and 200 women. Notice that there are more women than men in the sample, which is appropriate because women are more numerous in the population. It is important to notice that the purpose of stratifying is *not* to compare men with women. Rather, the purpose is to obtain a sample of the entire population that is representative in terms of gender.[3] With stratified random sampling, we have retained the benefit of randomization (i.e., the elimination of bias) and gained the advantage of having appropriate proportions of men and women. If your hunch that men and women differ was correct, you would have increased the precision of the results by stratifying.[4]

Note that stratifying does not eliminate sampling errors. For instance, when drawing the women at random, you may, by chance, have obtained women for the sample who are not representative of all women in the population. The same, of course, holds true for men. However, you have eliminated sampling errors associated with gender because if you had used *simple random sampling,* you could have obtained a disproportionately large number of either men or women.

For large-scale studies, ***multistage random sampling*** may be used. In this technique, you might draw a sample of counties at random from all counties in the country, then draw voting precincts at random from all precincts in the counties selected, and finally draw individual voters at random from all precincts that were sampled. In multistage random sampling, stratification can be incorporated into the sampling plan. For instance, you could first stratify the counties into rural, suburban, and urban, and then separately draw counties at random from these three types of counties—ensuring that all three types of counties are included.

---

[3]If the purpose was to compare men with women, then it would be acceptable to draw the same number of each and compare averages or percentages for the two samples.
[4]Of course, if your hunch that men and women differ in their opinions was wrong, the use of stratification would be of no benefit, but it would not introduce any additional errors beyond random errors.

An alternative sampling method is ***cluster sampling***, which is useful if it is done at random. For cluster sampling to be used, all members must belong to a cluster (i.e., an existing group). For instance, all Boy Scouts belong to a troop, all students belong to a homeroom, and so on. Unlike simple random sampling, in which individuals are drawn, in cluster sampling, *clusters* (i.e., groups) are drawn. To conduct a survey of Boy Scouts, for instance, you could draw a random sample of troops, contact the leaders of the selected troops, and ask them to administer the questionnaires.

The advantages of cluster sampling are obvious: There are fewer people to contact (only the Boy Scout leaders), and the degree of cooperation is likely to be greater if a leader asks the scouts to participate. There is a disadvantage, however, that results from the fact that clusters often are homogeneous in some way. For instance, suppose that you drew 10 troops (i.e., clusters) at random, and 9 of them, by chance, were in major urban areas. (Note that scouts in major urban areas may have different attitudes and skills from those in rural areas.) Even though there might be about 20 scouts in each troop, which would yield responses from about 200 scouts, the number 200 is misleading because the sample size is 10 and *not* 200. If you had drawn 200 Boy Scouts by simple random sampling, it is very unlikely that you would have selected such a disproportionate number of scouts from urban areas. Thus, when using cluster sampling, it is desirable to use a large number of clusters to overcome this disadvantage.

Terms to Review Before Attempting Worksheet 24

simple random sampling, table of random numbers, stratified random sampling, multistage random sampling, cluster sampling

Worksheet 24 A Closer Look at Sampling

> **Riddle: How are minds like parachutes?**

DIRECTIONS: To find the answer to the riddle, write the answer to each question in the space immediately below it. In the solution section, the word in parentheses next to the answer to the first question is the first word in the answer to the riddle, the word beside the answer to the second question is the second word, and so on.

1. Suppose that the size of a population is 50 and that the members of the population are numbered from 01 to 50. If you draw a sample starting at the beginning of the fifth row in Table 2 near the end of this book, what is the number of the second case drawn?

2. Referring to the information in Question 1, what is the number of the third case drawn?

3. Suppose that the size of a population is 352 and that its members are numbered from 001 to 352. If you draw a sample starting at the beginning of the first row in Table 2 near the end of this book, what is the number of the second case drawn?

4. Suppose that you want to use stratified random sampling to obtain a sample from a population in which there are 600 freshmen, 500 sophomores, 450 juniors, and 400 seniors. Should you draw the same number *or* the same percentage from each grade level?

Worksheet 24 (continued)

5. Suppose that you randomly draw 10% of the Democrats, then, separately, randomly draw 10% of the Republicans, and finally randomly draw 10% of all other registered voters from a population. Are you using simple random sampling, stratified random sampling, *or* cluster sampling?

6. Is the purpose of stratified random sampling, as described in this section, to produce two or more samples to be compared?

7. If you used cluster sampling and drew at random 30 clusters with 10 members each, is the sample size 30, 10, or 300?

8. If you take a master list of all class sections being taught on a college campus and draw 50 sections at random, are you using simple random sampling, stratified random sampling, *or* cluster sampling?

Solution section:

498 (lonely)   no (they)   same number (feeling)   30 (are)   10 (others)

cluster sampling (open)   stratified random sampling (when)   58 (jumping)

25 (they)   17 (will)   300 (prophet)   same percentage (function)   83 (run)

multistage random sampling (he)   088 (only)   simple random sampling (it)

Worksheet 24 (continued)

Write the answer to the riddle here, putting one word on
each line: _____ _____ _____ _____

_____ _____ _____ _____

"Whenever I'm overwhelmed by statistics
homework and I need a sunnier outlook,
I just turn up the brightness control."

Section 25   Introduction to Probability

Sampling at random from a population (see Sections 23 and 24) introduces random or chance errors, which are called **sampling errors**. Much of the rest of this book is concerned with how to assess the possible role of sampling errors on observations of a random sample from a population. Probabilities (the likelihood of something occurring) are used in this assessment.

Informally, we all use probabilities to make daily decisions. When we are considering crossing a street, we judge the odds (i.e., the probability) that we will make it safely to the other side before the approaching traffic reaches us. When we hear in the morning that the probability of rain that day is 60%, we make decisions about what to wear and whether to take an umbrella with us.

In a more formal manner, using probability theory, scientists make decisions after assessing the odds that random errors may have created the differences or relationships that they are examining.

Here are a few basic **principles of probability**:

1. Mutually exclusive events that are the result of chance are independent of each other.

When applied to events, the term **mutually exclusive** means that they are completely separate and have no bearing on each other. To understand this meaning, consider a state lottery in which the numbers 1 through 46 may be drawn. Suppose that the number 39 is drawn first one week. What were the odds that a 39 would be the first number drawn? Obviously, the odds were 1 in 46, or 1/46, which is equivalent to .02 (obtained by dividing 1 by 46). The following week, all 46 numbers are again in play (a mutually exclusive event). What are the odds that 39 will be the first number drawn again? They are still 1 in 46, or .02. Thus, knowledge of what was drawn one week gives a player no advantage in selecting numbers the next week because the events are mutually exclusive.

2. Summing the probabilities of separate (mutually exclusive) events determines the probability that any of them will occur.

In a lottery with 46 numbers, the odds that 39 will be drawn are 1/46, or .02.

The odds that 24 will be drawn are also 1/46 when all numbers are in play. Thus, the odds that 39 *or* 24 will be drawn are 1/46 + 1/46 = 2/46 = 1/23, or .04. Clearly, the probability that *either* 39 *or* 24 will be drawn is twice as great as the odds that just one of the numbers will be drawn.

3. If something is certain to occur, the probability of its occurrence is 1.00.

In a lottery with 46 numbers, the probability that any one of the 46 numbers will be drawn is 1.00.

4. If something is certain *not* to occur, the probability of its nonoccurrence is 0.00.

If a lottery is canceled and no numbers are drawn, the probability that any of them will be drawn is 0.00.

5. Calculating the product of the separate probabilities determines the probability of their successive occurrence.

To keep it simple for instructional purposes, assume that after a number is drawn in a lottery, it is placed back in play so that there are 46 numbers that may be drawn each time a draw is made. What is the probability that 39 *and* 24 will both be drawn in a given lottery? The fifth principle indicates that it is 1/46 × 1/46, which equals 1/2116, or .00047. This is a highly unlikely event. If you have to correctly select 6 numbers out of the 46 that will be drawn in a given lottery in order to win, you can determine your odds of success by multiplying 1/46 by itself six times. Using a typical calculator to do this (multiplying .02 by .02 by .02, etc.), you will find that your calculator will very quickly run out of decimal places for zeros. In other words, your calculator will run out of room to hold all the zero place holders and tell you that your odds are essentially zero. Of course, there is an extremely small probability that you will win, but a typical calculator cannot show such a small probability.

In Section 26, we will examine how probabilities relate to the normal curve, which is important for understanding concepts covered later in this book.

Terms to Review Before Attempting Worksheet 25

sampling errors, principles of probability, mutually exclusive

"I used a $3,000 computer, a $1,200 laser printer,
and a $300 data-processing program—
and I still got a D on my statistics project!"

Worksheet 25 Introduction to Probability

Riddle: **What principle applies to both levying taxes and shearing sheep?**

DIRECTIONS: To find the answer to the riddle, write the answer to each question in the space immediately below it. In the solution section, the word in parentheses next to the answer to the first question is the first word in the answer to the riddle, the word beside the answer to the second question is the second word, and so on.

1. If something is certain to occur, what is the probability that it will occur, expressed as a proportion (express the answer to four decimal places)?

    1.0000

2. If it is certain that something will not occur, what is the probability that it will not occur, expressed as a proportion?

    0.0000

3. What is the probability that 2 *and* 8 will be drawn in a given lottery in which there are 20 numbers in play on each draw?

    0.0025

4. What is the probability that 2 *and* 8 will be drawn in a given lottery in which there are 10 numbers in play on each draw?

    0.0100

5. Assume that a deck of 52 cards is shuffled, and a king of hearts is drawn. Then the king of hearts is put back in the deck, the 52 cards are shuffled again, and another card is drawn. Is the probability that a king of hearts will be drawn the second time the same as the probability that it would be drawn the first time?

    yes

Worksheet 25 (continued)

6. If you know that 2 was drawn in a lottery one week, does this help you select numbers in an independent lottery the next week?

NO

7. If a deck of 52 cards is shuffled, what is the probability, expressed as a proportion, that a jack of diamonds will be drawn?

1/52 , 0.0192

8. If a deck of 52 cards is shuffled, what is the probability, expressed as a proportion, that any of the four aces will be drawn?

0.0769

9. If the probability that Event A will occur is .005 and the probability that Event B will occur is .01, which event has a greater probability of occurring?

event B

Solution section:

Event A (government)   1/52 (painful)   Event B (skin)   1.0000 (you)

0.2500 (kill)   0.0000 (should)   0.0025 (stop)   0.0500 (Congress)

0.0100 (when)   yes (you)   0.0192 (to)   no (get)   100% (likely)

0.0769 (the)   0.0050 (broke)   probability (screaming)

Write the answer to the riddle here, putting one word on each line: you   should   stop   when   you   get   to   the   skin

Notes

Section 26   Probability and the Normal Curve

With the empirical approach to knowledge, we make observations and, based on them, make decisions. From previous observations, we can establish probabilities regarding the occurrence of specific events in the future. Weather forecasting is based on this approach. Events such as high- and low-pressure systems are observed, and predictions are based on previous observations of their effects on the weather.

Fortunately, for many problems, empirical probabilities are easy to determine because many distributions are normal.[1] Suppose that we conducted a large national survey to determine knowledge of basic math skills. Suppose we found that the distribution of math scores was normal, the mean was 50.00, and the standard deviation was 7.00. This information can be used to establish probabilities. To do so, we will need to use z-scores. (See Section 18 to review z-scores.) You may recall that the formula for them is

$$z = \frac{X - M}{S}$$

In this example, what is the probability of drawing an individual who has a score of 64 or higher at random from the population? To answer the question, first calculate the corresponding z-score (keeping in mind that the mean is 50.00 and the standard deviation is 7.00).

$$z = \frac{64 - 50.00}{7.00} = \frac{14}{7} = 2.00$$

X – score
M – mean
S – standard deviation

Second, look up the z-score in Table 1 near the end of this book. There, we find that the proportion of scores at or less than 2 is .9772. Because we are interested in scores that are higher than 2, we can subtract .9772 from 1 to get .0228 (or 2.28%). Our probability of .0228 indicates that there are only slightly more than 2 chances in 100 of drawing a person with a score of 64 or higher from the population. This is referred to as a ***one-tailed probability*** because we asked the question about

---

[1]The normal curve was first introduced in Section 10 and was discussed in Sections 15 through 20.

only the upper tail of the normal distribution—the right-hand tail of the distribution in Figure 1.

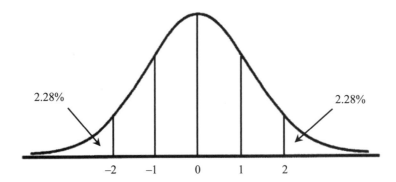

Figure 1. Normal distribution with selected *z*-scores.

Suppose, instead, that we asked this question: What is the probability of randomly drawing an individual with a *z*-score as high as 2.00 (or higher) *or* as low as –2.00 (or lower)? Obviously, the odds of doing so are double those of drawing just one of these. Thus, the odds are $2 \times .0228 = .0456$, which is a little more than 4 in 100. This is called a ***two-tailed probability*** because we are asking about the odds of drawing an individual at either tail of the normal distribution (see the percentages associated with each tail in Figure 1). The importance of distinguishing between one-tailed and two-tailed probabilities will become clear in later sections of this book.

The probabilities for both events described above represent ***unlikely events***. In most sciences, conventional wisdom indicates that any event that has a probability of occurrence of .05 or less is usually classified as unlikely to occur at random. A *z*-score of 1.96 has only a 2.5% chance of occurrence as a one-tailed probability. As a two-tailed probability, it has a 5.0% chance of occurrence $(2 \times 2.5\% = 5.0\%)$. Thus, an event with a *z*-score of 1.96 or greater or –1.96 or less (such as 1.97 or –1.97) is classified as an unlikely event.

A *z*-score of 2.58 or higher has only a .49% (or just less than 1/2 of 1%) chance of occurrence. The corresponding two-tailed probability is .98%, or almost 1%, for *z*-scores of 2.58 or –2.58. Some researchers only classify an event as unlikely if its likelihood is 1% or less.

There is no rule of nature that says at what point an event should be classified as unlikely. However, the 5% and 1% guidelines have evolved over time as the two most widely used. The only universally accepted rule is that a researcher must decide *in advance* of examining the data what guideline will be followed for declaring an event unlikely. Theoretically, any percentage may be specified, but to be accepted in most scientific circles, 5% or lower is generally used.

Identifying unlikely events is the basis of many of the tests of statistical significance presented in later sections of this book.

Terms to Review Before Attempting Worksheet 26

one-tailed probability, two-tailed probability, unlikely events

**"I have a photographic memory—
I just seem to be out of film today."**

Worksheet 26   Probability and the Normal Curve

> **Riddle:** What did George Washington do when he was asked for his ID?

DIRECTIONS: To find the answer to the riddle, write the answer to each question in the space immediately below it. In the solution section, the word in parentheses next to the answer to the first question is the first word in the answer to the riddle, the word beside the answer to the second question is the second word, and so on.

1. What is the one-tailed probability of drawing a subject with a z-score of 1.35 or higher at random from a normal distribution?

$$1- 0.9115 = 0.0885$$

2. What is the one-tailed probability of drawing a subject with a z-score of -1.70 or lower at random from a normal distribution?

$$0.0446$$

3. What is the two-tailed probability of drawing a subject with a z-score as extreme as 1.80 *or* -1.80 at random from a normal distribution?

$$0.0359 \times 2 = 0.0718$$
$$0.9641$$

4. For a normal distribution with a mean of 100.00 and a standard deviation of 16.00, what is the one-tailed probability of drawing a subject with a score of 124 or greater at random from a normal distribution?

$$z = \frac{124 - 100}{16} = 1.5 = 0.9332$$
$$1- 0.9332 = 0.0668$$

5. For a normal distribution with a mean of 40.00 and a standard deviation of 8.00, what is the one-tailed probability of drawing a subject with a score of 30 or <u>less</u> at random from a normal distribution?

$$z = \frac{30 - 40}{8} = -1.25 = 0.1056$$

Worksheet 26 (continued)

6. According to the information in Question 5, what is the probability of drawing a subject with a score as extreme as 30 or 50 at random from a normal distribution?

$$0.1056 \times 2 = 0.2112$$

7. According to the 5% guideline, should the answer to Question 2 be classified as an unlikely event?

yes

8. According to the 1% guideline, should the answer to Question 5 be classified as an unlikely event?

NO

Solution section:

.4554 (Congress)	no (it)	.0359 (public)	yes (showed)	.0718 (out)✗
.2112 (and)✗	.1336 (fooling)	.1056 (quarter)✗	.1770 (deficit)	
.0668 (a)✗	.0885 (he)✗	.9554 (politicians)	.0446 (whipped)✗	.4115 (saying)

Write the answer to the riddle here, putting one word on each line: __He__ __whipped__ __out__ __a__ __quarter__ __and__ __showed__ __it__

155

Notes

Section 27   Percentiles and the Normal Curve

The major advantage of using standard scores is that you can use them to compare measures from different scales. For instance, suppose Hannah takes two college entrance exams—one has a total possible of 36 points (the ACT) and the other has a total possible of 2,400 points (the SAT). She can convert her raw scores to standard scores to compare the two. However, sometimes the comparison is more intuitive when using percentile ranks. A ***percentile rank*** is the percentage of scores at or below a given score. If Hannah's ACT score is in the 95th percentile, then 95% of the people who took the same test scored at or below Hannah. If her SAT score is in the 81st percentile, then we know that she did better on the ACT than the SAT.

Sometimes we need to convert from a percentile rank to a raw score. For instance, assume that Noah wants to apply to a college that only accepts students who score above the 90th percentile on the SAT. He has not taken the exam yet and wants to know what his target SAT score is. We can find that number by reversing the steps we used in the previous section.

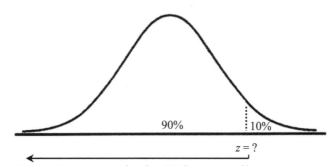

Figure 1. A score in the 90th percentile.

To review the use of Table 1 near the end of this book, we use both the left-most column and the top row as labels for z. For instance, the proportion of scores to the left of a z-value of 0.12 can be found in the row for .010 and the column for .02 (a proportion of .5478).

In Noah's case, the 90th percentile is above the mean (i.e., the 50th percentile), so we look in the positive values section of Table 1. Instead of using the row and column labels as we did when we knew the value of z, we will now search through the proportions in the middle of the table. The 90th percentile will have a value of .9000, and we want to find a value as close to that number as possible. There are two proportions that come very close: .8997 and .9015. Because .8997 is closest to our target, we use the row and column labels to identify the associated z-value of 1.28. At this point, we are not finished because we still want to know the SAT score (i.e., the raw score, or X-value) that Noah needs to obtain.

Recall that when calculating z-scores from X-values, we used the following formula:

$$z = \frac{X - M}{S}$$

To solve for X, the equation is changed to the following:

$$X = z(S) + M$$

If we know that the mean SAT score is 1,500 with a standard deviation of 100, then we can find the raw score necessary for Noah to earn on the SAT test:

$$X = 1.28(100) + 1,500 = 1,628$$

Term to Review Before Attempting Worksheet 27

percentile rank

Worksheet 27   Percentiles and the Normal Curve

> ### *Riddle*: Why are math books always unhappy?

DIRECTIONS: To find the answer to the riddle, write the answer to each question in the space immediately below it. In the solution section, the word in parentheses next to the answer to the first question is the first word in the answer to the riddle, the word beside the answer to the second question is the second word, and so on.

1. A percentile rank is the percentage of scores _____ a given score.

2. What equation do we use when finding the raw score?

Assume that the mean height is 70 inches with a standard deviation of 6 inches.

3. If Anne is 82 inches tall, what is her percentile rank?

4. If Kendra is 64 inches tall, what is her percentile rank?

5. If James is in the 77th percentile, what is his height?

6. If Alex is in the 25th percentile, what is his height?

7. What percentage of people is between 66 and 82 inches?

Worksheet 27 (continued)

8. What percentage of people is between 64 and 76 inches?

Solution section:

76 (puzzle)   98 (always) $(X - M)/S$ (never)   16 (have)   near (rather)   73 (of)

68 (problems) $z(S) + M$ (they)   2 (the)   64.5 (binder)   66 (lot)

at or below (because)   50 (since)   74 (a)

Write the answer to the riddle here, putting one word on each line: _____   _____   _____   _____
_____   _____   _____   _____

Section 28   Standard Error of the Mean

Suppose there is a large population with a mean of 100.00 and a standard deviation of 16.00 on a standardized test. Further, suppose that we do not have this information but wish to estimate the mean and standard deviation by testing a sample. When we draw a random sample and administer the test to just the sample, will we correctly estimate the population mean as 100.00? Probably not. Remember that random sampling introduces random or chance errors, which are called *sampling errors*.

Even though we cannot be sure the sample has provided accurate results, we have the advantage of using an unbiased, random sample—meaning that no factors are systematically pushing the estimate in the wrong direction. In addition, by using a large sample, the likelihood of getting a good estimate of the population from a sample is increased.[1]

When using random sampling, the **central limit theorem** is of great importance. To understand this theorem, first consider the **sampling distribution of means**. Suppose that we drew not just one sample but many samples at random. That is, we drew a sample of 60, tested the subjects, and computed the mean…then drew another sample of 60, tested the subjects, and computed the mean…then drew a third sample of 60, tested the subjects, and computed the mean…and so on. We would have a very large number of means—known as the *sampling distribution of means*. The central limit theorem says that the distribution of these means is normal in shape. The normal shape will emerge even if the underlying distribution is skewed, provided that the sample size is reasonably large (about 60 or more). The mean of an indefinitely large sampling distribution of means will equal the population mean. The standard deviation of the sampling distribution is known as the **standard error of the mean** (SE_m). Keep in mind that the means vary from each other only because of chance errors created by random sampling. That is, we are drawing random samples from the same population and administering the same test over and over, so all of the means should have the same value except for the effects of random errors. Therefore, there is variation among the means only because of

---

[1] See Sections 23 and 24 for more information on sampling.

sampling errors. For this reason, the standard deviation of the sampling distribution is known as the *standard error of the mean.*

In practice, we usually draw a single sample, test it, and calculate its mean and standard deviation.[2] Therefore, we are not certain of the value of the population mean, nor do we know the value of the standard error of the mean that we would obtain if we had sampled repeatedly. Fortunately, we do know two very useful things:

1. The larger the sample, the smaller the standard error of the mean.
2. The less the variability in the population, the smaller the standard error of the mean. For instance, consider a population in which there is no variability— that is, in which all subjects are identical. In this case, the standard error of the mean (i.e., the standard deviation of the sampling distributions of means) equals 0.00 (i.e., all the means will be identical and their standard deviation will be zero). In practice, we cannot be certain how much variability there is in a population from which we have only sampled. However, we can use the standard deviation of the sample that we have drawn as an estimate of the amount of variability in the population. For instance, if we observed a very small standard deviation for a random sample, it would be reasonable to guess that the population has relatively little variation.

Using these two facts and some statistical theory that is not covered here, statisticians have developed the following formula for estimating the standard error of the mean, based only on the information we have about a given random sample from a population:[3]

$$SE_m = \frac{s}{\sqrt{n}}$$

Consider the application of the formula in the following three examples to see how it works.

---

[2]Use the second formula in Appendix A near the end of this book when estimating the standard deviation of a population from a sample.

[3] A more precise estimate can be obtained by subtracting 1 from n. This adjustment is especially appropriate when a sample size (n) is less than 60.

Example 1

For a randomly selected sample, $m = 75.00$, $s = 16.00$, and $n = 64$. If we divide 16.00 by the square root of 64 (i.e., 8), we estimate that the standard error of the mean equals 2.00. This is an estimate of a ***margin of error*** that we should keep in mind when interpreting the sample mean of 75.00.

Keep in mind, too, that the standard error of the mean is an estimate of the standard deviation of the sampling distribution of the means, which is normal in shape when the sample size is relatively large. You may recall from your study of the standard deviation that about 68% of the cases lie within one standard deviation unit of the mean. Thus, we would expect about 68% of all sample means to lie within 2.00 points of the true (or population) mean. If we used the mean of 75.00—which was actually obtained—as an estimate of the population mean based on a random sample, we could estimate that odds are 68 out of 100 that the population mean lies between 73.00 ($75.00 - 2.00 = 73.00$) and 77.00 ($75.00 + 2.00 = 77.00$). The values 73.00 and 77.00 are known as the ***limits of the 68% confidence interval for the mean***. That is, the true mean lies between 73.00 and 77.00 for 68% of all possible samples.

Example 2

For a randomly selected sample, $m = 75.00$, $s = 16.00$, and $n = 128$. If we divide 16.00 by the square root of 128 (i.e., 11.314), we estimate that the standard error of the mean equals 1.41. Notice that this is substantially smaller than the standard error we obtained in Example 1. This is because the sample size is twice that of Example 1. However, notice also that the standard error has not been cut in half. This is because we are dividing by the *square root* of n.[4]

The limits of the 68% confidence interval for Example 2 are 73.59 ($75.00 - 1.41 = 73.59$) and 76.41 ($75 + 1.41 = 76.41$). The larger sample size in Example 2 has given us a smaller confidence interval than in Example 1.

---

[4]You may recall from Section 23 that increasing the sample size produces diminishing returns, which is clearly illustrated here.

Example 3

For a randomly selected sample, $m = 75.00$, $s = 5.00$, and $n = 128$. If we divide 5.00 by the square root of 128 (i.e., 11.314), we estimate that the standard error of the mean equals 0.44. The limits of the 68% confidence interval are 74.56 and 75.44. The smaller standard deviation in Example 3 has given us a smaller confidence interval than in Example 2.

A small confidence interval is desirable because it indicates that the sample mean is probably close to the true population mean. Of the two variables that affect the size of the standard error of the mean—the sample size and the variability of the sample—we often have direct control of the sample size. By using reasonably large samples, we can minimize the standard error of the mean.

Of course, 68% confidence is far short of certainty. The next section covers how to build 95% and 99% confidence intervals—intervals within which we can have much greater confidence in where the population mean lies.[5]

It is important to keep in mind that the confidence limits are valid only if we analyze the results obtained with unbiased (random) sampling. Each bias has its own unique and usually unknown effect on the results, and there are no generalizable techniques for estimating the amount of error created by them.

---

[5] Appendix F near the end of this book presents the formulas for calculating the standard error of a median and the standard error of a percentage.

Terms to Review Before Attempting Worksheet 28

**central limit theorem, sampling distribution of means,
standard error of the mean, margin of error,
limits of the 68% confidence interval for the mean**

GLASBERGEN

**"Statistics show that to prevent a heart attack, you should
take one aspirin every day. Take it out for a jog,
then take it to the gym, then take it for a bike ride…."**

Worksheet 28 Standard Error of the Mean

> *Riddle*: According to Frank Lloyd Wright, how are
> the truth and the facts related?

DIRECTIONS: To find the answer to the riddle, write the answer to each question in the space immediately below it. In the solution section, the word in parentheses next to the answer to the first question is the first word in the answer to the riddle, the word beside the answer to the second question is the second word, and so on.

1. What is the name of the theorem that says a large sampling distribution of means will be normal in shape?

2. "Other things being equal, the larger the sample size, the larger the standard error of the mean." Is this statement true *or* false?

3. "Other things being equal, the greater the variability in a population, the greater the amount of error that can be expected when we sample." Is this statement true *or* false?

4. If we double the size of a sample, can we expect to have half the amount of error due to random sampling?

5. For a randomly selected sample, $m = 50.00$, $s = 10.00$, and $n = 64$. What is the value of the standard error of the mean?

Worksheet 28 (continued)

6. For a randomly selected sample, $m = 50.00$, $s = 10.00$, and $n = 144$. What is the value of the standard error of the mean?

7. For a randomly selected sample, $m = 100.00$, $s = 16.00$, and $n = 100$. What are the limits of the 68% confidence interval for the mean?

8. For a randomly selected sample, the mean equals 90.00 and the standard error of the mean equals 5.22. What are the limits of the 68% confidence interval for the mean?

Solution section:

84.78–95.22 (facts)   standard error theorem (justice)   98.40–101.60 (the)

yes (Bible)   1.25 (important)   5.00 (lawyer)   0.15 (court)

no (more)   true (is)   false (truth)   central limit theorem (the)   0.83 (than)

4.17 (being)   6.25 (building)   0.16 (commandment)   84.00–116.00 (seeking)

Write the answer to the riddle here, putting one word on each line: _____ _____ _____ _____

_____ _____ _____ _____

Notes

Section 29 Confidence Interval for the Mean

The previous section of this book showed how to compute the standard error of the mean (SE_m) and how to use it to calculate the limits of the 68% confidence interval for a mean. Often, it is desirable to calculate limits in which we can have more than 68% confidence. This section shows how to do this for reasonably large sample sizes (about 60 or more).[1]

To determine the limits of the **95% confidence interval** (95% CI) for a mean, first multiply the standard error of the mean by the constant 1.96. Then, both add the product to the mean and subtract it from the mean. This process is illustrated in Example 1.[2]

Example 1
If $m = 40.00$ and $SE_m = 1.50$, then the limits of the 95% confidence interval for the mean are obtained as follows:

First: $(1.50)(1.96) = 2.94$

Second: $40.00 - 2.94 = 37.06$

Third: $40.00 + 2.94 = 42.94$

Thus, the limits of the 95% confidence interval are 37.06 and 42.94. The **lower limit** is 37.06, and the **upper limit** is 42.94. Therefore, we can state with 95% confidence that the true (i.e., population) mean lies between 37.06 and 42.94.

The process followed in Example 1 to obtain the 95% confidence interval is expressed by this formula:

$$95\% \text{ CI} = m \pm (1.96)(SE_m)$$

Note that the limits of the 68% confidence interval for Example 1 are 38.50 ($40.00 - 1.50$) and 41.50 ($40.00 + 1.50$). Thus, the 95% confidence interval

---

[1] With 60 or more, answers will be very close to the precise answer. Refer to Appendix G near the end of this book to learn how to build intervals when the sample size is less than 60.

[2] You may recall the value of 1.96 from the table of the normal curve (see Table 1 near the end of this book). Going out 1.96 standard deviation units from the mean in both directions captures 95% of the cases in a normal distribution (see explanation in Section 17).

(37.06 – 42.94) is larger than the 68% confidence interval. In more general terms, to obtain a greater degree of confidence for a given set of data, we have to allow for a larger interval as our estimate of where the true mean lies. Having a larger interval means more possibilities are included, which results in more confidence that one of these possibilities is the true mean.

To determine the limits of the ***99% confidence interval*** (99% CI) for a mean, first multiply the standard error of the mean by the constant 2.58. Then both add the product to the mean and subtract it from the mean. This process is illustrated in Example 2.[3]

Example 2

If m = 40.00 and SE_m = 1.50, then the limits of the 99% confidence interval for the mean are obtained as follows:

First: (1.50)(2.58) = 3.87

Second: 40.00 – 3.87 = 36.13

Third: 40.00 + 3.87 = 43.87

Thus, the limits of the 99% confidence interval are 36.13 and 43.87. The lower limit is 36.13, and the upper limit is 43.87. We can state with 99% confidence that the true (i.e., population) mean lies between 36.13 and 43.87.

The process followed in Example 2 to obtain the 99% confidence interval is expressed by this formula:

99% CI = $m \pm (2.58)(SE_m)$

Notice that the interval for 99% confidence is larger than the interval for 95% confidence, illustrating again that for a higher degree of confidence, we have to allow for a greater range of possibilities.

In review, if m = 40.00 and SE_m = 1.50, then

68% CI = 38.50 – 41.50 (an interval 3.00 points wide)

95% CI = 37.06 – 42.94 (an interval 5.88 points wide)

99% CI = 36.13–43.87 (an interval 7.74 points wide)

---

[3]You may recall from Table 1 near the end of this book that if you go out 2.58 standard deviation units on both sides of the mean in a normal distribution, you capture 99% of the cases.

At first, some may wonder why researchers do not use intervals in which they can have *100% confidence*. Brief reflection on the problem reveals that this is impossible if the answer is to be useful. Because random sampling introduces errors whose effects can only be estimates, the only way to have 100% confidence is to build an interval that includes all of the possibilities. Thus, if we administer a test with possible scores from 0 to 100, we can have 100% confidence that the population mean is either 0, 100, or somewhere in between. (Therefore, the 100% confidence interval would be from 0 to 100.) Researchers know this before testing a single subject, so this result is not useful.

Appendix G near the end of this book describes how to build confidence intervals when small samples (e.g., samples of 60 or less) are used. Note that the smaller the sample, the larger the standard error of the mean (see Section 28).

Terms to Review Before Attempting Worksheet 29

**95% confidence interval, lower limit,
upper limit, 99% confidence interval**

Worksheet 29   Confidence Interval for the Mean

> *Riddle*: According to Seneca, why have many people failed to attain wisdom?

DIRECTIONS: To find the answer to the riddle, write the answer to each question in the space immediately below it. In the solution section, the word in parentheses next to the answer to the first question is the first word in the answer to the riddle, the word beside the answer to the second question is the second word, and so on.

1. For a given set of data, will the 95% *or* the 99% confidence interval be larger?

2. For a given set of data, will the 68% *or* the 95% confidence interval be smaller?

3. "Other things being equal, the larger the sample size, the smaller the confidence interval for the mean." Is this statement true *or* false?

4. If $m = 50.00$ and $SE_m = 3.00$, what are the limits of the 95% confidence interval for the mean?

5. If $m = 50.00$ and $SE_m = 3.00$, what are the limits of the 99% confidence interval for the mean?

6. Is the interval larger in the answer to Question 4 *or* Question 5?

Worksheet 29 (continued)

7. If $m = 40.00$, $s = 12.00$, and $n = 144$, what are the limits of the 95% confidence interval for the mean? (You will need to calculate the standard error of the mean in order to answer this question. See Section 28 for information on how to calculate it.)

8. For the data in Question 7, what are the limits of the 99% confidence interval for the mean?

9. Is the interval smaller in the answer to Question 7 *or* Question 8?

Solution section:

95% (youngster) false (wisdom) Question 4 (silly) 99% (because)	
true (foolishly) 68% (they) Question 5 (they) 42.26–57.74 (that)	
44.12–55.88 (assumed) 28.00–52.00 (birthday) Question 7 (it)	
Question 8 (helpless) 37.42–42.58 (possessed) 38.04–41.96 (already)	

Write the answer to the riddle here, putting one word on each line: _____ _____ _____ _____

_____ _____ _____ _____ _____

Notes

Section 30   Appropriate Figures

When reporting statistical results, one should try to include a figure whenever possible because a figure can grab people's attention and reveal statistical patterns in an easily understandable way. While a good figure can simplify complicated statistical findings, a bad figure can leave a viewer very confused. There are two main challenges in figure creation: (1) determining which figures best communicate the statistical patterns of interest and (2) designing the figures so that viewers can quickly and easily discern those patterns.

Let us assume that students have just taken their first exam, and the instructor wants to communicate how well the class performed as a whole. Instead of reporting just the class average (73%), a **_histogram_** (see Section 8) would convey much more information. Figure 1 shows us that only one student failed the exam (earning between 35% and 39%), only one student received an A (90–94%), the mode was a low B (80–84%), and the median is a low C (70–74%). In general, most students did well, though there is still some room for improvement.

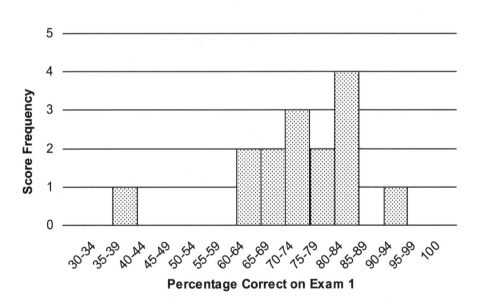

Figure 1. Distribution of grades for Exam 1.

Let us further assume that the instructor wants to know whether there is a relationship between class attendance and exam grades. When examining a relationship, a ***scattergram*** (also known as a scatterplot [see Section 22]) is appropriate. From Figure 2, we can see that the student with the lowest exam grade missed a few classes but did not miss the most classes. Also, the student with the highest exam grade did not have perfect attendance. However, the general trend shows that as students attend more classes, their exam grades increase.

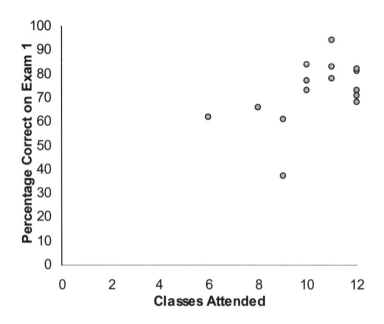

Figure 2. Relationship between attendance and exam scores.

Perhaps the instructor wants to compare first exam grades across different semesters to see how the current class compares. A ***line graph*** (as shown in Figure 3 on the next page) is well suited for showing such changes across time. Note that the variability captured here illustrates how the means vary rather than how the individual scores vary. Figure 3 indicates that it is typical for scores to vary from year to year. They have ranged from about 75 to 90 over the past 13 years.

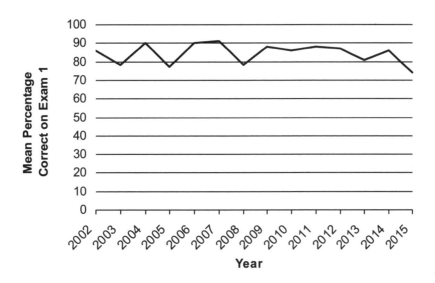

Figure 3. Mean exam performance from 2002 to 2015.

Suppose that after seeing Figure 3, the instructor notices the sharp decline from 2014 to 2015 and observes that the mean exam performance in 2015 is the minimum across the 13-year span. The instructor decides to take a closer look at the mean differences between 2014 and 2015 by examining their confidence intervals (see Figure 4).

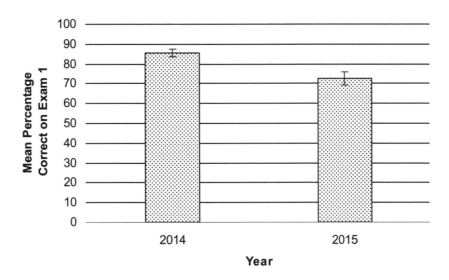

Figure 4. Mean exam performance for 2014 and 2015 with 68% confidence intervals.

Figure 4 is *a **bar graph***, which is particularly helpful when displaying mean values. The values shown here are the same ones shown in Figure 3 for 2014 and 2015, with the addition of confidence intervals (shown as small black bars that extend above and below the top of each shaded bar). Recall that a 68% ***confidence interval*** indicates that that the true mean lies within the interval of scores for 68% of all possible samples (for 2014, the interval is about 84%–88% and for 2015, the range is about 69%–76%). Confidence intervals are based on ***standard error***, which is a measure of variability that takes the sample sizes into account. The confidence intervals in Figure 4 tell us that there is more variability in 2015 than in 2014.

We can look even more closely at the mean differences between 2014 and 2015 by changing the scale of the *y*-axis and examining the 95% confidence intervals, as in Figure 5 on the next page. When comparing Figures 4 and 5, we see that they are both bar graphs and display the same mean scores, but the *y*-axis in Figure 4 provides the full range of possible scores (from 0–100), while Figure 5 emphasizes a smaller range, drastically changing the visual appearance of the figure even though the data are exactly the same in Figures 4 and 5. Both figures show variability around the means with confidence intervals, but the 95% confidence intervals in Figure 5 are twice as large as the 68% confidence intervals in Figure 4. Upon inspection of Figure 5 on the next page, it is clear that the confidence intervals between the two means do *not* overlap, which is a hint that the two means each represent different *true* means. That is, there appears to be a ***statistical difference*** between the scores in 2014 and 2015.

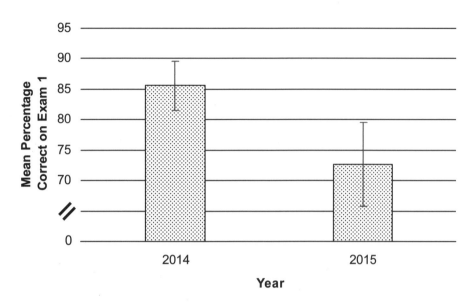

Figure 5. Mean exam performance for 2014 and 2015 with 95% confidence intervals.

In this section, we have seen how figures can highlight statistical patterns and enable a researcher to tell a story with data. To tell a good statistical story, one must (1) clearly label all aspects of the figure and (2) accompany each figure with a verbal description that points to specific patterns of interest. Consider how one might view the panels in Figure 6 on the next page if they appeared without any context. In Panel A, we see a scattergram that seems to show a correlation, but we have no idea what the two variables of interest are (e.g., percent humidity and monthly rainfall in Hawaii, weight and height for chimpanzees, number of online compliments and complaints for a local coffee bar?). In Panel B, it is obvious that we are comparing the years 2014 and 2015, but we do not know the range of values for the *y*-axis. Even worse, we cannot identify the variable being measured. Without additional information, the figures would likely leave a viewer quite perplexed.

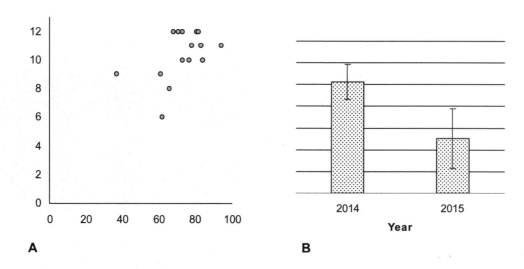

Figure 6. (A) A scattergram. (B) A bar graph showing the years 2014 and 2015.

Terms to Review Before Attempting Worksheet 30

histogram, scattergram, line graph, bar graph, confidence interval, standard error, statistical difference

Worksheet 30   Appropriate Figures

Riddle: According to Benjamin Franklin, what is more difficult than saying the right thing in the right place?

DIRECTIONS: To find the answer to the riddle, write the answer to each question in the space immediately below it. In the solution section, the word in parentheses next to the answer to the first question is the first word in the answer to the riddle, the word beside the answer to the second question is the second word, and so on.

1. If we were to measure annual rainfall across time, the most appropriate figure would be a _____.

2. The problem with the figure below is that it does not have labels for the _____.

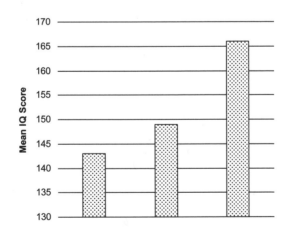

3. True or false: One can estimate the mean, median, mode, and outliers from a histogram.

Worksheet 30 (continued)

4. If two sample means have confidence intervals that _____, we can conclude that there is likely to be a statistical difference between the samples.

5. True or false: A 68% confidence interval helps us to estimate the sample mean with 68% confidence.

6. The standard error is a measure of variability that takes ____ into account.

7. True or false: Figures can do more harm than good if they do not include proper labels and verbal descriptions.

8. If we were to measure the mean weekly hours spent on the Internet for students in elementary school, middle school, high school, and college, which figure is most appropriate?

9. If we were investigating whether shoe size predicts IQ score, which figure is most appropriate?

Worksheet 30 (continued)

Solution section:

overlap (staying)   line graph (leaving)   sample size (at)   variability (time)

x-axis (unsaid)   true (the)   scattergram (moment)   histogram (never)

y-axis (forget)   do not overlap (wrong)   pie chart (matter)   error (who)

false (thing)   caption (a)   true (the)   bar graph (tempting)   confidence (say)

Write the answer to the riddle here, putting one word on each line: _____   _____   _____   _____

_____   _____   _____   _____   _____

Notes

Section 31   Introduction to the Null Hypothesis

In Section 1, we learned that statistics offers a way to determine whether our data show a true pattern from which we can draw general conclusions or display rare observations that are unlikely to recur in the future. In other words, statistics allow us to determine whether *something happened* or *nothing happened*.

Suppose that we drew a random sample of first-grade girls and a random sample of first-grade boys from a large school district in order to estimate the average reading achievement of each group on a standardized test. Furthermore, suppose these means were obtained:

<u>Girls</u>   <u>Boys</u>
$m = 50.00$ $m = 46.00$

The results suggest that girls, on average, have higher reading achievement. But do they? Remember that only a random sample of the boys and a random sample of the girls were tested. Thus, it is possible that the difference between the two means is due only to the errors created by random sampling, also called **sampling error** by statisticians. In other words, it is possible that the population mean for boys is identical to the population mean for girls, and a difference between the two sample means was found only because of the effects of random sampling. This possibility is known as the **null hypothesis**. For the difference between two means, it states:

The true difference between the means (in the population) is zero.

This statement can also be expressed with symbols, as follows:[1]

$H_0: \mu_1 - \mu_2 = 0$
    Where
        H_0 is the symbol for the null hypothesis,
        μ_1 is the symbol for the population mean for one group, and
        μ_2 is the symbol for the population mean for the other group.

---

[1]Another expression of the null hypothesis, which underlies a one-tailed test, is beyond the scope of this section but is discussed in Section 42.

Another way to state the null hypothesis is:

There is no true difference between the means.

The null hypothesis may also be stated in the positive:

The observed difference between the means was created by sampling error.

Most researchers search for differences among individual cases and for explanations for the differences they find. Therefore, most researchers do not undertake their studies in the hope of confirming the null hypothesis. Yet once they have sampled at random, they are stuck with the null hypothesis as a possible explanation for any observed differences. They may also have their own personal hypotheses (i.e., their ***research hypotheses***) that are not consistent with the null hypothesis. For instance, they might hypothesize that the average reading achievement of girls is higher than that of boys. In this case, the research hypothesis is an *alternative* to the null hypothesis.

When a research hypothesis specifies that one particular group's average is higher than that of another group, it is called a ***directional hypothesis*** because it indicates the direction of the difference. Expressed as symbols, this hypothesis is

$H_1: \mu_1 > \mu_2$

Where

H_1 is the symbol for an ***alternative hypothesis*** (i.e., an alternative to the null hypothesis),

μ_1 is the symbol for the population mean for the group hypothesized to have a higher mean (in this case, the girls), and

μ_2 is the symbol for the population mean for the other group (in this case, the boys).

Another researcher may hold a ***nondirectional hypothesis*** as his or her research hypothesis. That is, the researcher believes there is a difference between boys' and girls' reading achievement but that there is insufficient information to hypothesize as to which group's achievement is higher. In other words, such a researcher is hypothesizing that there is a difference—that the two groups are not equal—but is not willing to speculate in advance on the direction of the difference. Following is how to state a nondirectional research hypothesis in symbols:

$H_1: = \mu_1 \neq \mu_2$
Where

H_1 is the symbol for an alternative hypothesis (i.e., an alternative to the null hypothesis),

μ_1 is the symbol for the population mean for one group, and

μ_2 is the symbol for the population mean for the other group.

In review, reconsider the possibilities. A researcher may conduct research in which two means are compared because he or she hypothesizes one of three things:

1. There is no difference. (This assertion is consistent with the null hypothesis but is not frequently held.)

2. One specific group's mean is higher than the other group's mean. (This is the most frequently held. It is a *directional* hypothesis.)

3. There is a difference between the two groups' means in an unspecified direction. (This assertion is not frequently held. It is a *nondirectional* hypothesis.)

Whichever hypothesis an investigator believes is true at the onset of the study is his or her *research hypothesis*. As you can see, a directional research hypothesis is the one most frequently held.

Suppose that the two means we considered at the beginning of this section (i.e., $m = 50.00$ for girls and $m = 46.00$ for boys) were obtained by a researcher who started with the directional research hypothesis that girls, on the average, read better than boys. Clearly, the observed means support the research hypothesis, but is the researcher finished? Obviously not—because he or she has two possible explanations for the observed difference:

1. Girls have higher reading achievement than boys. (This is the research hypothesis.)

2. The observed difference in the sample is the result of the effects of random sampling. Therefore, there is no true difference. (This is the null hypothesis.)

Notice that the researcher must address the possibility raised by the null hypothesis. Because only random samples were studied, the researcher may be observing a difference that is the result of sampling error. Thus, the null hypothesis is a possible explanation for the difference. If the researcher stops at this point, he or she has two explanations for a single difference of four points (a mean of 50 for girls and a mean of 46 for boys). This is not a definitive result. To make it definitive, the researcher should try to rule out the null hypothesis and leave only the original research hypothesis. With the aid of inferential statistics (covered in detail in the remainder of this book), the researcher may test the null hypothesis to determine whether it is reasonable to rule it out as an explanation for the difference.

Terms to Review Before Attempting Worksheet 31

**sampling error, null hypothesis, research hypotheses,
directional hypothesis, alternative hypothesis, nondirectional hypothesis**

Worksheet 31 Introduction to the Null Hypothesis

> *Riddle*: According to Mark Twain, why is it better to keep your mouth shut and appear stupid?

DIRECTIONS: To find the answer to the riddle, write the answer to each question in the space immediately below it. In the solution section, the word in parentheses next to the answer to the first question is the first word in the answer to the riddle, the word beside the answer to the second question is the second word, and so on.

1. An investigator has studied *all* the girls and boys in a population. She has found a difference between the mean for boys and the mean for girls. Is the null hypothesis a viable hypothesis?   No

2. What is the name of the hypothesis that says "The true difference between the means equals zero"?   Null hypothesis

3. What is the alternative hypothesis that states that Group X, on average, is different from Group Y in an unspecified direction?   nondirectional hypothesis

4. What is the alternative hypothesis that is most frequently held by investigators?   directional hypothesis

5. What is the symbol for the null hypothesis? H_0

6. What is the symbol for an alternative hypothesis? H_1

189

Worksheet 31 (continued)

7. For what does the symbol μ stand?

population mean

8. Is the assertion that "there is no difference" an *infrequently* held research hypothesis?

yes

9. What term is defined as *errors created by random sampling?*

Sampling error

Solution section:

> alternative hypothesis (cows)   H (marriage)   *M* (tractor)
>
> sampling errors (doubt)   yes (all)   no (if)   null hypothesis (you)
>
> nondirectional hypothesis (open)   population mean (remove)
>
> H₁ (might)   directional hypothesis (it)   H₀ (you)

Write the answer to the riddle here, putting one word on each line: ___*If*___ ___*you*___ ___*open*___ ___*it*___ ,

___*you*___ ___*might*___ ___*remove*___ ___*all*___ ___*doubt*___

Section 32   Decisions About the Null Hypothesis

As indicated in the previous section, the null hypothesis states that there is no true difference between two means—that in the population, the difference is zero.[1] In other words, a difference between means was obtained only because of sampling errors created by random sampling. As you will see later in this book, the same null hypothesis applies when comparing a variety of other statistics, such as two frequencies (e.g., the frequency that said *yes* vs. the frequency that said *no*).

The sections that follow deal with how to test the null hypothesis. The tests vary according to which statistics are being compared, but all tests have the same underlying logic, which is described next.

An inferential test of a null hypothesis yields, as its final result, a ***probability of obtaining the current data set, given that the null hypothesis is true***. An alternative definition for the probability-value (or *p*-value) is the *probability of a **Type I error*** (i.e., the error of failing to reject the null hypothesis when it is false, also known as a false alarm). The symbol for the probability is a lowercase ***p***. Thus, if an inferential test indicates that the probability of a Type I error is less than 5 in 100, this result would be expressed as $p < .05$. How should this be interpreted? What does it indicate about the null hypothesis? Quite simply, it indicates that it is *unlikely* that there is a Type I error. If it is unlikely to be true, then we should conclude that it is probably *not* true.

To understand the point of the previous paragraph, consider an analogy: Suppose the weather forecaster reports that the probability of rain tomorrow is less than 5 in 100. What should we conclude? First, we know that there is some chance of rain—but it is very small. Because of its low probability, most people would conclude that it probably will *not* rain and would not make any special preparations for rain. By *not* making any special preparations, they are acting as though it will not rain. For practical purposes, they have rejected the hypothesis that it will rain tomorrow.

There is always some probability that the null hypothesis is true. If researchers wait for certainty, they will never be able to make a decision. Thus, statisticians and

---

[1]For one-tailed tests described in Section 42, the null hypothesis is expressed in a different form.

applied researchers have settled on the .05 level as the level at which it is appropriate to reject the null hypothesis. (The probability at which researchers are willing to reject the null hypothesis is known as the **alpha** level.) When an alpha of .05 is used, researchers are, in effect, willing to be wrong 5 times in 100 in rejecting the null hypothesis. Consider the rain analogy. If we make no special preparations for rain over 100 days for which the probability of rain is .05, it will probably rain 5 of those 100 days. Thus, in rejecting the null hypothesis, we are taking a calculated risk that we might be wrong. This type of error is known as a Type I error: the error of rejecting the null hypothesis when it is, in fact, correct (also referred to as a "false alarm"). On those 5 days in 100, when we are caught in the rain without rain gear, we will get wet because we made five Type I errors. Recall that the probability of a Type I error is the final result of an inferential test.

In review, when there is a low probability of a "false alarm," the null hypothesis should be rejected. A synonym for rejecting the null hypothesis is declaring a result to be **statistically significant**. In journals that report on research, a statement such as this can be found: *The difference between the means is statistically significant*. This statement indicates that the researchers have rejected the null hypothesis.

In journals, you will frequently find p values of less than .05 reported. The most common are $p < .01$ (less than 1 in 100) and $p < .001$ (less than 1 in 1,000). When a result is statistically significant at these levels, investigators can be more confident that they are making the right decision in rejecting the null hypothesis than they could be by using the .05 level. Clearly, if there is only 1 chance in 1,000 that something is true, it is less likely that it is true than if there are 5 chances in 100 that it is true. For this reason, the .01 level is a *higher* level of significance than the .05 level, and the .001 level is a *higher* level of significance than the .01 level. In review,

> **.06+ level**: *not* significant—do *not* reject the null hypothesis.
>
> **.05 level**: significant—reject the null hypothesis.
>
> **.01 level**: more significant—reject the null hypothesis with more confidence than at the .05 level.
>
> **.001 level**: highly significant—reject the null hypothesis with even more confidence than at the .01 or .05 levels.

So what probability level should be used? Remember that most researchers are looking for significant differences (or relationships). Thus, they are most likely to use the .05 level because this is the easiest to achieve.[2]

Should you decide to use some level other than .05, the decision should be made in advance of examining the data. Keep in mind, though, that when you require a lower probability before rejecting the null hypothesis (e.g., .01 instead of .05), you are increasing the likelihood that you will make a ***Type II error***, which is known as ***beta***. A Type II error is the error of failing to reject the null hypothesis when it is false. This type of error can have serious consequences. Suppose a drug company developed a new drug for a serious disease and that, in reality, the new drug is effective. If, however, the null hypothesis is not rejected because the drug company selected a level of significance that is too high, the results of the study will have to be described as insignificant, and the drug may not receive government approval.

In review, there are two types of errors that can be made when making a decision about the null hypothesis:

> ***Type I error***: rejecting the null hypothesis when, in reality, it is true.

> ***Type II error***: failing to reject the null hypothesis when, in reality, it is false.

At first, this might seem frustrating—even with inferential statistical tests, we face the possibility of errors. While this is true, using probabilities will result in making informed decisions that are *probably* true in the face of uncertainty. Either decision about the null hypothesis (reject *or* fail to reject) may be wrong, but by using inferential statistics to make the decisions, researchers can report the probability that they have made a *Type I error* (indicated by the *p* value included in the report). By reporting the probability level that was used, researchers inform readers of their research of the likelihood that an incorrect decision was made when they rejected the null hypothesis.

---

[2]If researchers find that their result is significant at the .01 or .001 levels, they will report it at these levels for the readers' information. However, if it had only reached the .05 level, they still would have reported it as significant in many cases. Section 41 provides more information in this regard.

Section 41 shows how to conduct a significance test for the difference between two means. The results of the test will yield a value of p, and when it is equal to or less than .05 (or some other level selected in advance), the null hypothesis will be rejected.

Terms to Review Before Attempting Worksheet 32

**probability, Type I error, p, alpha,
statistically significant, Type II error, beta**

Worksheet 32   Decisions About the Null Hypothesis

> **Riddle**: What is the best exercise for losing weight?

DIRECTIONS: To find the answer to the riddle, write the answer to each question in the space immediately below it. In the solution section, the word in parentheses next to the answer to the first question is the first word in the answer to the riddle, the word beside the answer to the second question is the second word, and so on.

1. What is the symbol for probability?

    p

2. What is the name of the error of rejecting the null hypothesis when it is true?

    type I error

3. If a difference is declared to be statistically significant, is the null hypothesis rejected?

    yes

4. Is the .05 level *or* the .01 level a higher level of significance?

    0.01

5. "When $p = .10$, the null hypothesis is usually rejected." Is this statement true *or* false?

    false

6. "When $p = .05$, the null hypothesis is usually rejected." Is this statement true *or* false?

    true

Worksheet 32 (continued)

7. Is it possible to reject the null hypothesis with 100% certainty?

NO

8. What is the name of the error of failing to reject the null hypothesis when it is, in reality, false?

type II error

9. Is a difference usually regarded as statistically significant *or* statistically insignificant when $p < .01$?

Statistically significant

Solution section:

> statistically significant (back)   Type II (pushing)   P (jumping)
>
> .05 level (running)   no (and)   p (placing)   Type I (both)
>
> statistically insignificant (eating)   true (table)   false (the)
>
> .01 level (against)   yes (hands)   null hypothesis (calories)   .10 (feast)

Write the answer to the riddle here, putting one word on each line:

placing   both   hands   against   the   table   and   pushing   back

Section 33   Introduction to the Pearson *r*

A statistician named Karl Pearson developed a widely used statistic for describing the relationship between two sets of scores. His statistic is often simply called the **Pearson r**. Its full, formal name is the *Pearson product-moment correlation coefficient,* but you might find variations on this term, such as the *Pearson correlation coefficient* or the *product-moment correlation coefficient,* in research literature.[1]

Begin by considering the following basic properties of a Pearson *r*:

- It can range only from −1.00 to 1.00.

- −1.00 indicates a **perfect negative relationship**—the strongest possible *inverse relationship.*

- 1.00 indicates a **perfect positive relationship**—the strongest possible *direct relationship.*

- 0.00 indicates the complete absence of a relationship.

- The closer a value is to 0.00, the weaker the relationship.

- The closer a value is to −1.00 or 1.00, the stronger the relationship.

Thus, the *Pearson r* varies from −1.00 to 1.00, as illustrated below:

−1.00				0.00				1.00
⇑	⇑	⇑	⇑	⇑	⇑	⇑	⇑	⇑
perfect	strong	moderate	weak	none	weak	moderate	strong	perfect

Notice the labels *strong, moderate,* and *weak* are used in conjunction with both positive and negative values of *r*. Also, exact numerical values are not given for the intermediate values. This is because the interpretation and labeling of an *r* may vary from one investigator to another and from one type of investigation to another.

---

[1]Pearson devised *r* for describing linear relationships (see Section 22). It should be used only for describing such relationships. When erroneously applied to a curvilinear relationship, it may indicate that there is little or no relationship when, in fact, there is a strong curvilinear one.

Because negative values of *r* can be confusing at first glance, consider the following true statements concerning negative values:

- A value of $r = -.25$ is as strong as a value of $r = .25$.
- A value of $r = -.50$ is stronger than a value of $r = .25$.
- A value of $r = -.99$ represents an almost perfect relationship.
- A value of $r = -.01$ represents an extremely weak relationship.

The interpretation of the values of *r* is complicated by the fact that an *r* is *not a proportion*. Thus, an *r* of .50 is not half of anything. It follows that multiplying .50 by 100 does *not* yield a percentage. That is, .50 is *not* equivalent to 50%. This is important because we are accustomed to thinking of .50 as being halfway between 0.00 and 1.00. In Section 36, you will learn how to compute another statistic that is directly related to *r* but that may be interpreted as a proportion and is easily converted to a percentage.

See Appendix B for additional information on interpreting a Pearson *r*.

Terms to Review Before Attempting Worksheet 33

Pearson *r*, perfect negative relationship, perfect positive relationship

Worksheet 33   Introduction to the Pearson *r*

> **Riddle**: What is the wacky definition of a babysitter?

DIRECTIONS: To find the answer to the riddle, write the answer to each question in the space immediately below it. In the solution section, the word in parentheses next to the answer to the first question is the first word in the answer to the riddle, the word beside the answer to the second question is the second word, and so on.

1. What letter of the alphabet is used to stand for Pearson's correlation coefficient?

    r

2. "The closer a correlation coefficient is to –1.00, the weaker it is." Is this statement true *or* false?

    false

3. "The closer a correlation coefficient is to 0.00, the weaker it is." Is this statement true *or* false?

    true

4. What value of a correlation coefficient indicates a perfect direct relationship?

    1.00

5. Is a correlation coefficient of –.29 weaker than one of –.48?

    yes

6. Is a correlation coefficient of .68 stronger than one of –.89?

    no

Worksheet 33 (continued)

7. What value of a correlation coefficient indicates a perfect inverse relationship?

−1.00

8. What is the last name of the statistician who developed r?

pearson

Solution section:

b (baby)   0.00 (helps)   Pearson (television)   −1.00 (watch)   no (to)

r (a)   1.00 (gets)   100.00 (sleeping)   .68 (teenager)   true (who) c (cries)

false (person)   product (laughs)   10.00 (relies)   yes (paid)   .90 (expensive)

Write the answer to the riddle here, putting one word on each line: a   person   who   gets   paid   to   watch   television

Section 34   Computation of the Pearson *r*

The original formula for *r* was defined in terms of standard scores (i.e., *z*-scores).[1] This formula is presented in Appendix C near the end of this book for those students who want to study it in order to better understand the meaning of *r*.

For students who are using calculators, the following formula, known as the **computational formula for r**, is recommended (for an alternate equation, see Appendix J near the end of this book):

$$r = \frac{N \sum XY - (\sum X)(\sum Y)}{\sqrt{[N \sum X^2 - (\sum X)^2][N \sum Y^2 - (\sum Y)^2]}}$$

To use the formula, first designate one set of scores as *X* and the other as *Y*. If one variable is measured before the other, it is customary to designate the first one measured as *X* and the second one as *Y*. However, the answer will be the same regardless of which one is called *X* and which one is called *Y*.

Table 1
Worktable for Computing r

Col. 1 Subject	Col. 2 X	Col. 3 Y	Col. 4 X^2	Col. 5 Y^2	Col. 6 XY
Bill	5	0	25	0	0
Liz	7	4	49	16	28
Carol	0	9	0	81	0
Stu	1	7	1	49	7
Frank	4	5	16	25	20
Brandy	2	6	4	36	12
$\Sigma =$	19	31	95	207	67

Table 1 is a worktable for computing *r*. The scores are shown in columns 2 and 3. Begin your work by completing the worktable as follows: Compute the values in column 4 by squaring each value of *X*. Compute the values in column 5 by squaring each value of *Y*. Finally, compute the values in column 6 by multiplying each *X* by each *Y*. (For instance, Brandy's score of 2 on *X* is multiplied by her score

---

[1]See Section 18 to review *z*-scores.

of 6 on Y to obtain the product 12 in column 6.) Then sum the values in columns 2 through 6 (as indicated by the Σ sign in the bottom row of the worktable).

The formula presented at the beginning of this section is rewritten here with column numbers to refer to the *sums* of the columns shown in the last row of Table 1 on the previous page.

$$r = \frac{N(Col.6) - (Col.2)(Col.3)}{\sqrt{[N(Col.4) - (Col.2)^2][N(Col.5) - (Col.3)^2]}}$$

$$r = \frac{6(67) - (19)(31)}{\sqrt{[(6)(95) - 19^2][(6)(207) - (31)^2]}}$$

$$r = \frac{402 - 589}{\sqrt{[570 - 361][1242 - 961]}}$$

$$r = \frac{-187}{\sqrt{[209][281]}} = \frac{-187}{\sqrt{58729}} = \frac{-187}{242.341} = -.772 = -.77$$

The answer is negative, which indicates that the relationship is inverse. With only a small number of scores, you can perform a quick check to see whether the answer should be negative. In this case, subjects such as Carol and Stu had low scores on X and high scores on Y. Also, subjects such as Bill and Liz had high scores on X and low scores on Y. Remember that

- in an ***inverse relationship***, high scores on one variable are associated with low scores on the other, resulting in a negative value of r; and

- in a ***direct relationship***, high scores are associated with high scores *and* low scores are associated with low scores, resulting in a positive value of r.

Note that if the value of r is going to be negative, it is the numerator of the fraction (e.g., −187 in the last row of the computations shown above) that will be negative. The denominator is never negative. If you obtain a negative in the denominator, you know you have made a mistake.

When subjects are *ranked* on both variables (e.g., ordinal data such as the most talented is given a rank of 1, the next-most talented is given a rank of 2, etc.), then a simpler formula developed by Spearman may be applied. This formula is presented in Appendix D near the end of this book.

Terms to Review Before Attempting Worksheet 34

computational formula for *r*, inverse relationship, direct relationship

"How many statisticians does it take to screw in a light bulb? Three: One to analyze the data, one to draw conclusions, and one to *skew* it in."

Worksheet 34 Computation of the Pearson r

> **Riddle:** In what footsteps do most boys follow?

DIRECTIONS: To find the answer to the riddle, write the answer to each question in the space immediately below it. In the solution section, the word in parentheses next to the answer to the first question is the first word in the answer to the riddle, the word beside the answer to the second question is the second word, and so on.

Questions 1 through 5 refer to the following data:

Col. 1 Subject	Col. 2 X	Col. 3 Y
Victor	2	0
Juliet	6	7
Romeo	4	5
Millie	3	6
Rob	5	4

1. What is the value of N?

2. What is the value of the sum of column 2 (i.e., what is the value of ΣX)?

3. What is the value of ΣX^2?

4. What is the value of ΣXY?

Worksheet 34 (continued)

5. What is the value of r?

Questions 6 through 9 refer to the following data:

Col. 1 Subject	Col. 2 X	Col. 3 Y
Ginny	12	1
Leslie	10	2
Steve	7	4
Clyde	8	3
Dave	6	6
Jose	5	5

6. What is the value of ΣY?

7. What is the value of ΣY^2?

8. What is the value of ΣXY?

9. What is the value of r?

Worksheet 34 (continued)

Solution section:

5 (those)	100 (father)	.94 (shoes)	145 (covered)	.75 (path)
−.94 (up)	91 (had)	89 (becoming)	25 (listening)	21 (he)
125 (watches)	20 (that)	.70 (thought)	−.64 (never)	90 (his)

Write the answer to the riddle here, putting one word on each line: _____ _____ _____ _____ _____ _____ _____ _____ _____

Section 35   Significance of a Pearson *r*

Often, researchers want to know whether a Pearson *r* is statistically significant. This issue arises when a random sample from a population has been drawn in order to estimate the correlation between two sets in a population. Following is an example:

> Twenty students were drawn at random from a population, and their GPAs were correlated with their heights. A Pearson *r* of .23 was obtained, indicating that those with higher GPAs are taller.

Before reporting this result, the researcher should consider that the ***observed value*** of *r* (.23) is based on a random sample of only 20 students. Therefore, the result (.23) may not be true in the entire population. Thus, the researcher needs to test the null hypothesis.[1]

The test of the null hypothesis for this type of problem is a special version of the *t* test. Fortunately, the value of *t* does not need to be computed. Instead, a researcher can determine the significance of a given correlation coefficient by referring to the values in Table 10 near the end of this book.[2]

To use Table 10, first compute the degrees of freedom, using this formula:

$$df = n - 2$$

> Where
>
> > *n* is the number of subjects.

Because there are 20 subjects in the example, $df = 20 - 2 = 18$.

Looking up 18 degrees of freedom in Table 10 indicates that a ***minimum value*** of *r* for significance at the .05 level is .444.

---

[1]In this case, we are concerned with the possibility that, in the population, there is a true correlation of 0.00. The null hypothesis for this situation says that the difference between 0.00 (the hypothesized true correlation) and 0.23 (the observed correlation) was caused by sampling errors resulting from random selection.

[2]The values in Table 10 were determined with the special *t* test.

Here is the decision rule:

If the *observed value of r is greater than the minimum value*[3] in Table 10, reject the null hypothesis. Otherwise, do not reject it.[4]

Because the observed value of .23 is *not* greater than the minimum value of .444, do *not* reject the null hypothesis and conclude that the difference is *not* statistically significant at the .05 level. The researcher has failed to demonstrate a significant correlation between GPA and height.

Terms to Review Before Attempting Worksheet 35

observed value, minimum value

"You can live a perfectly normal life if you accept the fact that statistics prove your life will never be perfectly normal."

---

[3]In the unlikely event that the observed value is exactly equal to the minimum value, reject the null hypothesis.

[4]Notice that in Table 10, only select values of *df* are given. If you obtain a *df* that is not shown in the table, use the next-lower value shown. For instance, if you have 52 degrees of freedom (which is not shown), use 50 (which is shown).

Worksheet 35   Significance of a Pearson *r*

Riddle: What is the trouble with American
            Thanksgiving dinners?

DIRECTIONS: To find the answer to the riddle, write the answer to each question in the space immediately below it. In the solution section, the word in parentheses next to the answer to the first question is the first word in the answer to the riddle, the word beside the answer to the second question is the second word, and so on.

1. For a random sample of 52 subjects, a Pearson *r* of .29 was obtained for the relationship between Variables A and B. What is the value of the degrees of freedom for determining the significance of this *r*?

2. What is the minimum value of *r* for significance at the .05 level for the study described in Question 1?

3. Is the value of *r* in Question 1 statistically significant at the .05 level?

4. Is the value of *r* in Question 1 statistically significant at the .01 level?

5. For a random sample of 14 subjects, a Pearson *r* of .29 was obtained for the relationship between Variables X and Y. What is the value of the degrees of freedom for determining the significance of this *r*?

Worksheet 35 (continued)

6. "The value of the Pearson r in Question 5 is statistically significant at the .05 level." Is this statement true *or* false?

7. For a random sample of 47 subjects, a Pearson r of .39 was obtained for the relationship between Variables X and Y. "This r of .39 is statistically significant at the .01 level." Is this statement true *or* false?

Solution section:

50 (two)	51 (eating)	52 (turkey)	true (again)	false (hungry)
14 (stuffed)	.273 (days)	yes (later)	13 (family)	no (you)
.354 (sleepy)	.29 (cooking)	12 (are)	.39 (sensation)	.01 (nervous)

Write the answer to the riddle here, putting one word on each line: _____ _____ _____ _____

_____ _____ _____

Section 36 Coefficient of Determination

The statistic known as the ***coefficient of determination*** is useful when interpreting a Pearson r. Its symbol, r^2, explains how it is computed: simply square r. Thus, for a Pearson r of .60, r^2 equals .36 (.60 × .60 = .36).

Although the computation is simple, its meaning is sometimes difficult to grasp. To understand its meaning, consider the example from Section 34, in which these scores were shown:

Table 1
Scores From Section 34

Col. 1	Col. 2	Col. 3
Subject	X	Y
Bill	5	0
Liz	7	4
Carol	0	9
Stu	1	7
Frank	4	5
Brandy	2	6

Notice that there are differences among the scores on Variable X. This is referred to as ***variance***. There is also variance in the scores on Variable Y. When interpreting a Pearson r, this is an important question to keep in mind: *What percentage of the variance on one variable is accounted for by the variance on the other?* If we are trying to predict Variable Y (which might be college GPAs) from Variable X (which might be scores on a college admissions test), the question might be phrased as follows: *What percentage of the variance on Y is <u>predicted</u> by the variance on X?* The answer to the question is determined simply by calculating r^2 and multiplying it by 100. For the scores shown in Table 1, $r = -.77$. Thus,

$$-.77 \times -.77 = .59 \times 100 = 59\%$$

This result indicates that 59% (*not* 77%) of the variance on one variable is accounted for by the variance on the other in this example.[1]

---

[1]*Variance accounted for* is sometimes referred to as *explained variance* or *predicted variance*.

Let us put the 59% in perspective. Suppose we are trying to predict how subjects will score on Variable Y. Further, suppose we naively put all of the subjects' names on slips of paper in a hat, draw a name, and declare that the first name drawn will probably perform best on Variable Y. Then we draw a second name and declare that this person will probably perform second best on Variable Y, and so on. What percentage of the variance on Y will we predict using this procedure? In the long run, with large numbers of subjects, the answer is about zero (0.00) percent. In the previous example, Variable X accounted for 59% of the variance on Variable Y, which is 59% better than using a random process to make predictions.

It follows, however, that if we can account for 59% of the variance, the remaining 41% (100% − 59% = 41%) of the variance is *not* accounted for. Thus, there is much room for improvement in our ability to predict.[2]

Consider Table 2. It shows selected values of r, the corresponding values of r^2, and the percentage of variance accounted for and not accounted for. Notice that small values of r shrink dramatically when converted to r^2, indicating that we should be very cautious when interpreting small values of r—they are further from perfection than they might seem at first.[3]

Table 2
Pearson r and Related Statistics

r	r^2	% accounted for	% not accounted for
.10	.01	1%	99%
.20	.04	4%	96%
.30	.09	9%	91%
.40	.16	16%	84%
.50	.25	25%	75%
.60	.36	36%	64%
.70	.49	49%	51%
.80	.64	64%	36%
.90	.81	81%	19%
1.00	1.00	100%	0%

[2]Notice that because r is negative (i.e., −.77), we need to predict that those who score high on X will score low on Y and that those who score low on X will score high on Y.

[3]Note that when there is no variance on either variable, the Pearson r will equal 0.00, and r^2 will also equal 0.00. This is easy to see by example. For instance, suppose a group of students all had identical SAT scores. Because these scores fail to differentiate among students, they cannot predict who will have high GPAs, who will have average GPAs, and so on.

Note that many researchers interpret values of r in the .20 to .40 range as being important. Indeed, they may be of some practical importance under certain circumstances. However, keep in mind that in this range, as indicated in Table 2 on the previous page, 84% to 96% of the variance on one variable is *not* accounted for by the other. Thus, considering a prediction study, an r of .40 or less leaves much room for improvement when attempting to predict Variable Y using Variable X.

Terms to Review Before Attempting Worksheet 36

coefficient of determination, r^2, variance

Worksheet 36   Coefficient of Determination

> *Riddle*: Why is the government certain that there is no life on Mars?

DIRECTIONS: To find the answer to the riddle, write the answer to each question in the space immediately below it. In the solution section, the word in parentheses next to the answer to the first question is the first word in the answer to the riddle, the word beside the answer to the second question is the second word, and so on.

1. "For an r of .55, 55% of the variance on one variable is accounted for by the variance on the other." Is this statement true *or* false?

2. If $r = .24$, what is the value of r^2 (rounded to the nearest hundredths' place)?

3. If $r = .47$, what is the value of the coefficient of determination?

4. Is r or r^2 a more direct indicator of variance accounted for?

5. If $r = .88$, what percentage of the variance on one variable is accounted for by the variance on the other?

6. If $r = .66$, is the majority of the variance on one variable accounted for by the variance on the other?

Worksheet 36 (continued)

7. If $r = .78$, is the majority of the variance on one variable accounted for by the variance on the other?

8. If $r = .95$, what percentage of the variance on one variable is *not* accounted for by the variance on the other?

9. If $r = .25$, what percentage of the variance on one variable is *not* accounted for by the variance on the other?

Solution section:

> 94% (money)   90% (shuttle)   6% (walking)   10% (any)
>
> no (States)   true (astronaut)   yes (for) r (exploration)   .88 (not)
>
> false (they) r^2 (the)   .22 (asked)   .48 (green)   77% (United)
>
> .06 (haven't)   25% (overwhelmed)   95% (unconventional)

Write the answer to the riddle here, putting one word on each line: _____   _____   _____   _____

_____   _____   _____   _____   _____

Notes

Section 37   Multiple Correlation

Researchers are often interested in the extent to which two variables, in combination, predict a third variable. For instance, a researcher might want to know how well high school GPAs in combination with scores on a college admissions test predict college GPAs. In this instance, there are three variables and, thus, three scores per subject:

Variable 1: college GPAs (*the variable being predicted*)

Variable 2: high school GPAs (*a predictor*)

Variable 3: scores on a college admissions test (*a predictor*)

In order to use the formula presented on the next page, name the variable being predicted as Variable 1. It does not matter which of the others is named Variable 2 and which is named Variable 3.

Because there are three variables, three values of Pearson r should be computed, which will be identified with subscripts. For instance, r_{12} stands for the relationship between Variables 1 and 2. Consider these values of r:

$r_{12} = .55$

$r_{13} = .44$

$r_{23} = .38$

The value of r_{12} indicates how well high school GPAs predict college GPAs, while the value of r_{13} indicates how well scores on the admissions test predict college GPAs. Clearly, high school GPA is a better predictor than the admissions test. Finally, the value of r_{23} indicates the extent to which the two predictors are correlated. The .38 indicates that, to a modest extent, there is overlap between the two predictors.

Getting back to the original concern: The researcher wants to know the extent to which Variables 2 and 3, *in combination*, will predict Variable 1.[1] To answer the

---

[1]The formula presented here tells us how well the combination will work if combined in the best mathematical fashion. The mathematics of determining such a combination are beyond the scope of this book.

217

question, compute a *multiple correlation coefficient*, whose symbol is **R**. The formula for R (when the variable being predicted has been named Variable 1) is as follows:

$$R = \sqrt{\frac{r_{12}^2 + r_{13}^2 - 2r_{12}r_{13}r_{23}}{1 - r_{23}^2}}$$

$$R = \sqrt{\frac{.55^2 + .44^2 - 2(.55)(.44)(.38)}{1 - .38^2}}$$

$$R = \sqrt{\frac{.303 + .194 - .184}{1 - .144}}$$

$$R = \sqrt{\frac{.313}{.856}} = \sqrt{.366} = .605 = .60$$

For all practical purposes, the multiple R is interpreted in the same way as the Pearson r except in this case, R indicates how well two variables in combination predict a third variable.[2] Note that the variable being predicted is often called the *criterion variable*.

The example shown above illustrates an interesting point. Notice that if we just use high school GPAs to predict college GPAs, the Pearson r is .55. If we just use admissions test scores to predict college GPAs, the Pearson r is .44. In combination, the two predictors only bring us up to a multiple R of .60. At first, you might think that the .55 and .44 in combination might bring us close to 1.00 (keep in mind that correlation coefficients cannot exceed 1.00). The relatively modest increase in the ability to predict is due to the fact that the two predictors overlap—that is, they both tap some of the same skills, as indicated by the r of .38 for the relationship between the two predictors. In general, the greater the correlation between the two predictors, the smaller the increase obtained when using them in combination.

---

[2]The technique of multiple correlation can be expanded to include more than two predictors. However, the mathematics for doing this are cumbersome and beyond the scope of this book.

Terms to Review Before Attempting Worksheet 37

multiple correlation coefficient, *R*, criterion variable

"On average, I feel fine."

Worksheet 37   Multiple Correlation

Riddle: What should you do on the "keyboard of life"?

DIRECTIONS: To find the answer to the riddle, write the answer to each question in the space immediately below it. In the solution section, the word in parentheses next to the answer to the first question is the first word in the answer to the riddle, the word beside the answer to the second question is the second word, and so on.

1. How many scores must you have for each subject in order to compute a multiple correlation coefficient using the formula given in this section? (In other words, how many variables must you have?)

2. To use the formula for computing the multiple correlation coefficient presented in this section, should the variable being predicted be named Variable 1, Variable 2, *or* Variable 3?

3. What is the symbol for the multiple correlation coefficient?

4. "As defined in this section, r_{23} indicates the extent to which the best predictor variable is correlated with the criterion variable." Is this statement true *or* false?

5. "The formula for the multiple correlation coefficient presented in this section indicates the extent to which two variables in combination predict a criterion variable." Is this statement true *or* false?

Worksheet 37 (continued)

6. Is a criterion variable a *predictor variable or* the *variable being predicted?*

7. What is the value of the multiple correlation coefficient given these values of Pearson r?

$$r_{12} = .30, r_{13} = .20, r_{23} = .10$$

8. What is the value of the multiple correlation coefficient given these values of Pearson r?

$$r_{12} = .61, r_{13} = .60, r_{23} = .47$$

Solution section:

.34 (escape)   number 2 (labor)   .12 (shaking)   .71 (key)   true (on)

variable being predicted (the)   number 3 (pain) r (crying)   .50 (small)

3 (always) r^2 (one)   predictor variable (visible)   false (finger)

Variable 1 (keep)   .30 (hurt) r_{23} (spank)   .10 (doctor)   .47 (hospital)

Write the answer to the riddle here, putting one word on each line: _____   _____   _____   _____

_____   _____   _____   _____

Notes

Section 38   Introduction to Linear Regression

In the previous sections, we have been considering relationships *across groups of subjects*—that is, to what extent variables are correlated when the scores of groups are examined.

Frequently, when we know that there is a moderate to strong correlation across a group of subjects, we want to make predictions for new individuals who will be subsequently tested. For instance, suppose that last year we administered an algebra aptitude test to a group of subjects during the first week of an algebra course. The test measured basic math skills needed to learn algebra. Then we administered an algebra achievement test at the end of the course and constructed the scattergram shown in Figure 1.[1]

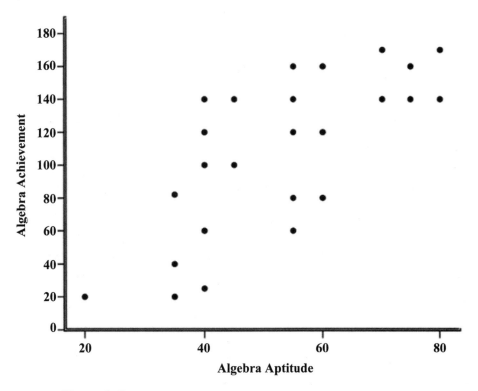

Figure 1. Scattergram.

[1]To review scattergrams, see Section 22.

How could we use the information in the scattergram to make predictions for students enrolling in algebra this year? We could make rough predictions, of course. For instance, if Frank obtains an algebra aptitude score of 25, we can see from the scattergram that he probably will not do well because his aptitude score puts him in the lower-left corner. If Sarah obtains a score of 75 on the measure of aptitude, we can predict that she probably will do well on achievement because those who scored about 75 last year obtained high achievement test scores.

We can make more specific predictions by using the technique of **linear regression**. In this technique, we determine the equation for a single straight line that best describes the dots.[2] Then when we make predictions, we use the equation to get a single predicted score.

First, consider the general equation for any straight line. It is

$Y = a + bX$

Where

Y is the score on Variable Y (the score to be predicted),[3]

a is the **intercept** (the point where the straight line meets the y-axis),

b is the **slope** (which determines the angle of the line), and

X is the score on Variable X.

Figure 2 on the next page shows a solid line with an intercept (a) of 2 and a slope (b) of .5 units. The intercept is easy to see: It is the point at which the line meets the y-axis. The slope indicates the ratio of change that produces the angle of the line. In this figure, the dashed lines show that for every one-unit increase on X (whether it is an inch or a mile!), we need to go up .5 units on Y to reach the solid line. Put another way, the vertical dashed line is one-half (i.e., .5) the length of the horizontal line. Thus, the formula for the solid line in Figure 2 is $Y = 2 + .5X$. Given the intercept and slope, we can make predictions for individuals once we know their score on X. Following are two predictions (see next page):

---

[2] Obviously, no single straight line can go through all the dots when there is scatter on the scattergram. The *best line* is defined as the one that minimizes the squared differences of the dots from the line.
[3] The symbol Y' (pronounced *Y prime*) is sometimes used to signify the predicted score.

John has a score of 14 on *X*. His predicted score on *Y* is

$$Y = 2 + (.5)(14) = 2 + 7 = 9$$

Joan has a score of 6 on *X*. Her predicted score on *Y* is

$$Y = 2 + (.5)(6) = 2 + 3 = 5$$

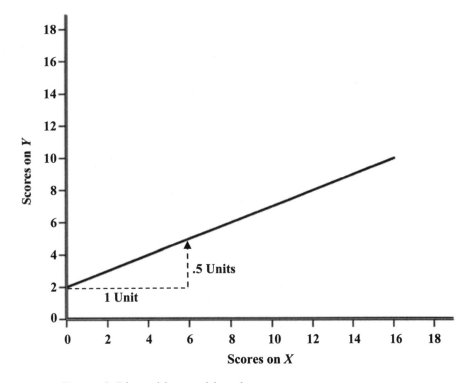

Figure 2. Line with a positive slope.

Figure 3 on the next page shows a line with a negative slope. Because the intercept is 12 and the slope is –1.5, the formula is $Y = 12 + (-1.5X)$. Notice that because the slope is negative, when we go right one unit, we go *down* 1.5 units.

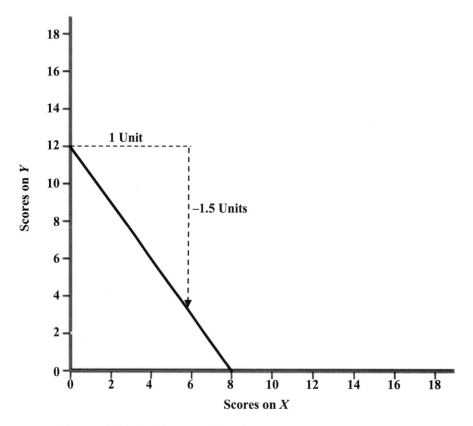

Figure 3. Line with a negative slope.

The following is a prediction based on the line in Figure 3:

Juliet has a score of 4 on *X*. Her predicted score on *Y* is

$$Y = 12 + (-1.5)(4) = 12 + (-6) = 6$$

Keep in mind that linear regression is useful only if the dots form a pattern that follows a straight line (i.e., a linear relationship—*not* a curvilinear one).[4]

In the next section, you will learn how to compute the values of *a* and *b* (values in the formula for a straight line) based on a given set of data.

---

[4]See Section 22 to review the distinction between *linear* and *curvilinear* relationships.

Terms to Review Before Attempting Worksheet 38

linear regression, intercept, slope

IF ONE PAIR OF LIPS LEAVES AT 8:45 AND TRAVELS 2.3 MILES AT 3.3 MPH AND ANOTHER PAIR OF LIPS LEAVES AT 8:53 AND TRAVELS AN EQUAL DISTANCE IN THE OPPOSITE DIRECTION AT 3.7 MPH, HOW LONG WILL IT TAKE FOR THEM TO KISS?

GLASBERGEN

Alan gets a love letter from the president of the Statistics Club.

Worksheet 38 Introduction to Linear Regression

DIRECTIONS: To find the answer to the riddle, write the answer to each question in the space immediately below it. In the solution section, the word in parentheses next to the answer to the first question is the first word in the answer to the riddle, the word beside the answer to the second question is the second word, and so on.

1. Is the letter X or the letter Y defined as the score to be predicted?

2. Is the point where the line meets the y-axis called the *slope* or the *intercept*?

3. "The purpose of linear regression is to determine the direction and strength of relationships between two variables across a group of subjects." Is this statement true *or* false?

4. In $Y = a + bX$, is a or b the slope?

5. If a line has a negative slope, will the line slope up *or* down (from left to right)?

6. If $Y = 3.1 + 1.6X$, and if Richard has a score of 12 on X, what is his predicted score on Y?

Worksheet 38 (continued)

7. If $Y = 50.2 + (-2.4X)$, and if Anne has a score of 20 on X, what is her predicted score on Y?

8. Is the technique described in this section appropriate for use with curvilinear relationships?

9. "In general, the lower the correlation between two variables, the greater the error that will be made when using linear regression." Is this statement true *or* false?

Solution section:

```
56.40 (charity)   no (Revenue)   true (Service)   –2.20 (external)   2.20 (Internal)

98.20 (like)   yes (home)   Y (in)   X (visible)   a (helpful)

22.30 (the)   down (like)   up (lift)   slope (silly)   intercept (case)

false (heaven)   b (is)   47.80 (helpless)   4.70 (people)
```

Write the answer to the riddle here, putting one word on each line: _____ _____ _____ _____

_____ _____ _____ _____ _____

Notes

Section 39   Computations for Linear Regression

The formulas for calculating linear regression will be illustrated using the scores from Table 1 in Section 34, which is reproduced here as Table 1.

Table 1
Worktable for Computing r

Col. 1 Subject	Col. 2 X	Col. 3 Y	Col. 4 X^2	Col. 5 Y^2	Col. 6 XY
Bill	5	0	25	0	0
Liz	7	4	49	16	28
Carol	0	9	0	81	0
Stu	1	7	1	49	7
Frank	4	5	16	25	20
Brandy	2	6	4	36	12
$\Sigma =$	19	31	95	207	67

The correlation coefficient (Pearson r) for the relationship between scores on X and Y was calculated to be $-.77$ in Section 34. This indicates that those who have high scores on X tend to have low scores on Y, and those who have low scores on X tend to have high scores on Y. If we wish to predict scores on Variable Y from scores on Variable X, we need to determine the equation for the straight line that maximizes the predictability of the scores.[1] As you know from the previous section, this means that we need to calculate the *slope* (b) and the *intercept* (a).

To calculate the slope (b), use this formula (or, for an alternative formula, see Appendix J near the end of this book):

$$b = \frac{\sum XY - \left[(\sum X)(\sum Y)/N \right]}{\sum X^2 - \left[(\sum X)^2 / N \right]}$$

$$b = \frac{67 - \left[(19)(31)/6 \right]}{95 - \left[19^2 / 6 \right]} = \frac{67 - \left[(589/6) \right]}{95 - \left[361/6 \right]} = \frac{-31.167}{34.833} = -.8947 = -.89$$

---

[1]A precise estimate of the degree of accuracy in prediction can be made with the standard error of estimate, which is discussed in Appendix E near the end of this book. The formulas in this section define a line that minimizes the squared distance of the scores from the line.

The next step is to calculate the means of X and Y, as follows:

Mean of X (M_x) = 19/6 = 3.17

Mean of Y (M_y) = 31/6 = 5.17

Third, calculate the intercept (a) by substituting the values of the slope and the means into this formula:

$a = M_y - bM_x$

$a = 5.17 - (-.89)(3.17) = 5.17 - (-2.82) = 7.99 = 8.00$

Because the general formula for a straight line is

$Y = a + bX$,

the equation for the data in question is

$Y = 8.00 + (-.89X)$

Now we have an equation into which we can substitute a value of X for a new individual and obtain a predicted value of Y. For instance, suppose we test Robert using Test X, and he obtains a score of 6. His predicted score on Y would be calculated as follows:

$Y = 8.00 + (-.89)(6) = 8.00 + (-5.34) = 2.66$

In other words, we can use a group's performance on two variables in the past to predict new individuals' performances in the future.

You can perform a rough check of your work by making an estimate, as we will do here for Robert. Notice that he obtained a score of 6, which, in Table 1 on the previous page, is near the top of the group on Variable X. Does it make sense that his predicted score is 2.66? Consider two subjects who scored near him on X. The scores Bill and Liz earned on X and Y are in Table 2 on the next page.

Table 2
The Two Highest-Scoring Subjects on Test X From Table 1 Plus Robert,
Who Had a High Score on Test X

Subject	Test X	Test Y
Bill	5	0
Robert	**6**	**2.66**
Liz	7	4

Because Robert's score on X is between Bill and Liz's scores, it makes sense that the predicted score for Robert would be between Bill and Liz's scores on Y.

Terms to Review Before Attempting Worksheet 39

slope, intercept

Worksheet 39 Computations for Linear Regression

Riddle: How do marriage and celibacy differ?

DIRECTIONS: To find the answer to the riddle, write the answer to each question in the space immediately below it. In the solution section, the word in parentheses next to the answer to the first question is the first word in the answer to the riddle, the word beside the answer to the second question is the second word, and so on.

The questions are based on the following table.

Table 3
Worktable for Computing Slope and Intercept

Col. 1 Subject	Col. 2 X	Col. 3 Y	Col. 4 X^2	Col. 5 Y^2	Col. 6 XY
Carol	0	2			
Wayne	1	4			
Paula	4	5			
Bobby	3	7			
David	7	8			
$\Sigma =$					

1. What is the value of ΣX?

2. What is the value of ΣY?

3. What is the value of ΣX^2?

4. What is the value of ΣXY?

Worksheet 39 (continued)

5. What is the value of b (the slope)?

6. What is the value of the mean of Y?

7. What is the value of a (the intercept)?

8. If a new person obtains a score of 8 on Test X, what is the predicted value of Y for that person?

9. If a new person obtains a score of 2 on Test X, what is the predicted value of Y for that person?

Solution section:

75 (many)	101 (thorns)	3.000 (peacefully)	−29.810 (themselves)
4.433 (roses)	15 (marriage)	26 (has) 9.035 (no)	−4.36 (afterward)
158 (loving) 103 (funny)	16 (wary) .767 (but)	5.200 (celibacy)	2.899 (has)

Write the answer to the riddle here, putting one word on each line: _____ _____ _____ _____
_____ _____ _____ _____ _____

Notes

Section 40 *z* Test for One Sample

The national mean for the population that takes the College Board's SAT-Verbal test is 500.00, and the standard deviation is 100.00. Using the symbols for the population mean and standard deviation, we can say that

$$\mu = 500.00 \text{ and } \sigma = 100.00$$

(Note that μ is the symbol for the population mean and σ is the symbol for the population standard deviation.)

Suppose that researchers for the Department of Education of the State of Disrepair (the 51st state admitted to the Union) suspected that their students, on average, performed more poorly than the national population. (This is their *research hypothesis*.) Suppose they drew a random sample of 200 students who took the test and found that

$$m = 485.00 \text{ and } s = 101.00$$

At first glance, the data seem to support their *research hypothesis*: On average, the sample of students from the state scored 15 points below the national population. However, the *null hypothesis* also offers an explanation for the 15-point difference. It states that the difference was created by sampling errors due to the random sampling—that, in fact, the *true* difference is zero. (It asserts that this true difference of zero would have been obtained if the entire population, instead of just a random sample, had been studied.) Thus, we have one difference of 15 points for which we have two explanations:

1. the *research hypothesis*, and

2. the *null hypothesis*.

To determine whether the *null hypothesis* is viable, we can test it with a *z test*.

As indicated in Section 18, a *z*-score for an individual is computed with the following formula:[1]

$$z = \frac{X - M}{S}$$

The *z*-score formula determines how many standard deviations an individual is from the mean of his or her group. As it turns out, *z*-scores of greater than 1.96 and less than −1.96 occur less than 5% of the time in a normal distribution. Thus, we can say that the probability of drawing a person on a single random draw who has a *z*-score this extreme is an unlikely event.[2] The same logic (but a modified formula) can be used to determine whether the sample mean of 485.00 is an unlikely event: that is, whether it is unlikely to be obtained by random sampling from a population with a mean of 500.00. The formula we use for the *z* test is

$$z = \frac{m - \mu}{SE_m}$$

The denominator of the formula should look familiar. It is the symbol for the standard error of the mean, which is described in Section 28. Note that the earlier version of the formula included the sample standard deviation (*s*) in the numerator, and the current version includes the population standard deviation (σ). Although the standard error of the mean can be calculated either way, using the population standard error will produce a better result and should be used if it is available. To use the formula, first calculate the standard error of the mean as follows:

$$SE_m = \frac{\sigma}{\sqrt{n}} = \frac{100.00}{\sqrt{200}} = \frac{100.00}{14.142} = 7.071$$

Using 7.071 as the denominator in the formula for *z*, we obtain

$$z = \frac{485.00 - 500.00}{7.071} = \frac{-15.00}{7.071} = -2.121$$

---

[1]For a reference guide to all equations for the statistical tests used in the current textbook, please see Appendix J near the end of this book.
[2]See Section 26 to review this concept.

Now that we have the value of z for this z test, we evaluate it to determine if it is an unlikely event. If we determine that a mean of 485.00 is unlikely to be obtained by random sampling from a population with a mean of 500.00, we will reject the null hypothesis and declare the difference statistically significant.

Remember that the null hypothesis says that the mean difference of 15 points is merely due to random sampling errors. If we determine that this is unlikely, we will reject the hypothesis. In statistics, as in everyday life, if something is unlikely to be true, we reject it and act as though it is false.

To evaluate our z of −2.121, we will first use the constants 1.96 and −1.96. The table of the normal curve (see Section 26 and Table 1 near the end of this book) tells us that the probability of obtaining a z this extreme is .05, or 5 in 100. Because we obtained a z of −2.121, the odds of obtaining our particular result are *less than* 5 in 100. This result may be reported in one of two ways. Note that they both have the same meaning and implications:

1. The null hypothesis has been rejected at the .05 level.

2. The difference is statistically significant at the .05 level.

We can also evaluate our value of z using the constants 2.58 and −2.58. As you learned in Section 26, the odds of obtaining a z this extreme are .01, or 1 in 100. Because we obtained a z of −2.121, our result is *not* sufficiently extreme to classify this as an unlikely event at the .01 level. Thus, using this level, we report the following:

1. The null hypothesis has *not* been rejected at the .01 level. (Another way of saying this: We have failed to reject the null hypothesis at the .01 level.)

2. The difference is *not* significant at the .01 level. (We could also say this: The difference is insignificant at the .01 level.)

Before examining the data, you should select a level (usually .05 or .01) that will be used in the significance test. Had you chosen the .05 level in the above example, you would report to your audience that the difference is significant at that level. Had you initially chosen the .01 level, you would report that the difference is *not* significant at that level. Initially, you should choose only one level.

It is important to note that the decision to *not reject* the null hypothesis is not equivalent to *accepting* the null hypothesis. Recall that, at the beginning of this section, we had two hypotheses that might explain the difference: the null hypothesis and the research hypothesis. If we fail to reject the null hypothesis, we are still left with two hypotheses—the null hypothesis, which we have failed to reject, and the research hypothesis, which cannot be directly tested with statistics. Tests exist only for the null hypothesis. Therefore, if we fail to reject the null hypothesis, we have an inconclusive result because there are two hypotheses that could explain the difference.

Let us review the **_decision rules_** for the *z* test:

1. If the value of *z* that you computed is as extreme as[3]

1.96 or –1.96, then declare the difference significant at the .05 level (i.e., reject the null hypothesis).

2.58 or –2.58, then declare the difference significant at the .01 level (i.e., reject the null hypothesis).

2. If the value of *z* is *not* as extreme as 1.96 or 2.58, do *not* declare the difference significant and do *not* reject the null hypothesis.

Let us apply the decision rules to several cases. In each one, a random sample has been drawn and tested and the population mean and standard deviation are known:

Example 1

Researcher Smith obtained a value of *z* of 3.458 for the difference between two means. She chose the .05 level before starting her study.

1. Should she reject the null hypothesis?

Yes, because 3.458 is more extreme than 1.96.

---

[3]Select one of the two rules *before* examining the data.

2. Should she declare the difference statistically significant?

Yes.

Example 2

Researcher Doe obtained a value of *z* of 1.786 for the difference between two means. He chose the .05 level before starting his study.

1. Should he reject the null hypothesis?

No, because 1.786 is not as extreme as 1.96.

2. Should he declare the difference statistically significant?

No.

Example 3

Researcher Jones obtained a value of *z* of 2.966 for the difference between two means. She chose the .01 level before starting her study.

1. Should she reject the null hypothesis?

Yes, because 2.966 is more extreme than 2.58.

2. Should she declare the difference statistically significant?

Yes.

Example 4

Researcher Daly obtained a value of *z* of –1.999 for the difference between two means. He chose the .01 level before starting his study.

1. Should he reject the null hypothesis?

No, because –1.999 is not as extreme as –2.58.

2. Should he declare the difference statistically significant?

No.

The decision rules in this section apply to what are known as *two-tailed tests*. These are usually appropriate and, thus, are widely used. *Two-tailed tests* and *one-tailed tests* are defined and compared in Section 42.

Terms to Review Before Attempting Worksheet 40
z test, decision rules

Worksheet 40 z Test for One Sample

> **Riddle:** According to Voltaire, what does the length of an argument tell us about who is right?

DIRECTIONS: To find the answer to the riddle, write the answer to each question in the space immediately below it. In the solution section, the word in parentheses next to the answer to the first question is the first word in the answer to the riddle, the word beside the answer to the second question is the second word, and so on.

1. If the standard deviation of a population is 50.00 and a sample of 42 subjects is drawn at random, what is the value of the standard error of the mean?

2. In a study, the mean of a population equals 45.00, the mean of a random sample equals 48.00, and the standard error of the mean equals 2.540. What is the value of z?

3. In a study, the mean of a population equals 100.00, the mean of a random sample equals 90.00, and the standard error of the mean equals 4.110. What is the value of z?

4. What constants are used to determine if z is an unlikely event at the .05 level?

5. What constants are used to determine if a result is significant at the .01 level?

Worksheet 40 (continued)

6. For the type of study described in this section, should the null hypothesis be rejected at the .05 level if z equals 2.343?

7. For the type of study described in this section, should the null hypothesis be rejected at the .05 level if z equals 1.74?

8. "For the type of study described in this section, a value of z of 2.997 means that the null hypothesis should be rejected at the .01 level." Is this statement true *or* false?

9. "*Not rejecting the null hypothesis* is equivalent to *accepting the null hypothesis*." Is this statement true *or* false?

Solution section:

true (are)	7.715 (a)	1.58 and –1.58 (fighting)	yes (both)
1.181 (long)	6.480 (quarrel)	2.96 and –2.96 (nevertheless)	
1.59 (listening)	–2.433 (dispute)	2.58 and –2.58 (that)	
no (parties)	false (wrong)	1.96 and –1.96 (means)	0.243 (time)

Write the answer to the riddle here, putting one word on each line: _____ _____ _____ _____

_____ _____ _____ _____ _____

Section 41 When to Reject the Null Hypothesis

When deciding to reject the null hypothesis, many students become confused because there are two different methods for making the decision, and these methods can seem to contradict each other. The following **null decision rules** are commonly used:

1. Compare the obtained p-value with the pre-defined critical p-value (typically, .05). If the obtained p-value is *less* than the critical p-value, then reject the null hypothesis.

2. Compare the obtained statistic (e.g., the value of z) with its critical value (see tables near the end of this book). If the obtained statistic is *more extreme* than the critical value, then reject the null hypothesis.

Note that a **p-value** represents the probability of obtaining a false alarm (or Type I error, which is the error of failing to reject the null hypothesis when it is false). If we set our critical p-value to .05 and obtain a p-value of .03, then we should reject the null hypothesis because there is only a 3% probability that the given results reflect a false alarm. It is far more likely that the results represent a statistical pattern.

Unfortunately, determining the precise p-value for a set of data without the use of statistical software can be difficult. However, we can estimate p-values based on our understanding of frequency distributions because p-values are simply percentages found in those distributions. Because the z-test is based on the normal curve, we already know that 95% of the scores lie within about 2 standard units (1.96 units, to be precise) from 0. In other words, only 5% of scores are more than 1.96 standard units from zero (see Figure 1 on the next page). Therefore, a z-value of 1.96 is associated with a p-value of exactly .05.[1]

---

[1] The p-value of .05 would only be correct for a two-tailed test. In a one-tailed test, the p-value would be .025.

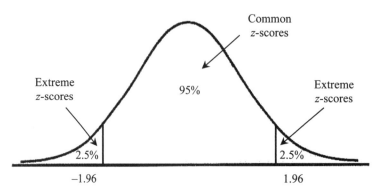

Figure 1. Extreme *z*-scores in the normal distribution.

In the figure, we see numbers on two different scales that should not be compared to each other. The numbers 95% and 2.5% represent the two-dimensional space under the curve. The numbers -1.96 and 1.96 are measures of the distance from zero and are found on a single line. Critically, these scales are inversely related: As the distance from zero increases, the percentage of scores beyond that point decreases. For instance, Figure 1 shows that only 5% (2.5% on each side) of the scores lie beyond a distance of 1.96 units from zero. If we increase the distance to 2.58 units from zero, the percentage drops to 1% (0.5% on each side). Because the percentages under the curve comprise the *p*-values, we can say that as the *z*-value becomes more extreme (farther from 0), the *p*-value decreases, thereby increasing the likelihood that the results are *not* due to chance alone. To reiterate, we should reject the null hypothesis when the *p*-value is very small, which necessarily means that the obtained statistical value is an extreme score.

Terms to Review Before Attempting Worksheet 41

null decision rules, *p*-value

Worksheet 41   When to Reject the Null Hypothesis

> *Riddle*: According to Mark Twain, what can you do after getting your facts first?

DIRECTIONS: To find the answer to the riddle, write the answer to each question in the space immediately below it. In the solution section, the word in parentheses next to the answer to the first question is the first word in the answer to the riddle, the word beside the answer to the second question is the second word, and so on.

1. Rachel obtained a *p*-value of .96. She should _____ the null hypothesis.

   fail to reject

2. Sam obtained a *z*-value of 3.63. He should _____ the null hypothesis.

   reject

3. If the *p*-value is .002, it is likely that the results are _____.

   not due to chance

4. As the *p*-value increases, the *z*-value _____.

   decreases, becomes less extreme

5. If you decide to reject the null hypothesis only if *z* is beyond 99% of the scores, your *p*-value would be _____.

   0.05

6. A *p*-value is the probability that a result is _____.

   due to chance

7. Approximately 95% of scores are within _____ standard unit(s) from zero.

   2

Worksheet 41 (continued)

Solution section:

0.1 (everything)   2 (please)   fail to reject (you)   reject (can)

not due to chance (distort)   1 (only)   0.01 (as)   becomes more extreme (one)

0.05 (if)   0.001 (truth)   stays the same (lie)   due to chance (you)

becomes less extreme (them)   3 (want)

Write the answer to the riddle here, putting one word on each line: <u>you</u> <u>can</u> <u>distort</u> <u>them</u>
<u>if</u> <u>you</u> <u>please</u>

Section 42 One-Tailed Versus Two-Tailed Tests

Section 40 showed how to conduct a two-tailed z test. The decision rule at the .05 level was to reject the null hypothesis when the value of z was as extreme as 1.96 *or* –1.96. The following figure illustrates that the rule is based on the two tails of the distribution, each of which contains 2.5% of the area under the normal curve. (Together, they contain 5%.)

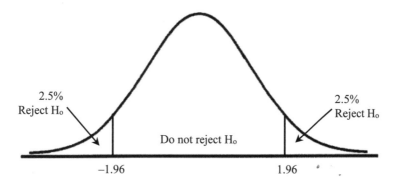

Figure 1. Two-tailed z test values for rejecting the null hypothesis at the .05 level.

In the example in Section 40, the population mean on the SAT-Verbal test was compared with the mean of a random sample of students from the State of Disrepair (the 51st state admitted to the union). By using a two-tailed test, we were expressing interest in one of two types of significant differences:

1. The sample mean is significantly lower than the population mean (as indicated by a z as extreme as –1.96).

2. The sample mean is significantly higher than the population mean (as indicated by a z as extreme as 1.96).

In other words, by using a two-tailed test, we were prepared to detect a difference in either direction—even though the investigators' research hypothesis was only that the students in the State of Disrepair were significantly below the national average. But does it not make sense that if they turned out to be significantly *above* the national average, the investigators from the Department of Education would want to be prepared to make this discovery? Had they selected a one-tailed test

249

initially (and the rules of the game state that a two-tailed or one-tailed test must be selected before the data are examined), they would have had to forgo conducting a significance test of this interesting difference even if their students, on average, had been vastly superior to the national average.

So, if a **two-tailed test** provides more flexibility in examining the outcomes of a study, why would someone choose a **one-tailed test**? One possible reason is that a one-tailed test makes it easier to reject the null hypothesis—but in one, and only one, direction. The following figure illustrates that for the .05 level, we would use a critical value of −1.65 to conduct a one-tailed z test. The entire 5 percent of the area is in one tail. (Compare the two figures in this section.)[1]

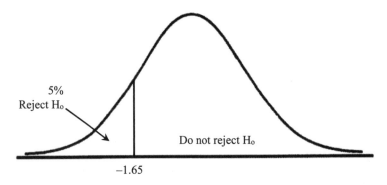

Figure 2. One-tailed z test value for rejecting the null hypothesis at the .05 level.

Notice that it is easier to reach −1.65 than −1.96 (the value for a two-tailed test).[2] In other words, −1.96 is a less likely event than −1.65 because it is farther from the mean. We will be examining a number of other tests in this book. The emphasis will be on two-tailed tests for the following reasons:

---

[1]The null hypothesis for the two-tailed test that we have been considering takes a familiar form. It states that, in truth, the sample mean equals the population mean. The null hypothesis for a one-tailed test states that, in truth, the sample mean is equal to or greater than the population mean.

[2]For a one-tailed z test of whether the sample mean is significantly higher than the population mean, use a critical value of 1.65. For corresponding one-tailed tests at the .01 level, use the critical values of 2.33 and −2.33.

1. Many consumers of research frown on a one-tailed test. They suspect that it may have been chosen only because it made it possible to report a significant difference and not because the underlying logic of the study justified a one-tailed test.

2. In most cases, it is difficult to justify a one-tailed test.[3] It can be justified only if you can convince your audience that there would be no interest in and no implications from a significant difference in a direction other than the one hypothesized in a directional research hypothesis. Usually, an astute consumer can imagine implications. Consider a couple of examples:

Example 1

A researcher hypothesizes that subjects who take Vitamin E supplements will, after a period of years, have fewer wrinkles. This is a directional hypothesis. (See Section 31 to review directional and nondirectional hypotheses.) This researcher might argue that she is interested in significance in only one direction (fewer wrinkles in the experimental group than in the control group) and, therefore, plans to use a one-tailed test.

But suppose the unexpected happened and those who took Vitamin E supplements had many more wrinkles than the control group. Would this be of interest? Would it have implications? Of course. People taking such supplements on their own might want to cut back their consumption of them as well as their consumption of foods rich in Vitamin E. Yet by specifying a one-tailed test in advance, the researcher would be ethically bound *not* to switch and test for significance in the other direction. (Remember, the statistical rules of the game are that by opting for a lower standard for rejecting the null hypothesis, a researcher must agree in advance of seeing the data to test only in one direction.)

---

[3]Some statisticians believe that a one-tailed test is justified whenever a researcher holds a directional research hypothesis (see Section 31). This is a much more liberal standard than is suggested in this section.

Example 2

A researcher hypothesizes that a new computer-assisted program for teaching remedial math is superior to an existing method. This is a directional hypothesis and might be used to justify a one-tailed test. The reasoning might be that if the program is not superior to the existing method, the school district will not switch to the program but will simply continue to use the existing method and ignore the program.

Suppose the unexpected happened and the students who used the computer program scored much lower than those who used the existing program. Would we want to know if this difference is statistically significant? Probably. The process of refining the educational process and keeping it up-to-date is ongoing. This process is accelerated if we not only know what procedures and programs are significantly better than traditional ones, but also which ones are significantly worse.

Should you ever use a one-tailed test? Yes, if you have a directional hypothesis *and* can convince yourself and your audience that a significant difference in the direction other than the one you hypothesized is of no interest.

Terms to Review Before Attempting Worksheet 42

two-tailed test, one-tailed test

Worksheet 42 One-Tailed Versus Two-Tailed Tests

> **Riddle:** Early to bed and early to rise does what?

DIRECTIONS: To find the answer to the riddle, write the answer to each question in the space immediately below it. In the solution section, the word in parentheses next to the answer to the first question is the first word in the answer to the riddle, the word beside the answer to the second question is the second word, and so on.

1. In a normal curve, what percentage of the area is above a *z*-score of 1.96?

    2.5%

2. If we are interested in whether a sample mean is either significantly higher or significantly lower than the population mean, should we use a one-tailed *or* a two-tailed test?

    two-tailed test

3. If we were only interested in whether a sample mean is significantly higher than the population mean, should we use a one-tailed *or* a two-tailed test?

    one-tailed test

4. In a normal curve, what percentage of the area is above a *z*-score of 1.65?

    5%

5. "If an investigator obtained a difference in the direction indicated by her research hypothesis, she would likely be more able to declare the difference significant if she used a one-tailed test than if she used a two-tailed test." Is this statement true *or* false?

    True

Worksheet 42 (continued)

6. "If a researcher declares a difference significant because the value of z is as extreme as 1.65, he is using a two-tailed test." Is this statement true *or* false?

false

7. If a researcher would be interested in a significant difference in either direction, should a one-tailed test be used?

NO

Solution section:

yes (seeing)   1% (dawn)   no (dead)   false (socially)   true (but)

0.005% (leads)   5% (healthy)   2.5% (makes)   two-tailed (a)

one-tailed (person)   maybe (good)   0.5% (night)   reject it (are)

Write the answer to the riddle here, putting one word on each line: *Makes*   *a*   *person*   *healthy*   *but*   *socially*   *dead*

Section 43   Introduction to the *t* Test

In this section, we will consider a frequently encountered problem: how to compare the means of two samples for statistical significance. Let us consider two examples:

Example 1

An investigator wanted to determine whether there were differences between male and female voters in their attitudes toward welfare. Samples of men and women were drawn at random and administered an attitude scale so that a score for each subject could be obtained. Means for the two samples were computed. Women had a mean of 40.00 (on a scale from 0 to 50, where 50 was the most favorable). Men had a mean of 35.00. What accounts for the 5-point difference? One possible explanation is the null hypothesis, which states that there is no true difference between men and women—that the observed difference is due to sampling errors created by random sampling.

Example 1 illustrates that two means may be obtained from a ***survey***—a descriptive study in which a sample is assessed so that inferences about its population can be drawn.

Example 2

A random sample of kittens are fed a vitamin supplement from birth to see if the supplement increases their visual acuity. Another random sample are fed a placebo that looks like the supplement but contains no vitamins. At the end of the study, both samples are tested for visual acuity, and an average acuity score is calculated for each sample. The kittens that took the supplement scored 4 points higher on average than the control group. What accounts for the 4-point difference? One possible explanation is the null hypothesis, which states that there is no true difference between the two samples of kittens—that the observed difference is due to sampling errors created by random sampling.

Example 2 illustrates that two means may be obtained from an ***experiment***—a study in which treatments are given in order that their effects may be observed.

Surveys and experiments are frequently conducted, and they often yield two means each. It is important to be able to test the null hypothesis for the difference between two sample means.[1] We cannot use a *z* test, which was covered in Section 40, because we do not know the standard deviation of the population, which is required to conduct that test. Fortunately, about 100 years ago, a statistician named William Gossett developed the ***t test*** for just the situation being considered. As a test of the null hypothesis, it yields a probability that a given null hypothesis is correct. When the probability that it is correct is low—say .05, or 5%, or less—researchers usually reject the null hypothesis.

The computational procedures for conducting *t* tests are covered in Sections 44 and 46. First, however, consider what makes the *t* test work. In other words, what leads the *t* test to yield a low probability that the null hypothesis is correct? Following are the three basic factors:

1. The larger the samples, the less likely that the difference between two means was created by sampling errors. You probably already intuitively know that larger samples have fewer sampling errors than smaller ones. Thus, when large samples are used, the *t* test is more likely to yield a probability low enough to allow us to reject the null hypothesis.[2]

2. The larger the difference between the two means, the less likely it is that the difference was created by sampling errors. Random sampling tends to create many small differences and few large ones. Thus, when large differences between means are obtained, the *t* test is more likely to yield a probability low enough to allow us to reject the null hypothesis.

3. The smaller the variance among the subjects, the less likely it is that the difference between two means was created by sampling errors. To understand this, consider a population in which all individuals are identical: They all look alike, think alike, and speak and act in unison. How many do you have to sample to get a good sample? Only one because they are all the same. Thus, when there is no variation among subjects, it is not possible to

---

[1]Other types of studies also yield two sample means that are to be compared.
[2]You may recall that increasing sample size yields diminishing returns in terms of reducing errors. (See Section 23.)

have sampling errors. As the variation increases, sampling errors are increasingly more likely to occur.[3]

There are two types of *t* tests: one is for ***independent data*** (sometimes called *uncorrelated data*), and one is for ***dependent data*** (sometimes called *correlated data*). Examples 1 and 2 in this section have independent data. Example 3 describes a study with dependent data.

Example 3

In a study of visual acuity, same-sex siblings (two brothers or two sisters) were identified. For each pair of siblings, a coin was tossed to determine which one received a vitamin supplement and which one received a placebo. Thus, in the control group, there is a subject who is the same-sex sibling of each subject in the experimental group.

The means obtained in the study in Example 3 are subject to less error than the means from Example 2. Remember that in Example 2, there was no matching or pairing of subjects before assignment to conditions. In Example 3, the matching of subjects assures us that the two groups are more similar than if just two independent samples were used. To the extent that genetics and gender are associated with visual acuity, the two groups in Example 3 will be more similar at the onset of the experiment than the two groups in Example 2.[4] The *t* test for dependent data takes this possible reduction of error into account. Thus, it is important to select the right *t* test.

Section 44 illustrates how to conduct a *t* test for independent data, Section 45 illustrates how to interpret the results of *t* tests in general, and Section 46 illustrates how to conduct a *t* test for dependent data. Students using computers to perform calculations may not need to master the calculations in Sections 44 and 46. How-

---

[3]In the types of studies being considered, we do not know the population standard deviation, which would indicate the amount of variation. The *t* test uses the standard deviations of the samples to estimate the variation of the population.

[4]Ideally, we would like to conduct an experiment in which the two groups are initially *identical* in their visual acuity. This would make it more likely that any differences in acuity at the end of the experiment were due to the vitamin supplement and not to initial group differences.

ever, examining the computations in these sections may give you a better understanding of how the *t* test works.

Terms to Review Before Attempting Worksheet 43

survey, experiment, *t* test, independent data, dependent data

Worksheet 43   Introduction to the *t* Test

> *Riddle*: According to Helen Rowland, why does a bachelor get tangled up with a lot of women?

DIRECTIONS: To find the answer to the riddle, write the answer to each question in the space immediately below it. In the solution section, the word in parentheses next to the answer to the first question is the first word in the answer to the riddle, the word beside the answer to the second question is the second word, and so on.

1. Is a study in which treatments are given in order for effects to be observed called a survey *or* an experiment?

   experiment

2. "Two sample means can be obtained only from experiments." Is this statement true *or* false?

   false

3. "The larger the difference between two means, the less likely it is that the difference was created by sampling errors." Is this statement true *or* false?

   True

4. Other things being equal, are large samples *or* small samples more likely to lead to rejection of the null hypothesis?

   large samples

5. Other things being equal, are samples with little variance *or* samples with much variance more likely to lead to rejection of the null hypothesis?

   little variance

Worksheet 43 (continued)

6. "A simple random sample of subjects was selected for the experimental group, and another simple random sample of subjects was selected for the control group." Will this design result in independent data *or* dependent data?

   independent

7. "Subjects were paired according to their ability, and then a coin was tossed for each pair to determine which subject was assigned to the experimental group. The remaining member of each pair was assigned to the control group." Will this design result in independent data *or* dependent data?

   dependent

8. In general, is there usually more sampling error in independent data than in dependent data?

   yes

Solution section:

> independent data (tied)✓ experiment (in)✗ survey (wedding)
>
> false (order)✗ yes (one)   no (argument)   dependent data (to)✗
>
> large samples (avoid)✗ small samples (can)   much variance (silly)
>
> little variance (getting)✓ true (to)✗ *t* (wisely)   sampling error (at)

Write the answer to the riddle here, putting one word on each line: _in_   _order_   _to_   _avoid_

getting _tied_   _to_   _one_

Section 44   Computation of *t* for Independent Data

As noted in the previous section, independent data are obtained when there is no matching or pairing of subjects across groups. In this section, we will first examine how to compute *t* for independent data and how to interpret it using the *t* table.

The formula for *t* is simple:

$$t = \frac{m_1 - m_2}{S_{Dm}}$$

   Where

   m_1 is the mean of the group with the higher mean,

   m_2 is the mean of the group with the lower mean, and

   S_{Dm} is the standard error of the difference between means.

The numerator of the formula is easy to understand. It is the difference between the two means. As you can see, the larger the difference, the larger the value of *t*.[1]

The denominator starts with the familiar symbol *S* (for standard deviation). The subscripts (*D* for *difference* and *m* for *means*) indicate that it is the standard deviation of the difference between means. This standard deviation is called the *standard error of the difference between means*.

In Section 28, we calculated the standard error of a single mean in order to interpret it in light of sampling errors. What we are interpreting in this section is the difference between two means. Thus, we need the standard deviation of this difference. Once we have it, we can use the technique that should be familiar to you by now—determining whether an event is unlikely to occur by chance in light of the number of standard deviations a given statistic is from the mean of the distribution. In this case, we want to know whether the difference between two means is an unlikely event. If it is unlikely (e.g., likely to occur fewer than 5 times in 100 due to chance alone), the difference will be declared statistically significant (i.e., unlikely to be the result of random errors).

---

[1]As you will see later in this section, the larger the value of *t*, the more likely it is that the null hypothesis can be rejected.

It is impractical to directly obtain the S_{Dm} for a given t test.[2] Instead, it must be estimated based on what we know about the sample size and the variance of the samples (remember that the *variance* is simply the square of the standard deviation, which has a symbol of s^2). The S_{Dm} can be estimated using this formula (an alternative equation is included in Appendix J near the end of this book):

$$S_{Dm} = \sqrt{\left[\frac{(n_1 - 1)(s_1^2) + (n_2 - 1)(s_2^2)}{n_1 + n_2 - 2}\right]\left[\frac{1}{n_1} + \frac{1}{n_2}\right]}$$

Where

n_1 is the number of cases in Group 1,

n_2 is the number of cases in Group 2,

s_1 is the standard deviation of Group 1 (which will be squared), and

s_2 is the standard deviation of Group 2 (which will be squared).

Note: When obtaining the standard deviations, you should use the second formula given in Appendix A near the end of this book.

Here is an example:

For Group 1, $m_1 = 24.000$, $s_1 = 1.500$, and $n_1 = 12$

For Group 2, $m_2 = 22.000$, $s_2 = 1.400$, and $n_2 = 11$

$$S_{Dm} = \sqrt{\left[\frac{(12 - 1)(1.500^2) + (11 - 1)(1.400^2)}{12 + 11 - 2}\right]\left[\frac{1}{12} + \frac{1}{11}\right]}$$

$$S_{Dm} = \sqrt{\left[\frac{(11)(2.250) + (10)(1.960)}{21}\right][.083 + .091]}$$

$$S_{Dm} = \sqrt{\left[\frac{(24.750 + 19.60)}{21}\right][.174]}$$

---

[2]If we were to draw an infinitely large number of two samples at random and each time compute the two means of the samples, then compute all the differences between the means, and finally compute the standard deviation of all the differences, we would have the standard error of the difference between means (S_{Dm}) for a given study. We could then compare the difference between means for a given study with this distribution of many differences between means in order to determine whether the difference in the study is unlikely to occur by chance. This is, of course, impractical.

$$S_{Dm} = \sqrt{\left[\frac{44.350}{21}\right][.174]} = \sqrt{[2.112][.174]} = \sqrt{.367} = .606$$

Thus, for the example, the value of S_{Dm} equals .606. We substitute it into the formula for *t* as follows:

$$t = \frac{m_1 - m_2}{S_{Dm}} = \frac{24.000 - 22.000}{.606} = \frac{2.000}{.606} = 3.300$$

The result is called the ***observed value of t***. Thus, in this example, we observed a value of 3.300. To evaluate its meaning, we need to take account of the number of cases that underlie it, using the following formula for the ***degrees of freedom (df)***:[3]

$df = n_1 + n_2 - 2$

Where

n_1 is the number of cases in Group 1,

n_2 is the number of cases in Group 2, and

2 is a constant for this type of problem. (Use it whenever you are conducting a *t* test on two means for independent data.)

For the example being considered,

$df = 12 + 11 - 2 = 21$

You know from previous sections that if a value of *z* as extreme as 1.96 is obtained, the result is declared an unlikely event. That is, it is declared unlikely to occur by chance because the odds are less than .05 that this is a chance deviation in a normal distribution. However, this is a *t* test, which is based on the fact that the underlying distributions are not normal in shape when the sample size is small. Thus, instead of using constants such as 1.96 to evaluate the value of *t*, we use the

---

[3]As you can see by studying this formula, degrees of freedom are directly related to the total number of cases. The name intrigues many students, although its mathematical derivation is not of use to students of applied statistics. For those who are interested, it comes from the fact that all but two of the cases can vary (take on any value), and the same means can be obtained if the remaining two are adjusted to appropriate values. Thus, all but two cases are "free to vary."

appropriate *critical value of t* found in the *t* table in Table 4 near the end of this book.[4]

Examining Table 4, we find that for an infinite number of degrees of freedom (at the bottom of the table), the familiar 1.96 is the critical value. However, in the example, the degrees of freedom equal 21. Look up 21 in the first column of Table 4, and then look at the .05 column to the right. There you find a *critical value* of 2.080. We have found that for 21 degrees of freedom, only values as extreme as 2.080 are unlikely events at the .05 level. The *observed value* is 3.300. Is this an unlikely event? Yes. Thus, we can reject the null hypothesis and declare the result statistically significant at the .05 level.[5]

Is the *observed value* of *t* of 3.300 an unlikely event at the .01 level? Yes, because the *observed value* of 3.300 exceeds the *critical value* for the .01 level for 21 degrees of freedom, which is 2.831. Thus, we can reject the null hypothesis and declare the result statistically significant at the .01 level.

Is the *observed value* of *t* of 3.300 an unlikely event at the .001 level? No, because the *observed value* of 3.300 does *not* exceed the *critical value* for the .001 level for 21 degrees of freedom, which is 3.819. Thus, we *cannot* reject the null hypothesis at the .001 level and cannot declare the result statistically significant at this level.

In review, here is how to use the *t* table (Table 4):

1. Look up the degrees of freedom for your problem in the first column.

2. Move to the right to the significance level you are interested in (.05, .01, or .001) to determine the *critical value*.[6]

3. If the observed value is greater than the critical value,[7] reject the null hypothesis. Otherwise, do not reject it.

---

[4]Table 4 near the end of this book is for a two-tailed *t* test. For a one-tailed test, use Table 5 near the end of this book. See Section 42 to review the differences between one-tailed and two-tailed tests.

[5]This probability is correct if the assumptions underlying the *t* test are met: (1) Random samples from populations with normal distributions are drawn, and (2) the variances of the two populations are similar. Mild violations of these assumptions have little effect on the probabilities. When there is serious doubt as to the tenability of the assumptions, use larger samples (say, 20 or more) to obtain relatively accurate probabilities in the face of violations of the assumptions.

[6]You should select the level you are interested in before examining any of the data.

[7]In the unlikely event that the observed value is equal to the critical value, reject the null hypothesis.

You may have noticed that not all possible values of degrees of freedom (*df*) are shown in Table 4. For instance, suppose you conducted a study in which there were 32 degrees of freedom. Table 4 shows the critical values of *t* for 30 *df* (2.042 for the .05 level) and 40 *df* (2.021 for the .05 level) but not for exactly 32 degrees of freedom. When this situation occurs, use the *lower value of df*. In the case under consideration, for a *df* of 32, use the critical value associated with 30 degrees of freedom.

Terms to Review Before Attempting Worksheet 44

observed value of *t*, degrees of freedom (*df*), critical value of *t*

Worksheet 44   Computation of *t* for Independent Data

> *Riddle*: According to Henry Wadsworth Longfellow, it takes less time to do a thing right than...

DIRECTIONS: To find the answer to the riddle, write the answer to each question in the space immediately below it. In the solution section, the word in parentheses next to the answer to the first question is the first word in the answer to the riddle, the word beside the answer to the second question is the second word, and so on.

Questions 1 through 3 refer to the information in this box.

> For Group 1, $m = 30.000$, $s = 2.100$, $n = 14$
>
> For Group 2, $m = 25.000$, $s = 1.900$, $n = 15$

1. What is the value of the standard error of the difference between means? (The answer in the solution section was obtained through rounding at each step to three decimal places. Allow for minor differences if you use a different procedure.)

2. What is the observed value of *t*? (Use the value of S_{Dm} in the solution section for Question 1.)

3. Based on a two-tailed test, is the difference statistically significant at the .05 level?

4. What is the critical value of *t* for a two-tailed test at the .05 level for a problem in which there are 6 degrees of freedom?

Worksheet 44 (continued)

5. For a problem in which the observed value of $t = 1.999$ with 21 degrees of freedom (two-tailed), may the null hypothesis be rejected at the .05 level?

6. "Based on the information in Question 5, the difference between the means is statistically significant at the .05 level." Is this statement true *or* false?

7. "For a problem in which the observed value of $t = 2.500$ with 26 degrees of freedom (two-tailed), the difference is significant at the .05 level but not at the .01 level." Is this statement true *or* false?

8. Using the information in Question 7, what decision should be made about the null hypothesis at the .05 level?

9. If $n = 30$ for one group and $n = 32$ for another group, what is the value of *df* for a *t* test on independent data?

Solution section:

false (you)	2.348 (mistake)	.872 (lengthy)	2.447 (explain)	true (did)
.742 (it)	6.739 (does)	no (why)	3.707 (always)	reject it (it) yes (to)
do not reject it (helpless)	62 (being)	60 (wrong)	61 (difficult)	

Worksheet 44 (continued)

Write the answer to the riddle here, putting one word on
each line: _____ _____ _____ _____

_____ _____ _____ _____ _____

"Now I have zero degrees of freedom."

Section 45   Reporting the Results of *t* Tests

We are considering the use of the *t* test to test the difference between two sample means for significance. Obviously, the values of the means should be reported in a research report before reporting the results of the *t* test conducted on them. In addition, the values of the standard deviations and the number of cases in each group should be reported. This may be done within the context of a sentence or in a table. Table 1 shows a typical table.

Table 1
Means and Standard Deviations

	m	*s*	*n*
Group A	2.50	1.87	6
Group B	6.00	1.89	6

Alternatively, we might include a bar graph (see Figure 1 below) to display the mean difference visually. While a bar graph may not communicate the standard deviations and sample sizes as clearly as a table does, Figure 1 includes 95% confidence intervals. Because the two confidence intervals do not overlap, we might conclude that each sample mean is drawn from a different population. Upon examination, the figure should agree with the results of the statistical test.

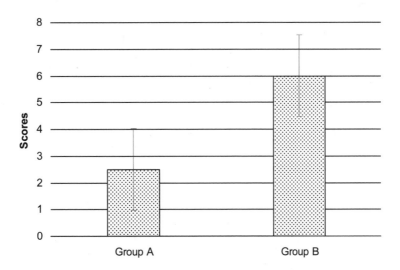

Figure 1. Means and 95% confidence intervals for Groups A and B.

The samples that formed Groups A and B were drawn at random. The null hypothesis states that the 3.50-point difference (6.00 – 2.50 = 3.50) between the means of 2.50 and 6.00 is the result of sampling errors (i.e., errors resulting from random sampling) and that the true difference in the population is zero.[1] Because the sampling error for each sample mean is represented by the 95% confidence intervals in the figure, we know that the null hypothesis is unlikely to be true.

The results of the *t* test may be described in several ways. Here are three examples for the results in Table 1 on the previous page:

Example 1

The difference between the means is statistically significant ($t = 3.22$, $df = 10$, $p < .01$, two-tailed test).

To a knowledgeable reader, the results in Example 1 indicate that the null hypothesis has been rejected because *statistically significant* is synonymous with *rejecting the null hypothesis*.

Example 2

The difference between the means is significant at the .01 level ($t = 3.22$, $df = 10$, two-tailed test).

In Example 2, the author has indicated that significance was obtained at the .01 level. This tells us that p was equal to or less than .01. Thus, the null hypothesis was rejected.

Example 3

The null hypothesis was rejected at the .01 level, $t (10) = 3.22$, $p < .001$, two-tailed test.

From Example 3, we know that the difference is statistically significant because rejecting the null hypothesis is the same as declaring statistical significance. Example 3 also shows the results in a format consistent with the guidelines of the American Psychological Association (APA).

---

[1]This statement of the null hypothesis is for a two-tailed test. See Section 42 to review the difference between one-tailed and two-tailed tests.

All of the three examples shown are acceptable. Authors of journal articles typically describe differences as either *statistically significant* or *statistically insignificant,* and they seldom mention the null hypothesis. In theses and dissertations, explicit references to the null hypothesis are more common.

When using the word *significant* in reporting the results of significance tests, you should always modify it with the adjective *statistically* because a result may be **statistically significant** but not be of any **practical significance**. For instance, suppose you found a statistically significant difference of 2 points in favor of a computer-assisted approach over a traditional lecture/textbook approach. While it is statistically significant, it may not be of practical significance if the school district would have to invest a sizable amount of money to buy new hardware and software in order to implement the computer-assisted program. In other words, the cost of acting on the difference may be too great in light of the absolute size of the benefit, making it of little practical significance.

Now, consider how to report a difference that is not significant. Table 2 presents results for which the difference between the two means is not significant. Examples 4 through 6 show some ways to express the results of the *t* test.

Table 2
Means and Standard Deviations

	m	*s*	*n*
Group X	8.14	2.19	7
Group Y	5.71	2.81	7

Example 4

The difference between the means is not statistically significant ($t = 1.80$, $df = 12$, $p > .05$, two-tailed test).

In Example 4, the fact that p is *greater than* (>) .05 suggests that we should not reject the null hypothesis and not declare statistical significance.

Example 5

For the difference between the means, $t = 1.80$ ($df = 12$, *n.s.*, two-tailed test).

The author of Example 5 has used the abbreviation *n.s.* to indicate that she has declared the difference not significant. Because a specific probability level is not given, most readers will assume that it was not significant at the .05 level—the most liberal of the widely used levels. Example 4 is preferable to Example 5 because Example 4 indicates the specific probability level in question.

Example 6

The null hypothesis for the difference between the means was not rejected at the .05 level ($t = 1.80$, $df = 12$, two-tailed test).

While reading journal articles, theses, and dissertations, you will find variations in the exact words used to describe the results of *t* tests. The examples in this section show models that you might use in your own writing.

Terms to Review Before Attempting Worksheet 45

statistically significant, practical significance

Worksheet 45 Reporting the Results of *t* Tests

Riddle: According to Ogden Nash, for a successful marriage, whenever you are wrong, admit it. What else should you do?

DIRECTIONS: To find the answer to the riddle, write the answer to each question in the space immediately below it. In the solution section, the word in parentheses next to the answer to the first question is the first word in the answer to the riddle, the word beside the answer to the second question is the second word, and so on.

Box A

The difference between the means is statistically significant, $t(26) = 2.12$, $p < .05$, two-tailed test.

1. For Box A, was the null hypothesis rejected at the .05 level?

yes

Box B

The null hypothesis was rejected at the .05 level ($t = 3.145$, $df = 6$, two-tailed test).

2. "For Box B, the difference is statistically significant at the .05 level." Is this statement true *or* false?

true

3. Is the statement in Box A *or* the statement in Box B in the form more often used by the American Psychological Association?

Box A

Worksheet 45 (continued)

Box C

> The difference between the means is not statistically significant ($t = 1.72$, $df = 25$, two-tailed test).

4. What important type of information is missing from Box C?

probability level

5. For Box C, has the author rejected the null hypothesis?

NO

6. The abbreviation *n.s.* stands for what two words?

not significant

Solution section:

true (you) probability level (right) Box B (cowardice) no (shut)

null significance (last) not significant (up) Box A (are) yes (whenever)

Box C (running) false (bloody) standard deviation (cry)

Write the answer to the riddle here, putting one word on each line: *whenever* *you* *are* *right*, *shut* *up.*

Section 46   Computation of t for Dependent Data

This section shows how to test the null hypothesis for the difference between two means when dependent data are being analyzed. Dependent data are obtained when each score in one set of scores is paired with a score in another set. See Section 43 to review the difference between dependent and independent data.

The formula for t looks almost the same as the formula for a t test for independent data that was presented in Section 44. It is

$$t = \frac{m_1 - m_2}{S_{mD}}$$

Where

   m_1 is the mean of the group with the higher mean,

   m_2 is the mean of the group with the lower mean, and

   S_{mD} is the standard error of the mean difference.

The numerator is the difference between the two means. As you can see, the larger the difference, the larger the value of t.

The denominator starts with the familiar symbol S (for standard deviation). The subscripts (m and D) indicate that it is the standard deviation of the mean difference. Following is the formula for S_{mD} (an alternative equation is included in Appendix J near the end of this book):

$$S_{mD} = \sqrt{\frac{\sum D^2 - (\sum D)^2 \div n}{n(n-1)}}$$

Where

   D is the difference between a pair of means, and

   n is the number of *pairs* of cases.

To use this formula, first list the two sets of scores, making sure that two paired scores are on each line. Table 1 on the next page illustrates this. In column 1 are the names of the pairs. For instance, each pair could be identical twins, one of whom was randomly assigned to the experimental group, while the other was assigned to

Table 1

Scores for Pairs of Subjects

	Experimental (X_1)	Control (X_2)	D	D^2
Pair A	8	5	3	9
Pair B	12	10	2	4
Pair C	10	11	−1	1
Pair D	9	6	3	9
Pair E	18	15	3	9
Pair F	11	7	4	16
Pair G	8	2	6	36
SUMS	$\Sigma X_1 = 76$	$\Sigma X_2 = 56$	$\Sigma D = 20$	$\Sigma D^2 = 84$

the control group.[1] The difference between each pair of scores was computed and entered in the column under D. Then the differences were squared and entered in the column under D^2. Substituting into the formula for the standard error of the mean difference, we obtain

$$S_{mD} = \sqrt{\frac{\Sigma D^2 - (\Sigma D)^2 \div n}{n(n-1)}}$$

$$S_{mD} = \sqrt{\frac{84 - (20)^2 \div 7}{7(7-1)}}$$

(Notice that in the numerator, we divide before subtracting in the subsequent steps.)

$$S_{mD} = \sqrt{\frac{84 - 400 \div 7}{7(6)}}$$

$$S_{mD} = \sqrt{\frac{84 - 57.143}{42}} = \sqrt{\frac{26.857}{42}} = \sqrt{.639} = .799$$

Before solving for the value of *t*, we must first compute the two means: $m_1 = 76/7 = 10.857$ and $m_2 = 56/7 = 8.000$. We now have the three values required by the formula for *t*. These have been substituted into the following formula:

$$t = \frac{m_1 - m_2}{S_{mD}} = \frac{10.857 - 8.000}{.799} = \frac{2.857}{.799} = 3.576 = 3.58$$

---

[1]The members of the pairs do not have to be related. For instance, pairs could have been formed through matching the subjects on the basis of their scores on an achievement test.

In order to evaluate the observed value of *t* using the critical values of *t* in Table 4 near the end of this book, first compute the degrees of freedom (*df*).[2] For dependent data, the formula is

$$df = n - 1$$

Where

n is the number of *pairs* of scores.

In this instance, there are 14 scores but only 7 pairs. Therefore,

$$df = 7 - 1 = 6$$

Examination of Table 4 near the end of this book for 6 degrees of freedom reveals that the **critical value** for the .05 level is 2.447. Because our **observed value** of *t* (3.58) exceeds the critical value, the difference between the means is significant at the .05 level, and the null hypothesis may be rejected at this level.

Table 4 also reveals that the critical value for the .01 level is 3.707. Because the observed value of *t* (3.58) does *not* exceed the critical value, the difference between the means is *not* significant at the .01 level, and the null hypothesis may *not* be rejected at this level.[3]

Keep in mind that you should select the level at which you wish to test before examining any of the data. In this instance, if you had selected the .05 level, you would have been allowed to declare the result significant. If, however, you had selected the .01 level, you would not have been allowed to do so.

The next section shows how to analyze the differences among two *or more* means. As you can see, the formula for *t* allows you to enter the values for only two means—limiting the usefulness of the *t* test to studies in which only two means are to be compared.

---

[2]For a one-tailed test, use the critical values in Table 5 near the end of this book. See Section 42 to review the difference between a one-tailed and a two-tailed test.
[3]In the unlikely event that the observed value is equal to the critical value, reject the null hypothesis.

Terms to Review Before Attempting Worksheet 46

critical value, observed value

"The committee met to approve your proposed data analysis
for your thesis. But first, we had to approve the approval,
providing everyone agreed to disagree to approve the
agreement, which approved the approval agreement.
After that, things got complicated."

Worksheet 46 Computation of *t* for Dependent Data

> *Riddle*: According to Mark Twain, how do we know that most writers regard the truth as valuable?

DIRECTIONS: To find the answer to the riddle, write the answer to each question in the space immediately below it. In the solution section, the word in parentheses next to the answer to the first question is the first word in the answer to the riddle, the word beside the answer to the second question is the second word, and so on.

The questions refer to the information in this box.

	Experimental	Control
Pair A	8	5
Pair B	4	1
Pair C	3	4
Pair D	8	5
Pair E	9	5
Pair F	9	6

1. To three decimal places, what is the value of the difference between the two means?

2. To three decimal places, what is the value of the standard error of the mean difference? (The answer in the solution section was obtained by rounding to three decimal places at each step. Allow for minor differences if you use a different procedure.)

Worksheet 46 (continued)

3. To two decimal places, what is the observed value of t?

4. What is the critical value of t at the .05 level for this problem? (Use Table 4 near the end of this book.)

5. Is the difference between the means significant at the .05 level?

6. "The null hypothesis may be rejected at the .05 level." Is this statement true *or* false?

7. Is the difference between the means significant at the .01 level?

8. "The null hypothesis may be rejected at the .01 level." Is this statement true *or* false?

Solution section:

> 6.833 (as)   15.000 (lie)   false (use)   2.500 (because)   3.48 (are)   true (in)
>
> 53.00 (never)   2.571 (most)   yes (economical)   .719 (they)
>
> 37.500 (waver)   no (its)   .05 (argument)   .01 (discourse)   .001 (been)

Worksheet 46 (continued)

Write the answer to the riddle here, putting one word on each line: _____ _____ _____ _____

_____ _____ _____ _____

"For my statistical experiment, I'm going to drive downtown, get a great parking spot, and then I'm going to count how many people ask me if I'm leaving."

Notes

Section 47 Introduction to Analysis of Variance

Sections 43 through 46 described the t test, which tests the null hypothesis regarding the difference between *two* means. A closely related test is the analysis of variance (***ANOVA***), which is sometimes informally called the F test. ANOVA is used to test the difference(s) among *two or more means*.

First, ANOVA can be used to test the difference between two means. To do so, we calculate a statistic called F, calculate the degrees of freedom for F, and evaluate F using a table of critical values of F. (The computational procedures are described in the next section.) After doing this, the resulting probability will be the same as the probability that we would have obtained using a t test. However, the value of F will not be the same as the value of t. In fact, for a given set of data yielding two means to be compared, $F = t^2$. Because the end result of primary interest in significance testing is the probability, if you have already mastered the t test, you do not need to learn how to use ANOVA to test the difference between two means. However, ANOVA can also be used to test the differences among more than two means in a single test, which cannot be done with a t test.[1]

Consider Example 1 to see an illustration of the use of ANOVA.

Example 1

A new drug for treating migraine headaches was tested on three groups selected at random. The first group received 250 milligrams, the second received 100 milligrams, and the third received a placebo (an inert substance). The average reported pain level for the three groups (on a scale from 0 to 20, with 20 representing the most pain) was determined through calculating the means. The means for the groups were as follows:[2]

> Group 1: $m = 1.78$
> Group 2: $m = 3.98$
> Group 3: $m = 12.88$

---

[1]The assumptions underlying ANOVA are that the variances of the groups are similar (i.e., homogeneous), that the groups are independent, and that the subjects were selected at random.
[2]When reporting means, you should also report the associated values of the standard deviations.

In Example 1, there are three differences among the means: (1) The difference between Groups 1 and 2, (2) the difference between Groups 1 and 3, and (3) the difference between Groups 2 and 3. Instead of running three separate t tests,[3] we can run a single ANOVA to test the significance of this *set of differences*. There are two ways the results of Example 1 can be reported. Example 2 shows one of them:

Example 2

The differences among the means are statistically significant at the .01 level ($F = 58.769$, $df = 2, 36$)

Note that the method of reporting in Example 2 is similar to that for reporting the results of a t test.[4] This result tells us that there is a significant difference with $p <$ .01. Thus, the null hypothesis may be rejected at the .01 level. The null hypothesis for this test says that the *set of three differences* was created at random. By rejecting the null hypothesis, we are rejecting the notion that *one or more* of the differences were created at random. Notice that the test does not tell us which of the three differences is responsible for the rejection of the null hypothesis. It could be that only one or two of the three differences was responsible for the significance. Procedures for determining which individual differences are significant are described in Sections 49 and 50.

Example 3 on the next page shows another way that the results of an ANOVA are commonly reported in journals. It is called an *ANOVA table*. In the table, you see the values of F, df, and p that were reported in Example 2. You also see the values of the *sum of squares* and the *mean square*, which are intermediate values obtained in the calculation of F. (For instance, if you divide the mean square of 315.592 by the mean square of 5.370, you will obtain F.) Procedures for calculating these intermediate values are described in Section 48. For the typical consumer of research, however, these values are of little interest.[5]

---

[3]It would be inappropriate to run three separate t tests without an adjustment in the standard probabilities for t. Alternatives to doing this are presented in Sections 49 and 50.

[4]You probably noticed that there are two values reported as degrees of freedom for an ANOVA. The next section indicates how to obtain and use them in evaluating F.

[5]Those with advanced training in statistics can use these intermediate values to enhance their interpretation of the data. The typical reader is interested in whether or not the null hypothesis has been rejected, which is indicated by the value of p.

Example 3

Table 1

Analysis of Variance Table for the Data in Example 2

Source of variation	df	Sum of squares	Mean square	F
Between groups	2	631.185	315.592	58.769*
Within groups	36	193.320	5.370	
Total	38	824.505		

*$p < .01$

Notice that the probability in Example 3 is given in a footnote, which is common. However, sometimes it will be given in the table, and sometimes it will be given in the text that describes the table.

The technique we are considering can be generalized to a larger number of means. Consider Example 4:

Example 4

Four methods of teaching computer literacy were used in an experiment, which resulted in four means. This produced six differences:

1. The difference between Methods 1 and 2.
2. The difference between Methods 1 and 3.
3. The difference between Methods 1 and 4.
4. The difference between Methods 2 and 3.
5. The difference between Methods 2 and 4.
6. The difference between Methods 3 and 4.

A single ANOVA can determine whether the null hypothesis for this entire set of six differences should be rejected. If the result is not significant, the researcher is done. If the result is significant, he or she may test to see which of the six differences are significant by using the techniques described in Sections 49 and 50.

The examples we have been considering are examples of what is known as a ***one-way ANOVA*** (also known as a *single-factor ANOVA*). This term is derived from the fact that subjects were classified *one* way. In Example 1, they were classified only according to the drug group to which they were assigned. In Example 4, they were classified only according to the method of instruction to which they were exposed. In Section 51, you will be introduced to the **two-way ANOVA** (also known as a *two-factor ANOVA*), in which each subject is classified in two ways: (1) which drug group he or she was assigned to, and (2) whether he or she is male or female. A two-way ANOVA permits us to answer questions that are potentially more interesting.

In the next section, the computational techniques for a single-factor ANOVA are presented. If you are using a computer to perform calculations, you may not need to master the section, but you should examine it carefully to obtain a better understanding of ANOVA.

Terms to Review Before Attempting Worksheet 47

ANOVA, one-way ANOVA, two-way ANOVA

Worksheet 47 Introduction to Analysis of Variance

> *Riddle*: According to Ingrid Bergman, a kiss is a lovely trick designed by nature to do what?

DIRECTIONS: To find the answer to the riddle, write the answer to each question in the space immediately below it. In the solution section, the word in parentheses next to the answer to the first question is the first word in the answer to the riddle, the word beside the answer to the second question is the second word, and so on.

1. ANOVA can be used to test the differences among how many means?

    two or more

2. For two means, will ANOVA and the *t* test yield the same probability?

    yes

3. In a comparison of three means, there are three differences. If *F* is significant, does this mean that all three differences are significant?

    NO

4. As a result of an ANOVA, this conclusion was drawn: The difference between the means was significant at the .05 level. What decision has been made about the null hypothesis?

    reject it

5. For the typical consumer of research, what statistic in an ANOVA table is of greatest interest?

    p

Worksheet 47 (continued)

6. For four means in a one-way analysis of variance, how many differences among means result?

6

7. Does Example 1 in this section illustrate a one-way *or* a two-way ANOVA?

one-way

Solution section:

one-way (superfluous)   two-factor (love) F (affection) df (never)

reject it (when)   do not reject it (only)   two or more (to)   yes (stop)

no (speech)   4 (always)   6 (become) p (words)   accept it (vision)

Write the answer to the riddle here, putting one word on each line: *to   Stop   Speech   when   words   become   Superfluous*

Section 48 Computations for a One-Way ANOVA

In Table 1, subjects were classified according to the three groups they were assigned to in an experiment. Group A received large amounts of praise, Group B received moderate amounts of praise, and Group C received no praise for correct answers to math problems. Their scores on a posttest are shown in the first three columns of Table 1. At the bottom of these columns are the sums of the scores and the associated means (e.g., for column 1, 36/6 = 6.000). In column 4 are the squared scores for Group A, in column 5 are the squared scores for Group B, and in column 6 are the squares of the scores for Group C. The sums of the squared scores are shown at the bottom of columns 4 through 6.

Table 1
Scores for Three Groups on a Posttest and Related Statistics

Col. 1	Col. 2	Col. 3	Col. 4	Col. 5	Col. 6
Group A	Group B	Group C	A^2	B^2	C^2
7	4	3	49	16	9
6	6	2	36	36	4
5	4	1	25	16	1
8	7	3	64	49	9
3	5	4	9	25	16
7	7	1	49	49	1
$\Sigma X_A = 36$	$\Sigma X_B = 33$	$\Sigma X_C = 14$	$\Sigma X_A^2 = 232$	$\Sigma X_B^2 = 191$	$\Sigma X_C^2 = 40$
$m = 6.000$	$m = 5.500$	$m = 2.333$			

In order to test the significance of the differences among the three means, we need to compute the value of F and, using the associated values of the degrees of freedom, compare the computed value of F with the critical values of F in Table 6 near the end of this book (for the .05 level) or Table 7 near the end of this book (for the .01 level) in order to determine significance.[1] To compute the value of F, follow these steps (an alternative set of equations is included in Appendix J near the end of this book):

---

[1]This procedure is similar to the one used with the t test. Remember that we computed the value of t and the associated degrees of freedom and then compared the observed value of t with the critical values in Table 4 near the end of this book.

Step 1: Set up a table similar to Table 1 on the previous page. In this table, there are three sets of scores, resulting in six columns. The number of columns will depend on how many groups you have. If you have only two sets of scores, there will be four columns. If you have four sets of scores, there will be eight columns, and so on.

Step 2: Compute the ***total sum of squares*** (SS_T). This is the formula and its solution for the example under consideration:

$$SS_T = \sum X^2 - \frac{(\sum X_T)^2}{N}$$

> Where
>> $\sum X^2$ is the sum of the squared scores for each group (in this case, 232, 191, and 40),
>>
>> $\sum X_T$ is the sum of *all* the scores (in this case, the sum of all 18 scores, which can be obtained by adding the sums of the three sets of scores: $36 + 33 + 14 = 83$), and
>>
>> N is the total number of subjects (in this case, 18).

$$SS_T = 232 + 191 + 40 - \frac{83^2}{18} = 80.278$$

Step 3: Compute the ***between-groups sum of squares*** (SS_b). This is a measure of the variation between the groups and is needed in order to compute the value of F. The formula and its solution for the problem under consideration are shown here:

$$SS_b = \sum \frac{(\sum X)^2}{n} - \frac{(\sum X_T)^2}{N}$$

> Where
>> $\sum X$ is the sum of the scores of each group (in this case, 36, 33, and 14, which will be used separately),
>>
>> $\sum X_T$ is the sum of *all* of the scores (in this case, the sum of all 18 scores, which is $36 + 33 + 14 = 83$),
>>
>> n is the number of subjects in each group (in this case, 6), and
>>
>> N is the total number of subjects (in this case, 18).

$$SS_b = \frac{36^2}{6} + \frac{33^2}{6} + \frac{14^2}{6} - \frac{83^2}{18}$$

$$= 216.000 + 181.500 + 32.667 - 382.722$$

$$= 430.167 - 382.722 = 47.445$$

Step 4: Compute the ***within-groups sum of squares*** (SS_w). This is an estimate of the amount of variation within groups.[2] We can obtain it by subtracting the SS_b from the SS_T, as shown here:

$$SS_w = SS_T - SS_b = 80.278 - 47.445 = 32.833$$

Before proceeding, enter the values that have been calculated up to this point into an ANOVA table, which helps us to organize and keep track of our statistics. Here is the table with the values computed up to this point.[3]

Table 2
ANOVA Table With Sum of Squares

Source of variation	df	Sum of squares	Mean square	F
Between groups	?	47.445	?	?*
Within groups	?	32.833	?	
Total	?	80.278		

*p = ?

Step 5: Compute the df for between groups (df_b), which is the number of groups minus one:

$$df_b = n - 1 = 3 - 1 = 2$$

Step 6: Compute the df for the total (df_T), which is the total number of all subjects minus one:

$$df_T = N - 1 = 18 - 1 = 17$$

---

[2]The statistic F is a comparison of the variation within groups (which is the natural amount of variation among subjects) with the variation between groups (which, in this case, may have been caused by the experimental treatments). If the variation between is sufficiently greater than the variation within, the difference will be declared statistically significant.
[3]ANOVA tables were introduced in the previous section.

Step 7: Compute the *df* for within groups (df_w), which can be obtained by subtracting the df_b (for between) from the df_T (for the total):

$$df_w = df_T - df_b = 17 - 2 = 15$$

Before proceeding, enter the values of the degrees of freedom into this ANOVA table:

Table 3
ANOVA Table With Sum of Squares and df

Source of variation	df	Sum of squares	Mean square	F
Between groups	2	47.445	?	?*
Within groups	15	32.833	?	
Total	17	80.278		

*p = ?

Step 8: Compute the mean squares (*MS*). This is accomplished by dividing each sum of squares by its associated *df*. Thus, the **between-groups mean square** (*MS*b) is 47.445/2 = 23.723, and the **within-groups mean square** (*MS*w) is 32.833/15 = 2.189.

Step 9: Compute the value of *F* by dividing the mean square for between groups by the mean square for within groups, as shown here:

$$F = \frac{MS_b}{MS_w} = \frac{23.723}{2.189} = 10.837$$

Enter the results of Steps 8 and 9 into this ANOVA table:

Table 4
ANOVA Table With Sum of Squares, df, Mean Squares, and F

Source of variation	df	Sum of squares	Mean square	F
Between groups	2	47.445	23.723	10.837
Within groups	15	32.833	2.189	
Total	17	80.278		

*p = ?

At this point, all that is missing is the value of p. To obtain this, we must compare the observed value of F (10.837) with the appropriate critical value in Table 6 near the end of this book (for the .05 level) or Table 7 near the end of this book (for the .01 level). Assume that we decided before examining the data to use the .05 level. Thus, we should examine Table 6 near the end of this book.[4]

The columns in Table 6 near the end of this book are labeled with degrees of freedom associated with the "Between-Groups Degrees of Freedom" (df_b). As you can see in Table 4 on the previous page, this is 2. Thus, we should look at the column labeled "2." The rows are labeled with "Within-Groups Degrees of Freedom"—in this case, it is 15. Thus, we go to where the column labeled "2" meets the row labeled "15," where we find a ***critical value of F*** of 3.68.

Here is the decision rule:

If the observed value of F (in this case, 10.837) is greater than the critical value (in this case, 3.68),[5] reject the null hypothesis. Otherwise, do not reject it.

Using the decision rule, we reject the null hypothesis at the .05 level and report that $p < .05$. Thus, the set of differences among the three means is statistically significant at the .05 level.

Table 5 is an ANOVA table with all the values:

Table 5
ANOVA Table With Sum of Squares

Source of variation	df	Sum of squares	Mean square	F
Between groups	2	47.445	23.723	10.837
Within groups	15	32.833	2.189	
Total	17	80.278		

*$p < .05$

Although we now know that the set of differences among the three means (6.000, 5.500, and 2.333) is statistically significant at the .05 level, we do not know

---

[4]Table 7 is read in the same way as Table 6.
[5]In the unlikely event that the observed value is exactly equal to the critical value, reject the null hypothesis.

which individual pairs of differences (A vs. B, A vs. C, or B vs. C) are significant. However, we can gain insight by graphing the means in a figure. As we learned in Section 30, a bar graph is an appropriate way to display mean differences. The figure below displays the three means along with the 95% confidence intervals. By viewing where the confidence intervals do and do not overlap, we can deduce which differences are statistically significant. Figure 1 indicates that the group receiving no praise (i.e., Group C) performed worse than the other groups, which did not differ. This conclusion can be confirmed by using the procedure described in Section 49.

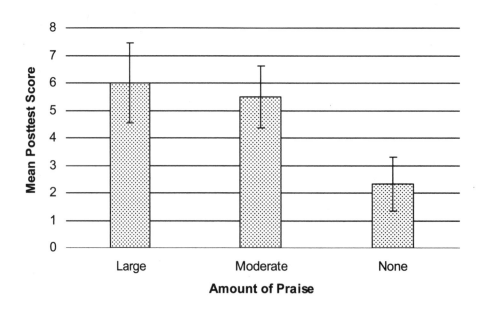

Figure 1. Mean posttest score as a function of praise amount.

Terms to Review Before Attempting Worksheet 48

**total sum of squares, between-groups sum of squares,
within-groups sum of squares, between-groups mean square,
within-groups mean square, critical value of *F***

Worksheet 48 Computations for a One-Way ANOVA

> *Riddle*: What does experience help you recognize?

DIRECTIONS: To find the answer to the riddle, write the answer to each question in the space immediately below it. In the solution section, the word in parentheses next to the answer to the first question is the first word in the answer to the riddle, the word beside the answer to the second question is the second word, and so on.

The questions on this worksheet refer to the scores in the following table.

Table 6
Scores for Three Groups on a Posttest

Col. 1	Col. 2	Col. 3	Col. 4	Col. 5	Col. 6
Group A	Group B	Group C	A^2	B^2	C^2
3	4	0			
2	5	1			
1	3	1			
5	4	2			
$\Sigma X_A =$	$\Sigma X_B =$	$\Sigma X_C =$	$\Sigma X_A^2 =$	$\Sigma X_B^2 =$	$\Sigma X_C^2 =$
$m =$	$m =$	$m =$			

1. What is the value of the mean for Group A?

2. What is the value of ΣX_C^2?

3. What is the value of the within-groups sum of squares?

Worksheet 48 (continued)

4. What is the value of the within-groups mean square?

5. What is the observed value of F?

6. Are the differences among the means significant at the .05 level?

7. What decision should be made about the null hypothesis at the .05 level?

Solution section:

2.750 (your)   6.000 (mistakes)   9.084 (ageless)   do not reject it (limitless)
30.917 (royalty)   18.167 (refuses)   reject it (again)   yes (them)
4.26 (my)   6.411 (make)   12.750 (when)   1.417 (you)   39 (never)
66 (interesting)   4.000 (well)   1.000 (younger)   11 (birthday)

Write the answer to the riddle here, putting one word on each line: _____ _____ _____ _____

_____ _____ _____

Section 49   Tukey's *HSD* Test

As noted in the previous section, when a one-way ANOVA is statistically significant, one cannot be sure which specific differences are significant. Thus, for the example in Section 48, there are three differences between pairs of means:

1. Group A versus Group B (6.000 – 5.500 = 0.500)

2. Group A versus Group C (6.000 – 2.333 = 3.667)

3. Group B versus Group C (5.500 – 2.333 = 3.167)

This *set of differences* was found to be statistically significant at the .05 level.

A number of tests have been suggested for determining the significance of the differences among pairs of means after obtaining an overall significant result using ANOVA.[1] One of these tests is ***Tukey's Honestly Significant Difference (HSD) test***. The formula is

$$HSD = q\sqrt{\frac{MS_{within}}{n}}$$

Where

q is the studentized range statistic (which will be obtained from Table 8 near the end of this book).

MS_{within} is the mean square for within groups calculated for the one-way ANOVA. (See Table 5 in Section 48, where you will find a value of 2.189 for the example.)

n is the number of individuals in *each* group (in the example from Section 48, there are 6 subjects in each group); thus, $n = 6$. (Note that Tukey's *HSD* test can be used only if there is the same number of individuals in each group.)

---

[1]Because the tests are conducted *after* an ANOVA, they are called *post hoc tests* and are designed for use when individual comparisons were not planned in advance based on theory. They are also known as *multiple-comparisons tests*. Although a *t* test may be used to test the difference between a pair of means, its use to make repeated comparisons involving the use of data more than one time makes the probabilities obtained with *t* inaccurate.

To use the formula, first determine the value of *q* as follows: Calculate the degrees of freedom associated with the within-groups mean square. For the example, it can be read from Table 5 in Section 48—where it is 15. Also determine the number of treatments—in the example, this is 3. Go to Table 8 near the end of this book, and read the value of *q* from the table: Where 3 *treatments* meet a *df* of 15, we find the value of *q* for our problem to be 3.67 for the .05 level.[2] Substituting this value of *q* and the other required values into the formula, the value of *HSD* is obtained:

$$HSD = 3.67\sqrt{\frac{2.189}{6}} = 2.217$$

Now compare the value of *HSD* (2.217) to the differences between the pairs of means, which are shown at the beginning of this section.

Here is the decision rule:

If the observed difference between a pair of means is greater than *HSD*, reject the null hypothesis. Otherwise, do not reject it.

Here are the results of the comparisons:

1. For Group A versus Group B, the observed difference is .500. Because this is *not* greater than 2.217, do *not* reject the null hypothesis at the .05 level. The difference is *not* statistically significant at this level.

2. For Group A versus Group C, the observed difference is 3.667. Because this is greater than 2.217, reject the null hypothesis at the .05 level. The difference is statistically significant at this level.

3. For Group B versus Group C, the observed difference is 3.167. Because this is greater than 2.217, reject the null hypothesis at the .05 level. The difference is statistically significant at this level.

Thus, the overall one-way ANOVA in Section 48 indicates that there is at least one significant difference in the entire set of differences. In addition, Tukey's *HSD* test

---

[2]Use Table 9 near the end of this book for the .01 level.

indicates that this is because of these significant differences: (1) the difference between Groups A and C, and (2) the difference between Groups B and C. The difference between Groups A and B is not significant.

Term to Review Before Attempting Worksheet 49

Tukey's Honestly Significant Difference (*HSD*) test

**"When our statistics professor isn't in the lab
to watch us, he loads up this screen saver."**

Worksheet 49   Tukey's *HSD* Test

> **Riddle:** According to Carey Williams, youth is that period when an adolescent knows what?

DIRECTIONS: To find the answer to the riddle, write the answer to each question in the space immediately below it. In the solution section, the word in parentheses next to the answer to the first question is the first word in the answer to the riddle, the word beside the answer to the second question is the second word, and so on.

Using the following information, conduct Tukey's HSD tests.

> Group A: $m = 2.000, n = 4$
> Group B: $m = 2.250, n = 4$
> Group C: $m = 6.500, n = 4$

Table 1
ANOVA Table

Source of variation	df	Sum of squares	Mean square	f
Between groups	2	51.167	25.583	12.973*
Within groups	9	17.750	1.972	
Total	11	68.917		

$*p < .05$

1. What is the size of the observed difference between the means for Groups A and B? (Subtract the smaller from the larger to get a positive value.)

2. What is the size of the observed difference between the means for Groups A and C? (Subtract the smaller from the larger to get a positive value.)

300

Worksheet 49 (continued)

3. What is the size of the observed difference between the means for Groups B and C? (Subtract the smaller from the larger to get a positive value.)

4. At the .05 level, what is the value of the studentized range statistic (from Table 8 near the end of this book) for this problem?

5. What is the value of *HSD*?

6. Is the difference between Groups A and B statistically significant at the .05 level?

7. Is the difference between Groups A and C statistically significant at the .05 level?

8. "The null hypothesis for the difference between Groups B and C may be rejected at the .05 level." Is this statement true *or* false?

Solution section:

> 4.500 (everything)   0.250 (almost)   false (school)   3.67 (intelligence)
>
> true (living)   yes (a)   no (make)   2.25 (never)   4.250 (but)   9 (helpful)
>
> 3.95 (how)   6.50 (something)   2.773 (to)   3.33 (energy)   12.973 (less)

Worksheet 49 (continued)

Write the answer to the riddle here, putting one word on each line: _____ _____ _____ _____

_____ _____ _____ _____

TOP TEN NEW LAWS THAT
STATISTICIANS FAVOR:

1. LIMIT DEVIATIONS
   FROM THE MEAN.
2. ARREST UNREPENTANT
   P-VALUES.
3. INCREASE THE DEGREES
   OF FREEDOM.
4. KEEP VARIANCE TO
   A MINIMUM.
5.

GLASBERGEN

Section 50   Scheffé's Test

As noted in the previous two sections, when a one-way ANOVA is statistically significant, a researcher cannot be sure which specific differences are significant. Thus, for the example in Section 48, there are three differences between pairs of means:

1. Group A versus Group B (6.000 – 5.500 = 0.500)

2. Group A versus Group C (6.000 – 2.333 = 3.667)

3. Group B versus Group C (5.500 – 2.333 = 3.167)

This *set of differences* was statistically significant at the .05 level.

A number of tests have been suggested for determining the significance of the differences between pairs of means after obtaining an overall significant result using ANOVA.[1] In Section 49, Tukey's *HSD* test was illustrated. An alternative test, known as **Scheffé's test**, is considered in this section. Scheffé's test is more conservative than Tukey's. That is, Scheffé's test is less likely to lead to rejection of the null hypothesis than is Tukey's.[2]

To conduct the test, apply this formula once for each difference:

$$F = \frac{(m_1 - m_2)^2}{MS_w(n_1 + n_2) \div (n_1)(n_2)}$$

Where

m_1 is the mean for one of the groups (to avoid negatives, call the larger of each pair of means m_1),

m_2 is the mean for the second group,

MS_w is the mean square for within groups computed for the one-way ANOVA (see Table 5 in Section 48, where the mean square for within groups equals 2.189),

n_1 is the number of cases in the first group, and

n_2 is the number of cases in the second group.

---

[1]Because the tests are conducted *after* an ANOVA, they are sometimes called *post hoc tests*. They are also known as *multiple comparison tests*.

[2]There is some disagreement among statisticians on how to make multiple comparisons. Some tests are more conservative than others.

Application of this formula for Groups A and B is shown below.

For the difference between Groups A and B

To determine the significance of the difference between the mean of Group A and the mean of Group B, calculate F using the formula shown on the previous page, as follows:

$$F_{AB} = \frac{(6.000 - 5.500)^2}{2.189(6+6) \div (6)(6)} = \frac{0.250}{2.189(12) \div 36} = \frac{0.250}{26.268 \div 36} = \frac{0.250}{0.730} = 0.342$$

We now need to compare this observed value of .342 with the critical value. Obtaining the critical value is slightly more complicated than it was for previous tests. First, recall that in Section 48, the degrees of freedom were 2 (for between groups) and 15 (for within groups). Using these, we found, in Table 6 near the end of this book (for the .05 level), that the critical value for the one-way ANOVA was 3.68. We use this formula:

$$CV_s = (CV_{ANOVA})(K - 1)$$

Where

CV_s is the critical value for Scheffé's test,

CV_{ANOVA} is the critical value for the one-way ANOVA, and

K is the number of groups (in this case, three: A, B, and C).

Applying it produces the following result:

$$CV_s = (3.68)(3 - 1) = (3.68)(2) = 7.36$$

The decision rule is as follows:

If the *observed value is greater than the critical value,*[3] reject the null hypothesis; otherwise, do not reject it.

Because the observed value (.342) is *not* greater than the critical value (7.36), we do *not* reject the null hypothesis at the .05 level. The difference between the means of Groups A and B is *not* statistically significant.

---

[3]In the unlikely event that the observed value is exactly equal to the critical value, reject the null hypothesis.

For the difference between Groups A and C

$$F_{AC} = \frac{(6.000 - 2.333)^2}{2.189(6+6) \div (6)(6)} = 18.421$$

To evaluate F, we use the same critical value that we calculated previously (7.36) and the same decision rule. Because the value of F_{AC} (18.421) exceeds the critical value (7.36), the null hypothesis is rejected at the .05 level. The difference between the means of Groups A and C is statistically significant.

For the difference between Groups B and C

$$F_{BC} = \frac{(5.500 - 2.333)^2}{2.189(6+6) \div (6)(6)} = 13.740$$

To evaluate F, use the same critical value calculated previously (7.36) and the same decision rule. Because the value of F_{BC} (13.740) exceeds the critical value (7.36), the null hypothesis is rejected at the .05 level. The difference between the means of Groups B and C is statistically significant.

Thus, we have arrived at the same conclusions regarding the significance of the difference between the pairs of means that we reached using Tukey's *HSD* test in Section 49. The overall one-way ANOVA in Section 48 indicated that the entire set of differences was statistically significant. Scheffé's test indicated that this was the result of the differences between (1) Groups A and C, and (2) Groups B and C. Furthermore, we should not discuss the difference between Groups A and B as being statistically significant.

Although the tests in Sections 49 and 50 led to the same conclusion in the example, they will not always do so. There may be times when Tukey's *HSD* results in the rejection of a null hypothesis for the difference between a pair of means when Scheffé's test does not. Use of either test is acceptable. However, a consumer of research may feel more comfortable with rejections of the null hypothesis when the more conservative Scheffé's test is used. Another consideration in selecting between the two tests is that Scheffé's test does not require that each category have the same number of subjects, while Tukey's *HSD* requires equal numbers.

Term to Review Before Attempting Worksheet 50

Scheffé's test

Worksheet 50 Scheffé's Test

> *Riddle:* According to Edward Gibbon, beauty is seldom despised except by whom?

DIRECTIONS: To find the answer to the riddle, write the answer to each question in the space immediately below it. In the solution section, the word in parentheses next to the answer to the first question is the first word in the answer to the riddle, the word beside the answer to the second question is the second word, and so on.

Use the data at the beginning of Worksheet 49. Conduct Scheffé's test at the .05 level.

1. What is the value of F for the difference between the means of Groups A and B?

2. What is the critical value for Scheffé's test at the .05 level?

3. Is the difference between the means of Groups A and B significant at the .05 level?

4. What is the value of F for the difference between the means of Groups A and C?

5. May the null hypothesis be rejected for the difference between the means of Groups A and C?

Worksheet 50 (continued)

6. What is the value of *F* for the difference between the means of Groups B and C?

7. "The difference between the means for Groups B and C is statistically significant."
   Is this statement true *or* false?

Solution section:

```
18.319 (been)   yes (has)   20.538 (it)   false (sudden)   0.986 (contest)

4.26 (willing)   true (refused)   4.564 (face)   8.52 (to)   0.064 (those)

no (whom)   0.255 (never)   15.333 (asking)   0.006 (truthfully)
```

Write the answer to the riddle here, putting one word on each line: _____ _____ _____ _____
_____ _____ _____

Section 51   Introduction to Two-Way ANOVA

In a ***two-way ANOVA*** (also known as a ***two-factor ANOVA***), subjects are classified in two ways. Consider Example 1, which illustrates a two-way ANOVA.

Example 1

A random sample of welfare recipients was assigned to a new job-training program. Another random sample was assigned to a conventional job-training program. (*Note*: The program to which they were assigned is one of the ways in which the subjects were classified. Subjects were also classified according to whether or not they had a high school diploma.) All of the subjects in each group found employment in the private sector at the end of their training. Their mean hourly wages are shown in the following table:[1]

	Type of Program		
	Conventional	New	Row means
H.S. diploma	$m = \$8.88$	$m = \$8.75$	$m = \$8.82$
No H.S. diploma	$m = \$4.56$	$m = \$8.80$	$m = \$6.68$
Column means	$m = \$6.72$	$m = \$8.78$	

First, consider the column means of $6.72 (for the conventional program) and $8.78 (for the new program). These suggest that, overall, the new program is superior to the conventional one. In other words, if we temporarily ignore whether subjects have a high school diploma, the new program seems superior to the conventional one. This difference ($8.78 − $6.72 = 2.06) suggests that there is what is called a ***main effect***. A *main effect* is the result of comparing one of the ways in which the subjects were classified while temporarily ignoring the other way in which they were classified.

---

[1]Note that income in large populations is usually skewed, making the mean an inappropriate average (see Section 13). For these groups, assume that it was not skewed. Also note that the row means and column means were obtained by adding and dividing by 2. This is appropriate only if the number of subjects in all cells is equal. If it is not, compute the row and column means using the original raw scores.

Because the concept of *main effect* is important, consider it another way. The column mean of $6.72 is for all subjects who had the conventional program (regardless of whether they had a high school diploma). The column mean of $8.78 is for all subjects who had the new program (regardless of whether they had a high school diploma). Thus, looking at the column means tells us that only the effects of the type of program (and *not* the effects of a high school diploma) are being considered. Looking at the effects of only one way in which the subjects were classified constitutes looking at a *main effect*.

Next, consider the row means of $8.82 (for those with a high school diploma) and $6.68 (for those with no high school diploma). This suggests that those with a diploma, on average, have higher earnings than those without one. This is also a *main effect*. This main effect is for the *diploma versus no diploma* variable—temporarily ignoring the type of training program.

Up to this point, two findings would be of interest to those studying the training of welfare recipients: (1) The new program is superior to the conventional program in terms of hourly wages, and (2) those with a high school diploma have higher hourly wages. (*Note*: We do not yet know whether these differences are statistically significant.)

You may have already noticed that there is a third interesting finding. Those with a high school diploma earn about the same amount regardless of the program. This statement is based on these means for those with a high school diploma, reproduced from the table shown for Example 1 on the previous page:

	Conventional program	New program
H.S. diploma	$m = \$8.88$	$m = \$8.75$

However, those with no high school diploma seem to benefit more from the new program than from the conventional one. This statement is based on these means for those with no high school diploma:

	Conventional program	New program
No H.S. diploma	$m = \$4.56$	$m = \$8.80$

Suppose you were the researcher who conducted this study. You are now an expert on the subject, and an administrator calls you for advice. She asks you, "Which program should we use? The conventional one or the new one?" You could, of course, tell her that there is a *main effect* that suggests that, overall, the new program is superior in terms of wages—but, if you stopped there, your answer would be incomplete. A more complete answer is as follows:

1. For those with a diploma, the two programs are about equal in effectiveness. Thus, the choice of program for them should probably hinge on other considerations, such as the cost of the two programs.

2. For those with no diploma, the new program is superior to the conventional one. Other things being equal, those without a diploma should be assigned to the new program.

Because you cannot give a complete answer about the two types of programs (one way in which the subjects were classified) without also referring to high school diplomas (the other way in which they were classified), the conclusion is that there is an **interaction** between the two. How well the two programs work depends, in part, upon whether the subjects have high school diplomas.

Here is a simple way to spot an interaction when there are only two rows of means: Subtract each mean in the second row from the mean in the first row. If the two differences are the same, there is no interaction. If they are different, there is an interaction. Here is how it works for the table in Example 1:

	Type of Program	
	Conventional	New
H.S. diploma	$m = \$8.88$	$m = \$8.75$
No H.S. diploma	$m = \$4.56$	$m = \$8.80$
Difference	$\$4.32$	$-\$0.05$

Because the two differences are *not* the same, there is an interaction.

Consider Example 2, in which there are no main effects but there is an interaction.

Example 2

A random sample of subjects from a population of those suffering from a chronic illness was administered a new drug. Another random sample from the same population was administered a conventional drug. Subjects were also classified as to whether they were male or female. At the end of the study, improvement was measured on a scale from 0 (for no improvement) to 10 (for complete recovery). These means were obtained:

	Drug		
	Conventional	New	Row means
Male	$m = 5.00$	$m = 7.00$	$m = 6.00$
Female	$m = 7.00$	$m = 5.00$	$m = 6.00$
Column means	$m = 6.00$	$m = 6.00$	

The two column means in Example 2 are the same. Thus, temporarily ignoring whether subjects are male or female, we would conclude that the two drugs are equally effective. To state it statistically, we would say that *there is no main effect for the drugs.*

The two row means are also the same. Therefore, if we temporarily ignore which drug was taken, we can conclude that males and females improved to the same extent. To state it statistically, we would say that *there is no main effect for gender.*

Of course, the interesting finding in Example 2 is the *interaction.* The conventional drug works better for females, and the new drug works better for males. Subtracting as in Example 1, we obtain the differences shown below. Because −2.00 is not equal to 2.00, there is an interaction.

Thus, Example 2 has an interaction but no main effects.

	Drug	
	Conventional	New
Male	$m = 5.00$	$m = 7.00$
Female	$m = 7.00$	$m = 5.00$
Difference	−2.00	2.00

Consider Example 3, in which there are two main effects but no interaction.

Example 3

Random samples of high and low achievers were assigned to one of two types of reinforcement during math lessons. Achievement on a math test at the end of the experiment was the outcome variable. The mean scores on the test are shown in this table:

	Type of Reinforcement		
	Type A	Type B	Row means
High achievers	$m = 50.00$	$m = 30.00$	$m = 40.00$
Low achievers	$M = 40.00$	$m = 20.00$	$m = 30.00$
Column means	$m = 45.00$	$m = 25.00$	

In Example 3, there is a main effect for type of reinforcement, as indicated by the difference between the column means (45.00 and 25.00). Thus, if we ignore achievement levels temporarily, Type A is more effective than Type B.

There is also a main effect for achievement level, as indicated by the difference between the row means (40.00 and 30.00). Thus, if we ignore the type of reinforcement, high achievers score higher on the math test than low achievers.

There is, however, no interaction, as indicated by the differences shown here:

	Type of Reinforcement	
	Type A	Type B
High achievers	$m = 50.00$	$m = 30.00$
Low achievers	$m = 40.00$	$m = 20.00$
Difference	$m = 10.00$	$m = 10.00$

What does this lack of an interaction indicate? It indicates that regardless of the type of reinforcement, high achievers are the same number of points higher than low achievers (i.e., 10 points). To put it another way, regardless of whether students are high or low achievers, Type A reinforcement is better.[2]

---

[2]The basis for this statement is that if you subtract across the rows, you get the same difference for each row. Earlier, you were told to subtract down columns. However, subtracting across the rows works equally well in determining whether there is an interaction.

In review, a two-way ANOVA examines two *main effects* and one *interaction*. Of course, because only random samples have been examined, the null hypothesis must be considered. For each of the main effects and for the interaction, the null hypothesis states that there is no *true* difference—that the observed differences were created by random sampling errors. A two-way ANOVA will, therefore, test the two main effects and the interaction for significance. This is done by computing three values of F (one for each of the three null hypotheses) and determining the probability associated with each. Typically, if a probability is .05 or less, the null hypothesis is rejected and the main effect or interaction is declared statistically significant.

Although the computational procedures for a two-way ANOVA are beyond the scope of this book, all standard statistical software packages permit such an analysis. Because computations for a two-way ANOVA are complex, use of statistical software is recommended.

Terms to Review Before Attempting Worksheet 51

two-way ANOVA (two-factor ANOVA), main effect, interaction

Worksheet 51   Introduction to Two-Way ANOVA

> *Riddle*: A banker is someone who will lend you an umbrella when the sun is out but...

DIRECTIONS: To find the answer to the riddle, write the answer to each question in the space immediately below it. In the solution section, the word in parentheses next to the answer to the first question is the first word in the answer to the riddle, the word beside the answer to the second question is the second word, and so on.

Assume there are equal numbers of individuals in each cell in all examples.

Questions 1 through 3 refer to the following information:

Random samples of those with headache pain and those with muscular pain were randomly assigned to two types of pain relievers. The means indicate the average amount of pain relief for each condition.

1. Does there seem to be a main effect for type of pain reliever?

	Type of Pain Reliever		Row means
	Type A	Type B	
Headache pain	$m = 20.00$	$m = 30.00$	$m =$
Muscular pain	$m = 15.00$	$m = 20.00$	$m =$
Column means	$m =$	$m =$	

2. Does there seem to be a main effect for type of pain (headache vs. muscular)?
   (Circle one letter.)

   A. yes

   B. no

315

Worksheet 51 (continued)

3. Does there seem to be an interaction? (Circle one letter.)

   A. no

   B. yes

4. If a two-way ANOVA was conducted, at what probability level would a null hypothesis typically be rejected (i.e., what is the lowest level at which significance is routinely declared)?

Questions 5 through 7 refer to the following information:

Two types of piano instruction were tried with random samples of individuals who either had previous instruction in playing or did not have previous instruction. The means indicate the proficiency in playing the piano at the end of the treatments.

	Type of Piano Instruction		
	Type A	Type B	Row means
Previous instruction	$m = 130.00$	$m = 100.00$	$m =$
No previous instruction	$m = 100.00$	$m = 130.00$	$m =$
Column means	$m =$	$m =$	

5. "There seem to be no main effects." Is this statement true *or* false?

6. "There seems to be no interaction." Is this statement true *or* false?

Worksheet 51 (continued)

7. Which of the following *F* tests would most likely be significant? (Circle one letter.)

    A. The test for the type of piano instruction

    B. The test for previous versus no previous instruction

    C. The test for the interaction

Questions 8 and 9 refer to the following information:

Random samples of rats were assigned to either a food reward or no reward. In addition, they were randomly assigned to run a maze either in darkness or in daylight. The means indicate the average number of seconds it took each group to run a standard maze.

	Type of Reward		Row means
	Food	No reward	
Darkness	$m = 2.4$	$m = 3.4$	$m =$
Daylight	$m = 1.4$	$m = 2.4$	$m =$
Column means	$m =$	$m =$	

8. There seems to be a main effect for (Circle one letter.)

    A. food versus no reward.

    B. darkness versus daylight.

    C. both A and B.

9. There seems to be (Circle one letter.)

    D. an interaction.

    E. no interaction.

Worksheet 51 (continued)

Solution section:

yes (wants) no (lender) A (it) 2 (money) H (rain) F (to)	
B (back) C (begins) false (it) true (minute) .05 (the)	
1 (being) G (checks) D (statement) E (sometimes)	

Write the answer to the riddle here, putting one word on each line: _____ _____ _____ _____

_____ _____ _____ _____ _____

"This is my relaxation tape—it's the sound of ocean waves
crashing onto the shore, snatching my statistics book off
my beach chair, and carrying it out to sea."

Section 52   Significance of the Difference Between Variances

Sections 40 through 51 dealt with testing the differences among means for significance. Occasionally, researchers are interested in the differences between variances. Here is an example:

> A randomly selected sample of students was assigned to learn elementary algebra using a new computer-assisted program (CAP). This was the experimental group. Another randomly selected sample was designated as the control group. It received elementary algebra instruction via a traditional textbook approach. The researcher hypothesized that the posttest scores of the experimental group would be more variable than those of the control group. The rationale for this research hypothesis was that the CAP allows students to move at their own pace so that high-achieving students could zip ahead while low-achieving students could move slowly. In contrast, the traditional approach would hold back the high achievers and pull up the low achievers, leading to less variability in the control group's scores. The following statistics were obtained:

Experimental	Control
$m = 43.22$	$m = 42.99$
$s = 7.88$	$s = 5.22$
$n = 21$	$n = 20$

You should recall that the standard deviation is the most widely used measure of variability. Comparison of the two standard deviations reveals an observed difference that is consistent with the research hypothesis: The standard deviation of the experimental group ($s = 7.88$) is greater than that of the control group ($s = 5.22$). However, before reporting the results, the researcher should consider the null hypothesis, which says that the observed difference was created by random sampling errors.[1]

To test the null hypothesis, first compute F using this formula:

$$F = \frac{s_L^2}{s_S^2}$$

Where

s_L^2 is the larger standard deviation squared, and

s_S^2 is the smaller standard deviation squared.

You might recall that the squared standard deviation has its own name: the **variance**. Hence, strictly speaking, we are testing the difference between the variances. Of course, the size of the variance is directly related to the size of the standard deviation.

When applying the formula to the example, this result is obtained:

$$F = \frac{7.88^2}{5.22^2} = \frac{62.09}{27.25} = 2.28$$

Thus, the **observed value** of F is 2.28. It needs to be compared with the **critical value** of F for significance to be determined. To obtain the critical value, first compute degrees of freedom. For the group with the larger variance,

$$df = n - 1 = 21 - 1 = 20$$

Thus, 20 is the degrees of freedom associated with the **numerator** of the formula for F.

For the group with the smaller variance,

$$df = n - 1 = 20 - 1 = 19$$

Thus, 19 is the degrees of freedom associated with the **denominator** of the formula for F.

---

[1]Note that in the term *random sampling errors*, the adjective *random* is superfluous because statisticians define *sampling error* as *error created by random sampling*. The redundant term is used here for instructional purposes.

For the .05 level,[2] use Table 6 near the end of this book to obtain the critical value of F. Notice that the columns are labeled "Between-Groups Degrees of Freedom (Numerator)." The word *numerator* is included to help you with this significance test. Look up the column for the degrees of freedom associated with the numerator, which is 20. Then look up the row for the degrees of freedom for the denominator, which is 19. Where column 20 intersects with row 19, there is a critical value of 2.15.

Here is the decision rule:

If the *observed value is greater than the critical value,*[3] reject the null hypothesis. Otherwise, do not reject it.

Because the observed value (2.28) is greater than the critical value (2.15), reject the null hypothesis and declare the difference between the two variances statistically significant at the .05 level.[4] Thus, we have ruled out the null hypothesis as an explanation for the difference between the variance of the experimental group and the variance of the control group.

Terms to Review Before Attempting Worksheet 52
variance, observed value, critical value,
numerator, denominator

---

[2]Use Table 7 near the end of this book for the .01 level.
[3]In the unlikely event that the observed value is equal to the critical value, reject the null hypothesis.
[4]You may have noticed that some of the possible degrees of freedom are missing in Table 6 near the end of this book. For instance, rows 66 through 69 are missing. This is because there are only very small differences in the critical values in this range. Suppose you had 67 degrees of freedom. Use the smaller of the ones shown—in this case, 65, which is conservative, meaning that you have very slightly reduced the odds of rejecting the null hypothesis.

Worksheet 52   Significance of the Difference Between Variances

Riddle: What is the loudest sound that you will ever hear?

DIRECTIONS: To find the answer to the riddle, write the answer to each question in the space immediately below it. In the solution section, the word in parentheses next to the answer to the first question is the first word in the answer to the riddle, the word beside the answer to the second question is the second word, and so on.

Questions 1 through 5 refer to the following information:

Experimental	Control
$m = 25.44$	$m = 26.99$
$s = 6.77$	$s = 5.89$
$n = 17$	$n = 15$

1. Which group (experimental *or* control) has more variance?

2. Which standard deviation (6.77 *or* 5.89) should you enter as the numerator of the formula for F?

3. To two decimal places, what is the observed value of F?

4. At the .05 level, what is the critical value of F for this problem?

Worksheet 52 (continued)

5. Should the null hypothesis be rejected at the .05 level?

Questions 6 through 8 refer to the following information:

Experimental	Control
$m = 100.48$	$m = 102.65$
$s = 10.03$	$s = 15.49$
$n = 30$	$n = 31$

6. To two decimal places, what is the observed value of F?

7. At the .05 level, what is the critical value of F for this problem?

8. Is the difference between the variances significant at the .05 level?

Solution section:

> yes (car)   control (breaking)   .76 (hearing)   experimental (the)
>
> 6.77 (first)   no (your)   2.39 (brand)   5.89 (shattering)   .41 (screams)
>
> 1.85 (new)   1.32 (rattle)   2.44 (in)   8.00 (listening)   9.00 (record)
>
> 10.00 (office)   7.89 (yelling)   2.00 (ears)   .51 (everything)

Worksheet 52 (continued)

Write the answer to the riddle here, putting one word on
each line: _____ _____ _____ _____

_____ _____ _____ _____

Statistics Laboratory
Hours 9AM - 9PM

GLASBERGEN

"And this button gives the computer a
mild electric shock when I need to punish it."

Section 53 Introduction to Chi-Square

Frequently, research data are nominal (i.e., naming data, such as subjects naming the political candidates for whom they plan to vote).[1] Such data do not directly permit the computation of means and standard deviations. Instead, researchers usually report the number of subjects who named each category (i.e., the frequency) and the corresponding proportions or percentages. Here is an example:

Example 1

A random sample of 200 registered voters was drawn, and voters were asked which of two candidates running for an elected office they planned to vote for. These data were obtained:

<u>Candidate Smith</u> <u>Candidate Doe</u>
$n = 110$ (55.0%) $n = 90$ (45.0%)

The data in Example 1 suggest that Candidate Smith is leading. However, only a random sample of voters was surveyed. It is possible, for instance, that the population of voters is evenly split and that a difference of 10 percentage points was obtained because of the sampling errors associated with random sampling. For this possibility, there is a null hypothesis that says there is no true difference in the population and that, in the population, the voters are evenly split. It is not possible to use a t test or ANOVA to test this null hypothesis because the result does not consist of means and standard deviations.

The appropriate test for the data under consideration (i.e., frequencies or numbers of cases) is ***chi-square***,[2] whose symbol is χ^2. Using computations described in the next section of this book, we determine that for these data, the probability that the null hypothesis is true is greater than 5 in 100 ($p > .05$). Thus, the null hypothesis cannot be rejected, and the difference is not statistically significant. In concrete terms, Candidate Smith cannot take comfort in the result

---

[1] See Section 3 to review scales of measurement, including the nominal scale.
[2] The tests on means (t and F) in earlier sections are based on the assumption that the underlying distributions are normal. These are examples of *parametric tests*. Because chi-square is not based on such an assumption, it is an example of a *nonparametric* (or *distribution-free*) test.

because it is not possible to rule out sampling errors as an explanation for the difference in her favor.

Example 1 illustrates a ***one-way chi-square*** (also known as a ***goodness-of-fit chi-square***). The subjects are classified in only one way: whom they plan to vote for. Example 2 illustrates a ***two-way chi-square***, in which samples from two populations of voters (i.e., males and females) were classified in terms of whom they plan to vote for.[3]

Example 2

A random sample of 200 male registered voters and a random sample of 200 female registered voters were drawn, and voters were asked which of two candidates running for elected office they planned to vote for. These data were obtained:

	Candidate Jones	Candidate Black
Males	$n = 80$	$n = 120$
Females	$n = 120$	$n = 80$

Inspection of the data in Example 2 suggests that Jones is a stronger candidate among females, and Black is a stronger candidate among males. If this pattern is true among all males and all females in the voting population, both candidates should take heed. For instance, Candidate Jones might consider ways to shore up her support among males without alienating the females, while Candidate Black might do the opposite. However, only a random sample was surveyed. Before taking action, the candidates should consider how likely it is that the observed differences between the two groups (males and females) were created by random sampling errors. Chi-square is the appropriate test because the data are at the nominal level. Using computations from Section 55 in this book, chi-square reveals that for the data in Example 2, p is less than 1 in 1,000 ($p < .001$). Thus, the probability that random errors created the differences is less than 1 in 1,000. In other words, it is very unlikely that this pattern of differences is due to sampling errors. Thus, with a

---

[3]There are two types of two-way chi-square tests. Example 2 illustrates a *chi-square test of homogeneity*. This test involves two or more populations (e.g., males and females) and their opinions on one outcome variable (e.g., which candidate they plan to vote for). Example 3 illustrates a *chi-square test of independence,* in which one population is classified in two ways.

high degree of confidence, the candidates can rule out random errors as an explanation.[4]

In Example 3, a sample from one population of subjects was asked two questions, each of which yielded nominal data.

Example 3

A random sample of college students was asked whether they think that IQ tests measure innate intelligence and whether they had taken a tests-and-measurements course in college. The following data were gathered:

	Took course	Did not take course
Yes, innate	$n = 20$	$n = 30$
No, not innate	$n = 40$	$n = 15$

The observed data in Example 3 suggest that those who did not take the course were more likely to perceive IQ tests as measures of innate intelligence (30 vs. 15) than those who took the course (20 vs. 40). In other words, there appears to be a relationship between whether subjects have taken the course and what they believe IQ tests measure. Once again, only a random sample was questioned and, thus, it is possible that the observed relationship is not true in the population. That is, the null hypothesis asserts that there is no *true* relationship (in the population). A chi-square test for these data produced this result:

$$\chi^2 = 11.455, df = 1, p < .001$$

Thus, the null hypothesis can be rejected with a high degree of confidence because the likelihood is less than 1 in 1,000 that it is a true hypothesis.

Section 54 illustrates the computational procedures for conducting a one-way chi-square, and Section 55 illustrates the procedures for a two-way chi-square.

---

[4]Notice that in these examples, the responses are independent. For instance, in Example 2, the gender of a person is not determined by his or her preference for a candidate. Also, each response is mutually exclusive. For instance, a subject is not allowed to indicate whether he/she is male or female. Independence and mutual exclusivity of categories are assumptions underlying chi-square.

Terms to Review Before Attempting Worksheet 53

chi-square, χ^2, one-way chi-square (goodness-of-fit chi-square),
two-way chi-square

**"Whenever I get a wrong answer to a statistics
problem, I just push this little button and restart.
I wish my whole life were like that!"**

Worksheet 53   Introduction to Chi-Square

> **Riddle:** What advice did Erma Bombeck offer about selecting a doctor?

DIRECTIONS: To find the answer to the riddle, write the answer to each question in the space immediately below it. In the solution section, the word in parentheses next to the answer to the first question is the first word in the answer to the riddle, the word beside the answer to the second question is the second word, and so on.

1. If you calculated the mean score for a sample of boys and the mean score for a sample of girls on a standardized test and wanted to compare the two means with an inferential test, would a chi-square test be appropriate?

   YES   NO

2. If you asked a random sample of subjects which of two brands of coffee they preferred and then wanted to compare the frequencies with an inferential test, would a chi-square test be appropriate?   ~~NO~~   *yes*

3. Suppose you asked subjects whether they had gotten a flu shot at the beginning of the flu season and then asked them at the end of the flu season whether they had gotten the flu in order to examine the relationship between getting a shot and getting the flu. Is this a one-way chi-square *or* a two-way chi-square problem?

   two way

4. Suppose you read that $\chi^2 = 4.001$, $df = 1$, $p < .05$. What decision should be made about the null hypothesis at the .05 level?

   reject it

Worksheet 53 (continued)

5. "If $\chi^2 = 10.999$, $df = 2$, $p < .01$, then the differences are statistically significant at the .01 level." Is this statement true *or* false?

true

6. "If $\chi^2 = 2.578$, $df = 1$, $p > .05$, then the differences are statistically significant at the .05 level." Is this statement true *or* false?

false

7. Suppose that as a result of a chi-square test, p is found to be less than .001 for a given set of data. This means that the likelihood that the null hypothesis is correct is less than 1 in ____.

1,000

8. If a difference is found to be statistically insignificant with chi-square, what decision should be made about the null hypothesis?

do not reject it

Solution section:

100 (wine) 10,000 (sleeping) one-way (nevertheless)		
do not reject it (died) 1,000 (have) false (plants) true (office)		
reject it (whose) two-way (doctor) no (avoid) yes (a)		

Write the answer to the riddle here, putting one word on each line:

Avoid   a   doctor   whose

office   plants   have   died

330

Section 54   Computations for a One-Way Chi-Square

As noted in the previous section, a one-way chi-square is one in which a random sample of subjects is classified on a single variable. For instance, three world history textbooks might be considered for use in a state's high schools. A random sample of the history teachers are asked to examine the three books and answer a number of questions about them. The crucial question is: Overall, which book do they prefer? Following are their preferences:

Textbook A	Textbook B	Textbook C
$n = 30$ (37.97%)	$n = 27$ (34.18%)	$n = 22$ (27.85%)

The results suggest that the teachers preferred Textbook A to Textbooks B and C and preferred Textbook B to Textbook C. But the researchers questioned only a random sample of all history teachers. Thus, it is possible that if all the teachers had examined the books, there would have been no difference in preference for the three books. This possibility leads to the null hypothesis that says there is no *true* difference in preference (in the population).[1] This null hypothesis can be tested with a chi-square test.

The frequencies obtained from the sample are called the ***observed frequencies*** (i.e., the frequencies actually observed in a study—in this case, 30, 27, and 22). The symbol for the observed frequencies is O. The frequencies that are expected based on the null hypothesis are called the ***expected frequencies*** (i.e., the frequencies that a researcher should expect to obtain if the null hypothesis is correct). The symbol for the expected frequencies is E. Because the null hypothesis for the example under consideration states that there is no difference in preference, a researcher would expect equal frequencies for the three textbooks. Because there are 79 subjects in

---

[1]In this instance, we are going to test the null hypothesis that the population of teachers is evenly split. A one-way chi-square may also be used to test the difference between observed frequencies and the frequencies that might be expected based on a theory or information at hand about a population. For instance, if we know that 60% of the voters in a state are registered Democrats and 40% are registered Republicans, and if we draw a random sample of 100 voters from one county in the state and obtain 55% Democrats and 45% Republicans, the question arises: Are the voters in the county significantly different from the voters statewide? The null hypothesis for this problem states that there is no true difference between the differences in registration in the sample and the differences in registration in the population.

the example ($30 + 27 + 22 = 79$), a researcher would expect 26.333 subjects to prefer each textbook (i.e., 79 subjects divided by 3 textbooks = 26.333).[2]

Review the steps up to this point for solving a one-way chi-square problem:

1. Select a random sample and classify subjects in a single way, such as on which textbook they prefer. There may be as many categories as needed for the research problem. In this instance, there are three categories. Call the frequencies (i.e., number of cases) in each category the *observed frequencies* (O).

2. Calculate the *expected frequencies* (E) for the null hypothesis under consideration. Because the null hypothesis states that there are no differences in the population, divide the total number of subjects in the sample by the number of categories. In this instance, there are 79 subjects and 3 categories, and $79/3 = 26.333$, which is the expected frequency for each category. These data are shown in Table 1.

Table 1
Observed and Expected Frequencies

	Textbook A	Textbook B	Textbook C
Observed	30	27	22
Expected	26.333	26.333	26.333

The next step is to apply the formula for chi-square, once for each textbook:

$$x^2 = \Sigma \frac{(O - E)^2}{E}$$

For Textbook A: $\dfrac{(30 - 26.333)^2}{26.333} = \dfrac{(3.667)^2}{26.333} = \dfrac{13.447}{26.333} = 0.511$

For Textbook B: $\dfrac{(27 - 26.333)^2}{26.333} = \dfrac{(0.667)^2}{26.333} = \dfrac{.445}{26.333} = 0.017$

---

[2]For the example in the first footnote, the expected frequencies would be 60 Democrats (60% of the 100 subjects in the sample) and 40 Republicans (40% of the 100 subjects in the sample).

For Textbook C: $\dfrac{(22-26.333)^2}{26.333} = \dfrac{(-4.333)^2}{26.333} = \dfrac{18.775}{26.333} = 0.713$

Summing the values for the three textbooks yields the value of chi-square:

$\chi^2 = 0.511 + 0.017 + 0.713 = 1.241$

Thus, 1.241 is the ***observed value of chi-square*** for the example.

Next, compute the degrees of freedom. For a one-way chi-square, the formula is

df = number of categories – 1

Because there are three categories of textbooks, the degrees of freedom for the example are

$df = 3 - 1 = 2$

To determine significance, compare the observed value of chi-square that we computed with the ***critical value of chi-square*** in Table 11 near the end of this book. The table shows that for 2 degrees of freedom, the critical value at the .05 level is 5.991.

Here is the decision rule:

If the *observed value of chi-square is greater than the critical value,*[3] reject the null hypothesis. Otherwise, do not reject it.

Because the observed value (1.241) is *not* greater than the critical value (5.991), do *not* reject the null hypothesis at the .05 level. The conclusion is that the differences are *not* statistically significant.

---

[3]In the unlikely event that the observed value is equal to the critical value, reject the null hypothesis.

Terms to Review Before Attempting Worksheet 54

observed frequencies (*O*), expected frequencies (*E*),
observed value of chi-square, critical value of chi-square

"I'm going to use hypnosis to help you confront repressed
traumatic memories of your last statistics class."

Worksheet 54 Computations for a One-Way Chi-Square

> *Riddle*: How do you calculate how much education you have?

DIRECTIONS: To find the answer to the riddle, write the answer to each question in the space immediately below it. In the solution section, the word in parentheses next to the answer to the first question is the first word in the answer to the riddle, the word beside the answer to the second question is the second word, and so on.

A random sample of 99 social workers was asked to indicate which of three welfare proposals they preferred. The following data were observed:

Proposal A	Proposal B	Proposal C
29	31	39

Compute chi-square and test the null hypothesis that there is no true difference in preferences in the population.

1. What is the expected frequency for Proposal A?

2. To three decimal places, what is the observed value of chi-square? (Allow for minor variations in the third place due to rounding.)

3. What is the value of the degrees of freedom?

4. At the .05 level, what is the critical value of chi-square?

Worksheet 54 (continued)

5. Is chi-square significant at the .05 level?

6. What decision should be made about the null hypothesis at the .05 level?

Questions 7, 8, and 9 refer to the following information:

These results were obtained for another research problem:
$\chi^2 = 10.22$, $df = 3$.

7. "Chi-square is significant at the .05 level." Is this statement true *or* false?

8. What decision should be made about the null hypothesis at the .05 level?

9. "Chi-square is significant at the .01 level." Is this statement true *or* false?

Solution section:

yes (college) 1.091 (degrees) no (forgotten) do not reject it (from)		
true (what) .485 (scholar) reject it (you) false (learned) 5.991 (have)		
2 (you) 1.697 (what) 33 (subtract) 29 (school) 99 (knowledge)		

Write the answer to the riddle here, putting one word on each line: _____ _____ _____ _____

_____ _____ _____ _____ _____

Section 55   Computations for a Two-Way Chi-Square

Suppose that three randomly selected groups were drawn from a population of people suffering from a chronic disease. One group was administered a large dose of an experimental drug, another was administered a small dose of the drug, and the third group, which served as a control, was administered a placebo that looked like the drug but was inert. Subjects were also classified as to whether their condition was improved. The following table shows the *observed frequencies* that resulted:[1]

Table 1
Observed Frequencies for Three Treatment Groups

	Large dose	Small dose	Placebo	Row totals
Improved	20	15	9	44
Not improved	10	14	20	44
Column totals	30	29	29	Grand Total = 88

Inspection of the frequencies suggests that the large dose was more effective than the small dose and that both dosage levels were more effective than the placebo. Because only random samples were observed, however, the null hypothesis needs to be tested.

Before using the formula for chi-square, calculate the *expected frequencies*. Here is the rule for calculating expected frequencies for a two-way chi-square:

> For each cell, multiply the associated row total by the associated column total and divide by the grand total.

Table 2 on the next page shows the application of this rule.

Some students have trouble mastering this rule at first, so consider a specific instance of its application. Specifically, consider the cell in Table 1 for the subjects who had the *large dose* and were *improved*. This cell is at the upper left and has an

---

[1]Normally, an investigator would assign the same number of subjects to each treatment group in an experiment of this type. However, some subjects may drop out, which would result in unequal numbers of subjects for analysis.

observed frequency of 20. The row total associated with this cell is 44 (shown at the right), and the column total associated with this cell is 30 (shown at the bottom). To apply the rule, multiply 44 by 30 and then divide by the grand total of 88. This computation is shown in the second column of Table 2. The computations for all the other cells are also shown.

Table 2
Computation of Expected Frequencies

	Large dose	Small dose	Placebo
Improved	$\dfrac{(44)(30)}{88} = 15.000$	$\dfrac{(44)(29)}{88} = 14.500$	$\dfrac{(44)(29)}{88} = 14.500$
Not improved	$\dfrac{(44)(30)}{88} = 15.000$	$\dfrac{(44)(29)}{88} = 14.500$	$\dfrac{(44)(29)}{88} = 14.500$

Now apply the formula for chi-square, which is

$$\chi^2 = \Sigma \frac{(O - E)^2}{E}$$

When applying the formula, apply it separately for each cell. In this case, there are 6 cells. For the cell for those who improved with the large dose (the upper left), the observed frequency (O) from Table 1 on the previous page is 20, and the expected frequency (E) from Table 2 is 15.000. These values are entered into the formula here:

For Improved/Large dose: $\dfrac{(20 - 15.000)^2}{15.000} = \dfrac{(5.000)^2}{15.000} = \dfrac{25.000}{15.000} = 1.667$

Then do the same thing for each of the other cells. These are the computations:

For Improved/Small dose: $\dfrac{(15 - 14.500)^2}{14.500} = \dfrac{(.500)^2}{14.500} = \dfrac{.250}{14.500} = .017$

For Improved/Placebo: $\dfrac{(9 - 14.500)^2}{14.500} = \dfrac{(-5.500)^2}{14.500} = \dfrac{30.250}{14.500} = 2.086$

For Not improved/Large dose: $\dfrac{(10-15.000)^2}{15.000} = \dfrac{(-5.000)^2}{15.000} = \dfrac{25.000}{15.000} = 1.667$

For Not improved/Small dose: $\dfrac{(14-14.500)^2}{14.500} = \dfrac{(.500)^2}{14.500} = \dfrac{.250}{14.500} = .017$

For Not improved/Placebo: $\dfrac{(20-14.500)^2}{14.500} = \dfrac{(5.500)^2}{14.500} = \dfrac{30.250}{14.500} = 2.086$

Summing the six values yields the value of chi-square:

$$\chi^2 = 1.667 + .017 + 2.086 + 1.667 + .017 + 2.086 = 7.540$$

Thus, 7.540 is the *observed value of chi-square*.

Next, compute the degrees of freedom. For a two-way chi-square, the formula is

df = (number of rows – 1)(number of columns – 1)

Because there are two rows (improved and not improved) and three columns (large dose, small dose, and placebo), the degrees of freedom for the example are

df = (2 – 1)(3 – 1) = (1)(2) = 2

To determine significance, compare the observed value of chi-square (computed above) with the *critical value of chi-square* in Table 11 near the end of this book. Table 11 indicates that for 2 degrees of freedom, the critical value at the .05 level is 5.991.

Here is the decision rule:
If the *observed value of chi-square is greater than the critical value,*[2] reject the null hypothesis. Otherwise, do not reject it.

Because the observed value (7.540) is greater than the critical value (5.991), we should reject the null hypothesis at the .05 level. A researcher should conclude that

---

[2]In the unlikely event that the observed value is equal to the critical value, reject the null hypothesis.

the differences are statistically significant because random sampling error has been ruled out as the explanation for them.

One note of caution: The probabilities obtained with chi-square will not be accurate if the expected frequency in any cell is small (i.e., less than about 10). In most cases, this can be prevented by using a reasonably large sample size. Another solution is to collapse adjoining cells when there is a logical basis for doing so. For instance, suppose you obtained the following expected frequencies for an experiment:[3]

	Experimental group	Control group
Major improvement	4	1
Minor improvement	12	10
No improvement	12	15

Collapsing (i.e., combining) the frequencies for major improvement with minor improvement (and simply calling them *improvement*) makes the expected frequencies for the analysis larger. This has been done for the following table of results. Note that when the results for major improvement and those for minor improvement are combined, all the cells have frequencies of 10 or more.

	Experimental group	Control group
Improvement	4 + 12 = 16	1 + 10 = 11
No improvement	12	15

Terms to Review Before Attempting Worksheet 55

observed frequencies, expected frequencies,
observed value of chi-square, critical value of chi-square

---

[3]Several modifications to the chi-square formula have been suggested for use when one or more expected frequencies is small. These are not universally accepted among statisticians and only apply to problems with one degree of freedom. One of the most popular modifications is the Yates' correction, which you may encounter when reading journal articles—especially older ones.

"I couldn't do my statistics homework because my computer has a virus and so do all my pens and pencils."

Worksheet 55   Computations for a Two-Way Chi-Square

Riddle: What proves that people are wrong to complain about the postal service?

DIRECTIONS: To find the answer to the riddle, write the answer to each question in the space immediately below it. In the solution section, the word in parentheses next to the answer to the first question is the first word in the answer to the riddle, the word beside the answer to the second question is the second word, and so on.

A random sample of subjects from a community were asked whether they favor or oppose welfare. They were also asked whether they had ever been on welfare. The following frequencies were obtained.

	Favor welfare	Oppose welfare
Had been on welfare	15	10
Never on welfare	50	60

1. Is someone who had been on welfare *or* someone never on welfare more likely to favor welfare?

2. What is the grand total of the frequencies?

3. What is the expected frequency for the Never on welfare/Favor welfare cell?

4. What is the expected frequency for the Never on welfare/Oppose welfare cell?

Worksheet 55 (continued)

5. To three decimal places, what is the observed value of chi-square? (Allow for minor variations in the third place due to rounding.)

6. What is the value of the degrees of freedom?

7. What is the critical value of chi-square at the .05 level?

8. Is chi-square significant at the .05 level?

9. "The null hypothesis should be rejected at the .05 level." Is this statement true *or* false?

Solution section:

> 4 (slowly) 5.991 (delivery) false (time) no (on) 3.841 (always)
>
> 1 (are) 1.726 (bills) never on welfare (postage) had been on welfare (phone)
>
> 135 (bills) 52.963 (and) 57.037 (electric) 2 (complain) 3 (left)

Write the answer to the riddle here, putting one word on each line: _____ _____ _____ _____

_____ _____ _____ _____ _____

Notes

Section 56   Cramér's Phi

A two-way chi-square (see Sections 53 and 55) tests whether there is a statistically significant relationship between two variables. In Section 55, the significance of the relationship between the two variables shown in Table 1 was determined.

Table 1
Observed Frequencies for Three Treatment Groups

	Large dose	Small dose	Placebo	Row totals
Improved	20	15	9	44
Not improved	10	14	20	44
Column totals	30	29	29	Grand total = 88

The observed frequencies in Table 1 suggest that there is a relationship between (1) improvement/no improvement and (2) dosage of drug taken. The larger the dosage, the more improvement. This relationship was found to be statistically significant as indicated by the fact that

$$\chi^2 = 7.540, p < .05$$

Thus, it was possible to reject the null hypothesis, which says that the relationship was created by sampling errors.

Note, however, that a significance test does not indicate how strong a relationship is. In fact, the chi-square test of significance indicates only that the relationship is reliable (i.e., significant), but even a weak relationship is sometimes reliable. Inspection of Table 1 clearly indicates that the relationship being considered is far from perfect. For instance, while 20 of the 30 who took the large dose (about 67%) improved, 9 of the 29 who received the placebo (about 31%) also improved. Thus, improvement is not entirely contingent on receiving the drug. The relationship between improvement and dosage level is, therefore, far less than perfect.

Cramér developed a statistic based on the Pearson r that describes the *strength* of the relationship between two variables examined in a two-way chi-square.[1] Here is the formula for **Cramér's phi,** whose symbol is ϕ.

$$\phi = \sqrt{\frac{\chi^2}{N(k-1)}}$$

Where

χ^2 is the value of chi-square,

N is the total number of cases (the grand total), and

k is the number of categories for the variable with the smaller number of categories. (In our example, there are two categories of improvement [improved and not improved] and three categories of drug usage [large dose, small dose, and placebo]; thus, $k = 2$ for our example.)[2]

Solving the example,

$$\phi = \sqrt{\frac{7.540}{(88)(2-1)}} = \sqrt{.0857} = .2927 = .29$$

To interpret Cramér's phi, keep in mind that 0.00 indicates no relationship and 1.00 indicates a perfect relationship. Thus, for this example, phi indicates that the relationship is weak.

When reporting the results, a researcher can now indicate that there is a statistically significant relationship, as indicated by chi-square, but that the relationship is weak, as indicated by Cramér's phi. Reporting the value of phi along with the results of the chi-square test gives consumers of research a more comprehensive report of results than one that contains only the results of a chi-square test.

---

[1]Remember that to compute a Pearson r, two sets of scores are needed (see Section 33). Here, the data are frequencies—not scores. It is possible to assign scores arbitrarily to the categories and compute a Pearson r as a measure of relationship. Cramér's method, however, is much easier if a chi-square test has already been computed.

[2]If both variables have the same number of categories, then use the number in either one as k. For instance, if there are two categories on Variable A and two on Variable B, use 2 as the value of k.

Term to Review Before Attempting Worksheet 56

Cramér's phi (ϕ)

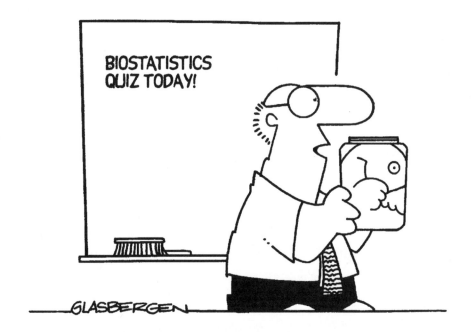

"Class, who can tell me what I have preserved in this jar?
No, it's not a pig or baby cow—it's the last student
who got caught cheating on one of my tests!"

Worksheet 56 Cramér's Phi

> *Riddle*: Why are people who live in the lap of luxury anxious?

DIRECTIONS: To find the answer to the riddle, write the answer to each question in the space immediately below it. In the solution section, the word in parentheses next to the answer to the first question is the first word in the answer to the riddle, the word beside the answer to the second question is the second word, and so on.

1. If there is no relationship between two variables, what will be the value of Cramér's phi?

2. If a relationship is statistically significant, is it necessarily a strong relationship?

Questions 3 through 5 refer to the information in the following table on gender-based preferences for two candidates. The cells contain frequencies (i.e., numbers of cases).

	Candidate A	Candidate B
Males	20	30
Females	30	20
$\chi^2 = 4.000$, $df = 1$, $p < .05$		

3. What is the value of N for use in the formula for Cramér's phi?

Worksheet 56 (continued)

4. What is the value of k for use in the formula for Cramér's phi? (See Footnote 2 on page 346.)

5. To two decimal places, what is the value of Cramér's phi?

Questions 6 through 8 refer to the information in the following box:

> Two hundred patients were randomly assigned to one of three treatments for a life-threatening disease. After 5 years, they were classified as either alive or dead. The relationship between type of treatment and survival was statistically significant ($\chi^2 = 25.991$, $df = 2$, $p < .001$).

6. What is the value of N for use in the formula for Cramér's phi?

7. To two decimal places, what is the value of Cramér's phi?

8. As indicated by Cramér's phi, is the relationship strong *or* weak?

Solution section:

> 1.00 (wealth)   .20 (might)   200 (suddenly)   .36 (stand)   .40 (but)
>
> 0.00 (they're)   100 (that)   strong (lift)   yes (golden)   no (afraid)
>
> 2 (luxury)   weak (up)   .04 (dependent)   50 (something)

Worksheet 56 (continued)

Write the answer to the riddle here, putting one word on

each line: _____ _____ _____ _____

_____ _____ _____ _____

Section 57   Median Test

Although the mean is the most frequently used average, it is sometimes inappropriate.[1] The most popular alternative is the median—the value that has half the scores above it and half the scores below it. In Section 13, you learned how to compute the median.

Use the ***median test*** to get the statistical significance of the difference between the medians for two groups from which two independent, random samples have been drawn. Here is an example:

Example 1

A random sample of subjects was drawn from the east side of town, and a random sample was drawn from the west side. They were asked to indicate their annual incomes to the nearest thousand dollars. These results were obtained (*Note*: 5 = $5,000.00, 6 = $6,000.00, and so on):

East side	West side
5	6
7	9
8	12
10	14
17	20
30	40
33	45
41	55
44	61
Median = 17	Median = 20

The medians suggest that those who live on the west side, on average, have higher incomes than those on the east side. However, only random samples have been drawn, forcing the researcher to consider the null hypothesis, which states that there is no *true* difference. To test this null hypothesis, calculate chi-square. To do so, follow these steps:

---

[1]The mean is inappropriate when a distribution of scores is highly skewed, in which case the median is preferred. Also, if the data are ordinal, the mean is inappropriate, and the median should be used. See Section 13 to review these concepts.

Step 1: Arrange *all* the scores in order from low to high.

5, 6, 7, 8, 9, 10, 12, 14, 17, 20, 30, 33, 40, 41, 44, 45, 55, 61

Step 2: Determine the median of the scores listed in Step 1.

Because there are 18 scores, count up 9 (half of 18) scores to reach the middle score of 17. Count down 9 scores to reach the middle score of 20. Thus, the median is halfway between 17 and 20 ($17 + 20 = 37/2 = 18.5$). The median of all the scores is 18.5.

Step 3: Determine how many subjects in *each* group are above and below the median of all the scores (i.e., 18.5), and arrange them in a table, as shown below.[2] For instance, among those on the east side, there are 4 subjects with incomes above 18.5.

Number above and below 18.5 in each group		
	East side	West side
Number above median	4	5
Number below median	5	4

Step 4: Conduct the usual two-way chi-square test using the method described in Section 55. Applying the method produces the following result:

$\chi^2 = .222$, $df = 1$, not significant at the .05 level.

Because the value of chi-square in the example is *not* significant, do *not* reject the null hypothesis, and do *not* declare statistical significance.

In the next section, an alternative to the median test is described.

Term to Review Before Attempting Worksheet 57

median test

---

[2]If a subject's score is equal to the median, include the subject in the *below*-median group. Do not use this test if there are 2 or fewer subjects in any group in your table.

Worksheet 57 Median Test

Riddle: What does an addicted shopper do at the end
of the day?

DIRECTIONS: To find the answer to the riddle, write the answer to each question in the space immediately below it. In the solution section, the word in parentheses next to the answer to the first question is the first word in the answer to the riddle, the word beside the answer to the second question is the second word, and so on.

The questions refer to these scores. You will need to use the technique described in Section 55 for conducting a two-way chi-square.

Group A	Group B
0	3
1	4
5	6
11	17
12	18
16	29
23	35
33	39
44	55
Median = 12	Median = 18

1. On average, which group has higher scores?

2. What is the median of *all* the scores?

Worksheet 57 (continued)

3. How many subjects in Group A are below the median of *all* the scores?

4. How many subjects in Group B are below the median of *all* the scores?

5. What is the value of chi-square?

6. Is chi-square statistically significant at the .05 level?

7. "The null hypothesis may be rejected at the .05 level." Is this statement true *or* false?

Solution section:

Group A (buys)   Group B (leaves)   16.50 (the)   6 (mall)   4 (runs)

yes (always)   .50 (cash)   3 (with)   no (but)   16.00 (credit)

2.00 (everything)   18 (fashions)   false (money)   15.00 (bankrupt)

Write the answer to the riddle here, putting one word on each line: _____ _____ _____ _____
_____ _____ _____

Section 58 Mann-Whitney *U* Test

The ***Mann-Whitney U test*** is an alternative to the median test presented in the previous section.[1] It tests whether the distribution of scores for one random sample is significantly different from the distribution of scores for another independent, random sample.[2]

The test will be illustrated with the following scores, which were also analyzed in the previous section:

Col. 1	Col. 2
East side	West side
(Group 1)	(Group 2)
5	6
7	9
8	12
10	14
17	20
30	40
33	45
41	55
44	61
Median = 17	Median = 20

Step 1: Rank all scores as though the two groups were a single group.

When ranking, give a rank of 1 to the lowest score, a rank of 2 to the next-lowest score, and so on.[3]

Although all scores were ranked as though they were a single group, list the ranks separately by group in columns 3 and 4, as shown on the next page.

---

[1] The Mann-Whitney *U* test is more powerful than the median test. It is more likely to lead to the rejection of the null hypothesis than the median test.

[2] If the two distributions have similar shapes, when significance is obtained with the Mann-Whitney *U* test, it is safe to assume that the two medians are significantly different.

[3] If there are ties, split the ranks among them. For instance, if the two lowest scores are 4 and 4 (i.e., two subjects have a 4), they are tied, and it is not possible to determine which should have a rank of 1 and which should have a rank of 2. Compromise by adding the ranks in question (1 + 2 = 3) and dividing by the number of tied scores (in this case, two scores). Thus, 3/2 = 1.5, which is the rank assigned to each score.

Col. 1	Col. 2	Col. 3	Col. 4
East side (Group 1)	West side (Group 2)	Ranks for Group 1	Ranks for Group 2
5	6	1	2
7	9	3	5
8	12	4	7
10	14	6	8
17	20	9	10
30	40	11	13
33	45	12	16
41	55	14	17
44	61	15	18
Median = 17	Median = 20	$\Sigma R_1 = 75$	$\Sigma R_2 = 96$
$n_1 = 9$	$n_2 = 9$		

Step 2: Sum the ranks in columns 3 and 4, and enter them at the bottom of the columns, as shown above. For instance, the sum of the ranks for Group 1 is $\Sigma R_1 = 75$, where R stands for the ranks.

Step 3: Solve for the value of U_1 for Group 1 using this formula:

$$U_1 = (n_1)(n_2) + \frac{n_1(n_1 + 1)}{2} - \Sigma R_1$$

$$= (9)(9) + \frac{9(9 + 1)}{2} - 75$$

$$= 81 + \frac{90}{2} - 75 = 81 + 45 - 75 = 51$$

Step 4: Solve for the value of U_2 for Group 2 using this formula:

$$U_2 = (n_1)(n_2) + \frac{n_2(n_2 + 1)}{2} - \Sigma R_2$$

$$= (9)(9) + \frac{9(9 + 1)}{2} - 96$$

$$= 81 + \frac{90}{2} - 96 = 81 + 45 - 96 = 30$$

356

Step 5: Inspect the results of Steps 3 and 4 to determine which value of *U* is *smaller*. (That is, determine whether U_1 or U_2 is smaller.)

In the example, U_2, which equals 30, is smaller than U_1.

Step 6: Evaluate the smaller value of *U* identified in Step 5 using Table 12 near the end of this book, for the .05 level, to determine significance.[4] To find the critical value, identify where the row for N_1 meets the column for N_2. For our example, the *critical value of U* is 17.

> **Here is the decision rule:**
>
> If the *observed value of U is less than the critical value,*[5] reject the null hypothesis. Otherwise, do not reject it.

Because the observed value (30) is *not* less than the critical value (17), do not reject the null hypothesis, and do *not* declare the difference statistically significant at the .05 level.

A note of caution: The Mann-Whitney *U* test, as illustrated in this section, should be used only when *n* = 20 or less for the larger of the two groups *and n* = 9 or more for the larger group. Application of the test for situations beyond these parameters is beyond the scope of this book.

Term to Review Before Attempting Worksheet 58

Mann-Whitney *U* test

---

[4]Use Table 13 near the end of this book for the .01 level. Tables 12 and 13 are for two-tailed tests.
[5]Be careful: In all of the previous decision rules, the observed value had to be *greater* than the critical value in order for significance to be declared. Also, in the unlikely event that the observed value is equal to the critical value, reject the null hypothesis.

"How to lose weight while doing statistics homework: Double-click mouse six million times between each data entry."

Worksheet 58   Mann-Whitney *U* Test

Riddle: According to R. E. Shay, what proves that a rabbit's foot is not lucky?

DIRECTIONS: To find the answer to the riddle, write the answer to each question in the space immediately below it. In the solution section, the word in parentheses next to the answer to the first question is the first word in the answer to the riddle, the word beside the answer to the second question is the second word, and so on.

Col. 1	Col. 2	Col. 3	Col. 4
East side (Group 1)	West side (Group 2)	Ranks for Group 1	Ranks for Group 2
1	0		
3	4		
5	6		
11	17		
12	18		
16	29		
23	35		
33	39		
44	55		
Median = 12	Median = 18	$\Sigma R_1 =$	$\Sigma R_2 =$
$n_1 = 9$	$n_2 = 9$		

1. What is the rank for a person with a score of 18?

2. What is the value of *U* for Group 1?

3. What is the value of *U* for Group 2?

Worksheet 58 (continued)

4. Should the value of U for Group 1 *or* Group 2 be used as the observed value for the test of significance?

5. What is the critical value of U at the .05 level?

6. Should the null hypothesis be rejected at the .05 level?

7. "The difference is statistically significant at the .05 level." Is this statement true *or* false?

Solution section:

Group 1 (fur)   yes (fortune)   true (being)   11 (it)   49 (did)   32 (not)

8 (animal)   false (rabbit)   no (the)   17 (for)   7 (money)

14 (windows)   Group 2 (work)   15 (charm)   10 (superstitious)

Write the answer to the riddle here, putting one word on each line: _____ _____ _____ _____

_____ _____ _____

360

Section 59   Wilcoxon's Matched-Pairs Test

The median test in Section 57 and the Mann-Whitney U test in Section 58 are used with independent data. ***Wilcoxon's matched-pairs test*** (also known as the ***matched-pairs signed-ranks test***) is for use when one subject in each group is matched with one subject in the other group.[1] An example of matched pairs follows:

Eighteen students were selected at random for an experiment on learning advanced basketball skills. Students were paired based on the results of a test of elementary basketball skills: The two subjects with the lowest elementary skills were designated as one pair, the two with the next-lowest elementary skills were designated as another pair, and so on. For each pair, a coin was flipped to determine which one would become a member of the experimental group. The other member of the pair became a member of the control group. Following are the scores they earned on a test of advanced skills at the end of the experiment:

Pair	Col. 1 Experimental	Col. 2 Control
A	3	6
B	7	1
C	9	8
D	15	13
E	26	19
F	30	22
G	35	31
H	20	9
I	16	6
	Median = 16	Median = 9

Inspection of the medians suggests that the performance of the experimental group was superior to that of the control group. However, because only a random sample was studied, the null hypothesis, which states that there is no *true* difference

---

[1]Thus, Wilcoxon's matched-pairs test is for *dependent* or *correlated* data while the tests in Sections 57 and 58 are for *independent* or *uncorrelated* data. All three tests are used with ordinal data or data that violate the assumptions of the *t* test or ANOVA.

between the distributions, needs to be considered. To test the null hypothesis, follow these steps:

Step 1: Calculate the *absolute* difference between each pair of scores. (The *absolute difference* is the difference without regard to sign. In practical terms, this means to record all differences as though they were positive. Do not record any negative signs.) Thus, subtract each score in column 2 from the score for its pair in column 1, ignore the sign of the answer, and enter the absolute differences in column 3, as shown in the following table:

Pair	Col. 1 Experimental	Col. 2 Control	Col. 3 Absolute difference
A	3	6	3
B	7	1	6
C	9	8	1
D	15	13	2
E	26	19	7
F	30	22	8
G	35	31	4
H	20	9	11
I	16	6	10

Step 2: Rank the differences in column 3, and record the ranks in column 4. When ranking, give the smallest difference a rank of 1, the next-smallest difference a rank of 2, and so on.[2] The ranks are shown in the following table:

---

[2]If there are ties, split the ranks among them. For instance, if the two lowest scores are 4 and 4 (i.e., two subjects have a 4), they are tied, and it is not possible to determine which should have a rank of 1 and which should have a rank of 2. We compromise by adding the ranks in question (1 + 2 = 3) and dividing by the number of tied scores (in this case, two scores). Thus, 3/2 = 1.5, which is the rank assigned to each score.

	Col. 1	Col. 2	Col. 3	Col. 4
			Absolute	
Pair	Experimental	Control	difference	Rank
A	3	6	3	3
B	7	1	6	5
C	9	8	1	1
D	15	13	2	2
E	26	19	7	6
F	30	22	8	7
G	35	31	4	4
H	20	9	11	9
I	16	6	10	8

Step 3: Subtracting column 2 from column 1 in each case, record in column 5 whether the difference between columns 1 and 2 *would have been* positive or negative. This is done in column 5 in the table that follows.

	Col. 1	Col. 2	Col. 3	Col. 4	Col. 5
			Absolute		Positive/
Pair	Exp.	Control	difference	Rank	negative
A	3	6	3	3	−
B	7	1	6	5	+
C	9	8	1	1	+
D	15	13	2	2	+
E	26	19	7	6	+
F	30	22	8	7	+
G	35	31	4	4	+
H	20	9	11	9	+
I	16	6	10	8	+

Step 4: Record the *ranks* associated with the positive signs in column 6 and the *ranks* associated with the negative signs in column 7, as shown in the table that follows. Then sum these two columns.

	Col. 1	Col. 2	Col. 3	Col. 4	Col. 5	Col. 6	Col. 7
			Absolute		Pos./	Rank+	Rank–
Pair	Exp.	Control	difference	Rank	neg.	$R+$	$R-$
A	3	6	3	3	–		3
B	7	1	6	5	+	5	
C	9	8	1	1	+	1	
D	15	13	2	2	+	2	
E	26	19	7	6	+	6	
F	30	22	8	7	+	7	
G	35	31	4	4	+	4	
H	20	9	11	9	+	9	
I	16	6	10	8	+	8	
						$\Sigma R+ = 42$	$\Sigma R- = 3$

Step 5: Determine whether $\Sigma R+$ or $\Sigma R-$ is smaller. The smaller value is the *observed value* of Wilcoxon's T statistic. Therefore, for this example,

Wilcoxon's $T = 3$

Step 6: Determine the *critical value* of Wilcoxon's T from Table 14 near the end of this book, using this formula for degrees of freedom:[3]

$df = N_{pairs} - 1 = 9 - 1 = 8$

Table 14 indicates that for 8 degrees of freedom at the .05 level, the *critical value* is 4.

Here is the decision rule:

If the *observed value of Wilcoxon's T is less than the critical value,*[4] reject the null hypothesis.

Because the *observed value* (3) is less than the *critical value* (4), reject the null hypothesis at the .05 level and declare the difference statistically significant.

---

[3]This table is for a two-tailed test.
[4]In the unlikely event that the observed value is equal to the critical value, reject the null hypothesis.

Term to Review Before Attempting Worksheet 59

Wilcoxon's matched-pairs test (matched-pairs signed-ranks test)

**"I forgot to make a backup copy of my brain, so everything
I learned in statistics last semester was lost."**

Worksheet 59   Wilcoxon's Matched-Pairs Test

> *Riddle*: According to Bierce's *Devil's Dictionary*, what is the definition of love?

DIRECTIONS: To find the answer to the riddle, write the answer to each question in the space immediately below it. In the solution section, the word in parentheses next to the answer to the first question is the first word in the answer to the riddle, the word beside the answer to the second question is the second word, and so on.

Pair	Col. 1 Exp.	Col. 2 Control	Col. 3 Absolute difference	Col. 4 Rank	Col. 5 Pos./ neg.	Col. 6 Rank+ $R+$	Col. 7 Rank– $R-$
A	10	3					
B	8	6					
C	7	10					
D	1	12					
E	6	2					
F	15	5					
G	10	9					
H	10	5					
						$\Sigma R+ =$	$\Sigma R- =$

1. What is the rank for Pair A?

2. What is the sum of column 6?

3. What is the sum of column 7?

Worksheet 59 (continued)

4. What are the degrees of freedom?

5. What is the critical value of Wilcoxon's *T* at the .05 level?

6. May the null hypothesis be rejected at the .05 level?

7. "The difference is statistically significant at the .05 level." Is this statement true *or* false?

Solution section:

> 8 (right) 4 (bliss) 25 (is) 6 (love) 11 (temporary) false (marriage)
>
> true (feelings) no (by) 2 (curable) yes (right) 7 (insanity)
>
> 15 (flowers) 20 (proof) 16 (wedding) 0 (heart) 1 (nothing)

Write the answer to the riddle here, putting one word on each line: _____ _____ _____ _____ ,
_____ _____ _____

Notes

Section 60   Descriptive Statistics: Their Value in Research

In Part A of this book (Sections 1 through 22), a wide variety of *descriptive statistics* was presented. They are of great value for three reasons. First, they help researchers to obtain overviews of selected characteristics of the groups they study. Second, they make it relatively easy to compare two or more groups on the characteristics (i.e., variables) being studied. Finally, they allow researchers to communicate their findings quickly and efficiently. These three reasons are illustrated in the examples that follow.

Example 1

A medical researcher assigned 180 patients with a potentially terminal illness to two groups at random. The experimental group ($n = 90$) received a new drug designed to treat the illness, while the other group ($n = 90$) received a placebo that looked and tasted like the new drug but was actually inert. At the end of the study, the researcher had collected these data:

Participant	Group	Outcome
Jill	Experimental	Alive
Fernando	Control	Deceased
Suzanne	Control	Deceased
Rachel	Experimental	Deceased
Roxanne	Control	Deceased
Wayne	Experimental	Alive

Plus additional results of the type shown above for the remaining 174 participants.

The researcher in Example 1 collected **nominal** data (see Section 3 of this book). It is nominal because, unlike scores, the data are *names,* such as *experimental* and *control* as well as *alive* and *deceased*. The researcher can use descriptive statistics to count the **frequencies** (see Section 4) of those who are alive and dead in each group. (The symbol for frequencies is f. However, frequencies are usually reported in research reports as *numbers of participants*, whose symbol is n. In other words, f and n are equivalent for all practical purposes.) The researcher can also compute the **percentages** or **proportions** (see Section 4) that correspond to the frequencies. These can be reported in sentences or in a statistical table, such as this one:

	Outcome	
	Deceased	Alive
Experimental group	42%	58%
	(n = 38)	*(n = 52)*
Control group	74%	26%
	(n = 67)	*(n = 23)*

The descriptive statistics in the table of results shown (1) provide an overview of the results, (2) make it easy to compare the outcome for the experimental group with the outcome for the control group, and (3) provide an efficient way to communicate the results of the experiment. Thus, Example 1 illustrates the three characteristics that make descriptive statistics exceptionally useful in research.

Example 2

In May of each year, administrators test the ability of all first-grade students in a school district to add and subtract one-digit numbers using a 20-item completion test with questions such as "3 + 4 = ___." For each of the 325 first graders in the three schools in the district this year, they obtained a number-right score, the name of the school attended, and the name of the class in which the students were enrolled, as identified by teachers' names (e.g., Marilyn = 14 right, School X, Teacher A). This is the beginning of the list of the 325 results, in no particular order (i.e., not yet analyzed with descriptive statistics):

Student	Number right	School	Teacher
Mary	15	Washington	Jones
Jose	19	Franklin	Black
Hillary	17	Bishop	Doe
Francis	21	Washington	Smith
Tom	8	Bishop	Doe
Smitty	3	Washington	Jones

Plus additional results for the remaining 319 participants (not shown here).

The results in Example 2 need to be organized so that the school administrators can get an overview of the data, compare the groups (e.g., comparing the various schools with each other), and communicate the results to interested parties (e.g., parents and the school board). While there are various ways to do this using descriptive statistics, the following steps are standard for these types of data:

Step 1: Determine the *scale of measurement* (see Section 3). Note that most researchers treat multiple-choice test scores as being at the *interval scale* (see Section 3) of measurement. This is based on the assumption that each correct answer on such a test represents about the same amount of knowledge as each other correct answer. Thus, researchers assume, for instance, that the interval between 10 correct and 11 correct is about the same size (in terms of amount of knowledge) as the interval between 11 correct and 12 correct (i.e., that data points generated with multiple-choice tests have *equal intervals*). Note that if the scores only ranked students (and did not measure them with equal units), the scale would be *ordinal* (see Section 3). Also, note that the assumption that the scores are at equal intervals will influence the selection of additional statistics in subsequent steps.

Step 2: Examine the shape of the distribution using a statistical table such as a *frequency distribution* (see Sections 5 and 6) and/or by constructing a statistical figure such as a *histogram* (see Section 8) or a *frequency polygon* (see Section 9).

Step 3: If the distribution is at least roughly symmetrical and not highly *skewed* (see Section 10), then select the *mean* (see Section 12) as the average. If the scale of measurement is ordinal, such as *ranks* (see Section 3 and Step 1 above), or if the distribution is highly skewed, select the *median* (see Section 13) as the average. Compute the average (i.e., mean or median) for all 325 students. Also, compute the average for each group the administrators want to compare, such as the students at each of the three schools (Washington, Franklin, and Bishop), so that the averages can be compared across schools.

Step 4: If the administrators also want to use the test scores to determine how each student performed in relation to the other students in the school or the district, compute *percentile ranks* (see Section 7) and/or *standard scores* (see Sections 18 and 19) for each student.

Step 5: Examine the variability in the scores. If the median was selected as the average, compute the *range* and *interquartile range* (see Section 14) as the measures of variability. If the mean was selected as the average, compute the *standard deviation* (see Sections 15–17). Note that important information can be obtained by comparing a measure of variability across schools and classes. For instance, if one school has a much larger standard deviation (i.e., students tend to be further from the mean in one school than in the other schools), the instructional techniques used in that school might need to be modified. For instance, when there is a wide variation in a group of students (as indicated by a very large standard deviation), individualized instruction is probably preferable to whole-class instruction, such as group lectures.

By following the five steps listed in this section, the school administrators will be able to (1) obtain an overview of the students' abilities to add one-digit numbers—at either the district, school, or classroom level, (2) compare various groups of students within the school district, and (3) concisely communicate important information, such as individual students' percentile ranks as well as information about the groups' averages and variability.

Consider Example 3, in which there is one set of scores for two groups of research participants.

Example 3

A research psychologist developed a new scale to measure depression. The scale consists of 30 true-false statements, such as, "I often feel sad when I wake up in the morning." The scale yields scores that can range from zero to 30. Both theory and research on depression indicate that anxiety is often associated with depression, which suggests that there should be a modest relationship between the two variables. Therefore, the psychologist administered the scale to 75 research participants. To the same group of participants, the psychologist administered a previously published standardized measure of anxiety that yields *T scores* (see Section 19). The *T* scores can range from 20 to 80. The following data were obtained:

Participant	Depression score	Anxiety score
Jose	29	55
Sally	5	25
Ling	15	45
Sammy	10	75

Plus additional results of the type shown above for the remaining 71 participants.

The research psychologist in Example 3 determined that the distributions of the two sets of scores were not highly skewed (see Section 10) by examining the *frequency distribution for grouped data* (see Section 6) and a frequency polygon (see Section 9), and she assumed that both variables were measured at the interval scale (see Section 3). She calculated the mean (see Sections 12 and 13) for each variable and the standard deviation (see Sections 15–17). Then, the psychologist constructed a *scattergram* (see Section 22) and determined that the relationship was reasonably close to being *linear* (see Section 22). However, she observed considerable scatter in the scattergram, which indicated a far-less-than-perfect relationship between the two sets of scores.

To obtain a single numerical value to represent this relationship, the psychologist computed the *Pearson r* (see Sections 33 and 34) and obtained an *r* of 0.44. To interpret this value, she computed the *coefficient of determination* (see Section 36), which is the square of *r* ($0.44 \times 0.44 = 0.19$). Multiplying the coefficient of determination by 100% ($0.19 \times 100\% = 19\%$), the psychologist determined that the amount of variance on anxiety accounted for by her new measure of depression is 19%, which indicates that her new measure operates as predicted by the theory and previous research on these variables (i.e., anxiety and depression are modestly related). She wrote a journal article that reported on the development of the new measure of depression. The article included a discussion of the descriptive statistics mentioned here, which provided readers with a concise overview, obviating the need to report the two scores for each of the 75 individual participants.

Terms to Review Before Attempting Worksheet 60

nominal (see Section 3), frequencies (see Section 4), percentages or proportions (see Section 4), scale of measurement (see Section 3), interval scale (see Section 3) ordinal (see Section 3), frequency distribution (see Sections 5 and 6), histogram (see Section 8), frequency polygon (see Section 9), skewed (see Section 10), mean (see Section 12), ranks (see Section 3), median (see Section 13), percentile ranks (see Section 7), standard scores (see Sections 18 and 19), range (see Section 14), interquartile range (see Section 14), standard deviation (see Sections 15–17), *T* scores (see Section 19), frequency distribution for grouped data (see Section 6), scattergram (see Section 22), linear (see Section 22), Pearson *r* (see Sections 33 and 34), coefficient of determination (see Section 36)

Engelbert Working on His Statistics Homework

Worksheet 60 Descriptive Statistics: Their Value in Research

Riddle: A clear conscience is usually a sign of what?

DIRECTIONS: To find the answer to the riddle, write the answer to each question in the space immediately below it. In the solution section, the word in parentheses next to the answer to the first question is the first word in the answer to the riddle, the word beside the answer to the second question is the second word, and so on.

1. According to the information in this section, descriptive statistics are of great value for how many reasons?

    TWO

2. The researcher in Example 1 collected data that were at what scale of measurement (nominal, ordinal, *or* interval)?

    NOMinal

3. What is the symbol for number of participants?

    n

4. In Example 1, which group (experimental *or* control) had a higher percentage of participants who had died by the end of the study?

    control

5. Most researchers treat multiple-choice test scores as being at what level (scale) of measurement?   interval

6. If the scale of measurement is interval and if the distribution is at least roughly symmetrical and not highly skewed, which average should be selected?

    mean

Worksheet 60 (continued)

7. To determine how each student performed in relation to other students, compute percentile ranks and/or what other types of scores?

Standard

8. If the mean was selected as the average, what statistic should be computed to examine the variability in a set of scores?

Standard deviation

9. There were two scores per research participant in which of the three examples (Example 1, Example 2, *or* Example 3)?

example 3

10. To interpret a value of a Pearson *r*, which statistic should be computed?

coefficient of determination

Solution section:

four (mindless)   nominal (is)   *p* (are)   % (strength)   *n* (very)   three (it)

range (people)   standard scores (of)   Example 1 (wrong)   frequencies (crazy)

experimental (beautiful)   mean (sign)   coefficient of determination (memory)

Example 3 (bad)   ratio (invent)   median (to)   standard deviation (a)

ordinal (heaven)   number-right scores (kindness)   two (death)   control (often)

interquartile range (clear)   Example 2 (weakness)   interval (the)

Worksheet 60 (continued)

Write the answer to the riddle here, putting one word on each line: <u>Death</u>   <u>is</u>   <u>very</u>   <u>often</u>   <u>the</u>   <u>sign</u>   <u>of</u>   <u>a</u>   <u>bad</u>   <u>memory</u>

Computer Repairs

"Your computer has high cholesterol and an overdose of statistics homework."

Section 61   Inferential Statistics: Their Value in Research

Inferential statistics are covered in Part B of this book (Sections 23 through 59). A wide variety of inferential statistics are used to interpret descriptive statistics in light of *sampling errors* (see Sections 23 and 24), which are defined as "errors created by random sampling." Consider Example 1 to review one application of inferential statistics.

Example 1

Members of the school board of a large school district asked researchers to estimate their high school seniors' knowledge of current events. Instead of administering a current-events test to all 1,950 seniors in the district, the researchers administered it to only 300 of the seniors, who were selected through simple random sampling (e.g., drawing names out of a hat). On the 50-item current-events multiple-choice test, the mean score was 35.0, which the researchers reported to the school board. The researchers cautioned the members of the board, however, that the mean of 35.0 was only an estimate of the average based on the simple random sample of 300 seniors. They also reported that a safer estimate of the seniors' knowledge was the ***95% confidence interval*** (see Section 29) for the mean, which the researchers calculated to be 31.0 to 39.0. Thus, board members were able to have 95% confidence that the true mean (which would have been obtained if the researchers had tested all seniors in the district) would have been between 31.0 and 39.0. Based on this information, the board members voted to hire consultants to advise the board on how to increase students' knowledge of current events.

The researchers in Example 1 reported the mean as a descriptive statistic, which directly describes only the seniors in the sample of 300. They calculated the 95% confidence interval using inferential statistics. Note that testing a random sample of only 300 is much more efficient and cost-effective than testing all 1,950 seniors in the district. However, without inferential statistics (such as the limits of the 95% confidence interval for the mean), it would be difficult to interpret the mean from a sample because there would be no estimate of the extent to which random errors affected the results. Thus, Example 1 illustrates the first major value of inferential statistics: They help us to interpret statistics that estimate population values (such as the mean of a population) based on studies of random samples.

The second major value of inferential statistics is a corollary of the first: Inferential statistics help in the interpretation of differences in descriptive statistics among various samples drawn at random. Consider Example 2 to review this valuable contribution of inferential statistics.

Example 2

A social science researcher conducted an experiment to explore the effectiveness of two corporate programs that helped laid-off employees find employment with other companies. Program A stressed individual job-placement counseling, while Program B stressed group job-placement counseling. The researcher selected a random sample of the laid-off employees and assigned them to Program A. He then assigned another random sample to Program B. After the programs were administered to the two samples, the researcher determined that 22% of those in Program A found new employment, while only 20% of those in Program B found new employment. By conducting an inferential test of statistical significance, the researcher determined the probability that the difference between 22% and 20% was not statistically significant. In light of this result, the researcher reported to the corporation's directors that the difference in the outcome between the two programs was statistically insignificant (i.e., an unreliable difference that could have been created by the random selection of the groups). On the basis of the researcher's experiment, the corporation's directors concluded that the two treatments appeared to be about equal in their effectiveness. Given this information, they selected Program B for future use because the group counseling component of that program was less expensive than the individual counseling component of Program A.

As you probably recall, a test of statistical significance tests the ***null hypothesis*** (see Sections 31 and 32). In general, the null hypothesis states that any differences that are obtained when using random sampling are the result of sampling errors. In Example 2, these errors would be those created by the random selection of participants for the two groups (i.e., the two groups might differ in ways, quite at random, that might affect the outcome of the experiment). The researcher found that the difference was not greater than what would be expected on the basis of random error alone. Hence, the result is insignificant.

In Example 2, the researcher tested for the significance of the difference between frequencies (and the corresponding percentages) using the inferential statistical test named the ***chi-square test*** (see Sections 53–55).

Now consider Example 3, in which a different test of significance was used in a nonexperimental study.

Example 3

A researcher wanted to know if there was a difference in job satisfaction between those who were hired before a new, less-generous retirement program was instituted and those who were hired after. The researcher drew a random sample of each group and administered a standardized job-satisfaction scale that yielded scores from 20 to 80. The researcher obtained a mean of 70.50 for the sample hired under the old retirement program and a mean of 62.75 for the sample of those hired under the newer one. A t test yielded a probability of $p < .001$, indicating that it was highly unlikely (the likelihood was less than 1 in 1,000) that the difference between the two means was the result of errors created by the random sampling. Because it was highly unlikely that the difference was due to sampling error, the researcher concluded that there was a statistically significant difference between the two means and, therefore, rejected the null hypothesis.

Notice that in Example 3, the ***t test*** (see Sections 43–46) helped in the interpretation of the descriptive statistics (i.e., the difference between the two means). Without an inferential test, the researcher could not determine whether the difference was greater than would be expected on the basis of chance alone (e.g., quite at random, the researcher might have selected more satisfied employees from those under the old retirement program).

In summary, inferential statistics help in the interpretation of descriptive statistics in light of possible errors created by random sampling. Studying only random samples is usually more efficient than studying whole populations, and inferential statistics help researchers make inferences about what populations are like based on random samples drawn from those populations.

Terms to Review Before Attempting Worksheet 61

sampling errors (see Sections 23 and 24), **95% confidence interval** (see Section 29), **null hypothesis** (see Sections 31 and 32), **chi-square test** (see Sections 53–55), *t* **test** (see Sections 43–46)

Worksheet 61 Inferential Statistics: Their Value
in Research

Riddle: What is the quickest way to double your
money in Las Vegas?

DIRECTIONS: To find the answer to the riddle, write the answer to each question in the space immediately below it. In the solution section, the word in parentheses next to the answer to the first question is the first word in the answer to the riddle, the word beside the answer to the second question is the second word, and so on.

1. According to the information in this section, is there a wide *or* a narrow variety of inferential statistics?

   wide variety

2. Inferential statistics are used to interpret what other type of statistics?

   descriptive statistics

3. Did the researchers in Example 1 administer the current-events test to all 1,950 seniors in the school district?

   NO

4. In addition to the standard deviation, what other descriptive statistic was reported in Example 1?

   mean (?)

5. The second major value of inferential statistics is that they help us to interpret differences in descriptive statistics among various samples drawn at _____.

   random

Worksheet 61 (continued)

6. When a difference is unreliable, is it statistically significant *or* insignificant?

   insignificant

7. In which Example (1, 2, or 3) was a *t* test used?

   example 3

8. What adjective is used before the word *hypothesis* to indicate that the hypothesis states that any differences obtained when using random sampling are the result of sampling error?

   Null

9. What is the name of the inferential statistical test used in Example 2 to determine whether the difference was statistically significant?

   Chi-square

10. When an inferential test indicates that $p < .001$, this means that the likelihood is less than 1 in how many others?

    1,000

11. What type of sampling was used in all three examples?

    random

Worksheet 61 (continued)

Solution section:

percentages (blackjack)   populations (climb)   descriptive (it)

100 (spend)   Example 2 (jumping)   insignificant (put)   errors (Nevada)

null (back)   no (in)   wide (fold)   significant (steal)   stratified (chips)

Example 1 (ladder)   1,000 (your)   random (and)   Example 3 (it)   mean (half)

inferential (were)   volunteers (bank)   efficient (casino)   chi-square (in)

research (having)   random (pocket)   yes (being)   frequencies (broke)

10,000 (lose)   deviation (dealer)

Write the answer to the riddle here, putting one word on each line: _fold_ _it_ _in_ _half_ _and_ _put_ _it_ _back_ _in_ _your_ _pocket_

Section 62   Limitations of Inferential Statistics: I

As you know from Part B (Sections 23–59) of this book, ***inferential statistics*** are used to interpret descriptive statistics in light of ***sampling errors***, which are defined as "errors created by random sampling" (see Sections 23 and 24). Specifically, inferential statistics are used to build ***confidence intervals*** (see Sections 28 and 29) as well as to interpret differences among descriptive statistics for various samples drawn at random (such as comparing the means of two samples drawn from two different populations).

As you probably recall, a test of statistical significance tests the ***null hypothesis*** (see Sections 31 and 32). The null hypothesis asserts that any differences obtained when using random sampling are the result of sampling errors created by the process of random sampling. Inferential statistics test this assertion. When they indicate that there is a low probability that the null hypothesis is true (such as $p < .05$, .01, or .001), it is conventional to reject the null hypothesis and conclude that it is unlikely that any difference being considered is the result of sampling errors.

Despite their great value in research, inferential statistics have two major limitations that are often insufficiently recognized. In this section, the first limitation will be considered, which is that the validity of inferential statistics is limited to data obtained only from *random samples. Nonrandom samples* (such as a sample of people who happen to be in a shopping mall as representatives of all shoppers in a city *or* the students in a single classroom as representatives of all students in a school because only one teacher agreed to allow the research to be conducted) are, by default, considered ***biased samples***. In other words, if a sample is not drawn at random, it is presumed biased (see Sections 23 and 24 to review types of bias and various methods of random sampling). Consider Example 1 as background material for a more detailed discussion of this first limitation of inferential statistics.

Example 1

A parent was interested in other parents' reactions to the possibility of requiring elementary school students in a large public school district to wear uniforms at school. The parent selected several nearby elementary schools and briefly interviewed some of the parents who were picking up their children at the end of the school day. In all, 50 parents were asked to rate the desirability of requiring uniforms on a scale from 10 (*extremely desirable*) to 1 (*extremely undesirable*). A mean of 7.25 was obtained for the 35 female parents, and a mean of 6.75 was obtained for the 15 male parents who were interviewed. These descriptive statistics were presented at an open meeting of the school board as evidence that parents (on average) favor requiring students to wear uniforms. It was also noted that the female parents were more in favor than the male parents.

Clearly, the samples of women and men in Example 1 are biased. Perhaps the most important source of bias results from selecting only parents at "nearby" elementary schools within the district's total area. Thus, the sample is biased against parents whose children attend "far-away" elementary schools. The geographical bias (i.e., the bias against parents at far-away schools) is potentially very serious because neighborhoods tend to differ in many important respects, such as socioeconomic status, political affiliation, cultural/ethnic/racial composition, number of immigrants, and so on. Thus, what was learned from parents whose children attended nearby schools might be very different from what would have been learned from studying a random sample drawn from all the schools in the district. Unfortunately, there are no inferential statistics to deal with specific biases (such as the bias against far-away schools).

Also, notice from Example 1 that the parent conducting the study interviewed only parents who were picking their children up from school. Parents who pick their children up might differ in many ways from those who do not. For instance, parents who do so might be more protective, have children who live beyond walking distance from the school, be unemployed (and thus have time to pick their children up), have younger children, and so on. Once again, there are no inferential statistical methods for interpreting errors due to biases. Inferential methods are designed for interpreting only descriptive statistics that may have been influenced by random errors.

It is important to note that inferential statistics can be calculated from any set of values (such as scores from 1 to 10 in Example 1), whether or not the scores were obtained from a random sample. Thus, it is *mathematically possible* to calculate confidence intervals for the two means in Example 1 as well as to perform the calculations necessary to conduct a *t* test of the significance of the difference between the means for female and male parents. However, these inferential statistics would be of limited value (from a strict point of view) because they would have been misapplied to descriptive statistics obtained from clearly biased samples of female and male parents.

Although researchers know the value of using randomly drawn samples, in practice, they often have great difficulty obtaining them when studying humans as participants in research. This is true for two reasons. First, sometimes it is impossible to identify all the members of a population, which makes it impossible to draw a random sample of all of them. (Note that researchers cannot put all the names in a hat in order to draw a random sample if they do not know the names of all the members of a population.) For instance, it is not possible to identify all individuals with a certain disease (partly because many people with the disease may be undiagnosed or because of privacy issues). Likewise, it is not possible to identify all successful (never arrested) burglars in a state, all the homeless in a city, all the married couples in abusive relationships, and so on.

The second reason why it is often difficult or impossible to obtain random samples is that in most settings, researchers must rely on the voluntary participation of subjects. For instance, a research psychologist might draw a random sample of all freshmen on a college campus (a known population) but be required by the college to use those in the sample who agree in writing to participate in the research. Those who do not agree and therefore do not participate in the research create a bias in the remaining sample (i.e., those who participate constitute a sample biased in favor of the type of people who tend to agree to participate in psychological research).

Despite the difficulties in obtaining random samples from important populations of human subjects in fields such as medicine, sociology, psychology, political science, and education, researchers nevertheless proceed with their investigations in order to obtain at least limited information on pressing problems in these fields. Furthermore, it has become conventional to apply inferential statistics in studies in which biased samples are used and to report these statistics in published research reports. In this way, inferential statistics provide information on a "what if" scenario. In other words, inferential statistics are being used to explore these questions: "What if the sample was random instead of biased?" "What confidence intervals and levels of significance would be obtained under this 'what if' condition?"

It is also important to note that when inferential statistics are applied to results obtained from biased samples, researchers and consumers of research should use great caution in interpreting these results because, in the strictest sense, inferential statistics should be limited to analysis of data obtained from random samples. Nevertheless, application of inferential statistics provides us with hints as to what might be obtained under more optimal circumstances. In addition, inferential statistics provide a common standard for comparing the results between studies (e.g., to identify which studies had low values of p and which did not), even if the studies were conducted with biased samples.

Because of the limitation considered in this topic, the results obtained with inferential statistics should be taken with a grain of salt whenever biased samples are used. When a sample is clearly biased, such as in Example 1, researchers should warn their readers of the limitation. In many cases, it is also a good idea to label studies with this weakness *pilot studies* in either the title or the introduction and conclusion of a research report.

Note that the limitation being considered in this section is *not* due to some mathematical flaw in the development of inferential statistics. Instead, the limitation results from the fact that inferential statistics were designed for interpreting only results that have errors due to random sampling. In the same sense that even the very best traditional automobile is of limited value for off-road driving, inferential statistics are of limited value in interpreting the results obtained from biased samples.

In the next section, another important limitation of inferential statistics is explored.

Terms to Review Before Attempting Worksheet 62

inferential statistics (see Section 61), **sampling errors** (see Sections 23 and 24), **confidence intervals** (see Sections 28 and 29), **null hypothesis** (see Sections 31 and 32), **biased samples** (see Sections 23 and 24)

"You are getting sleepier and sleepier. When I count to three, you will be able to answer all my statistics homework questions correctly."

Worksheet 62 Limitations of Inferential Statistics: I

Riddle: What does the wacky sign outside the
         muffler shop read?

DIRECTIONS: To find the answer to the riddle, write the answer to each question in the space immediately below it. In the solution section, the word in parentheses next to the answer to the first question is the first word in the answer to the riddle, the word beside the answer to the second question is the second word, and so on.

1. What adjective is used before the word *errors* to indicate errors that are created by random sampling?

   Sampling

2. Inferential statistics can be used to build confidence _____.

   Intervals

3. Is the null hypothesis rejected when the probability determined with a significance test is high *or* when it is low?

   low

4. If a sample is not drawn at random, it is presumed to be what?

   biased

5. Should the samples of male and female parents in Example 1 be presumed to be unbiased?

   NO

6. If a sample is biased, is it mathematically possible to calculate inferential statistics?

   yes

Worksheet 62 (continued)

7. What adjective might be put before the word *study* in either titles or introductions and conclusions of research reports in which biased samples are used?

pilot

Solution section:

inferential (cars)   intervals (appointment)   biased (we)   descriptive (free)

unbiased (used)   samples (noise)   calculate (cost)   high (sound)   default (ticket)

pilot (coming)   probability (shopping)   large (mechanic)   sampling (no)

confidence (driving)   published (moving)   no (hear)

low (necessary)   confidence (charge)   hypothesis (loud)

errors (check)   geographical (dangerous)   yes (you)

Write the answer to the riddle here, putting one word on each line: No   appointment necessary   we   near   you   coming

Notes

Section 63   Limitations of Inferential Statistics: II

From the previous section, you know that inferential statistics are of limited value in interpreting descriptive statistics obtained through the study of biased samples. Even if unbiased (i.e., random) samples are used, there is an additional limitation: Inferential statistical tests indicate only whether differences are **reliable**. They do *not* indicate whether differences are large. Individuals who mistakenly believe that all significant differences are large will often be misled.

To understand this limitation, first consider the difference between a reliable difference and a large difference. When a researcher says that a *reliable difference* has been identified, he or she is referring to consistency, not to whether the difference is large or small. Example 1 illustrates that a small difference can be reliable.

Example 1
Jackson arrives at work each morning in the nick of time, clocking in just before his pay would be docked. He would prefer to arrive a few minutes early and to not have to rush. However, he is the single parent of an elementary school child, and he waits until his daughter is on the school bus before leaving for work. This leaves him with just enough time to rush to work and clock in on time. His behavior is *reliable* because it is consistent from day to day. Sheila, on the other hand, arrives about five minutes early each day because the public bus that she takes arrives at that time. Sheila's behavior is also highly *reliable* because it is consistent from day to day.

Under most circumstances, a five-minute difference, such as the one between Jackson's and Sheila's arrival times in Example 1, would be considered small. In the example, the difference is not only small, but it is also unimportant because both employees arrive at work on time. Despite its smallness and unimportance, over a long enough period of observation, anyone would become convinced that this is a real difference and not one due to chance factors alone. In the same way, given a large enough sample, significance tests can identify reliable (i.e., statistically significant) differences—even if they are very small.

To better understand why small differences can be statistically significant, consider the three basic factors that underlie the *t test*. As you know from Section 43, they are

1. The size of the sample: *The larger the sample, the more likely that the difference will be found statistically significant.*

2. The difference between two means: *The larger the difference, the more likely that the difference will be found statistically significant.*

3. The ***variance*** (see Sections 14 and 15) among the subjects: *The smaller the variance, the more likely that the difference will be found statistically significant.*

Thus, while a result with a larger difference is more likely to be statistically significant (see Statement 2), the other two factors (sample size and variance) also contribute to determining whether the difference between two means is significant. In fact, if sample size is very large and variance is very small in a study that has a small difference between means, the sample size and variance can overwhelm the small difference and create a statistically significant result. It is important to note that this is not a flaw of significance testing. Rather, it is a limitation because significance testing was designed to help us identify only reliable (i.e., consistent) differences—not necessarily large differences. If this is confusing, consider Example 1 again, and use it as an analogy that illustrates that small differences can be reliable, and remember that significance tests were designed to test for reliability.

Individuals who do not understand this limitation of significance testing often make correct but potentially misleading statements such as:

1. Program A should be adopted because studies show that it is, on average, significantly superior to Program B.

2. The new college admissions test is valid because the scores on it are significantly correlated with freshman GPA. The test is a statistically significant predictor of college grades.

3. The new drug should be approved by the FDA because significantly more individuals in the experimental group than in the control group reported relief from their symptoms.

All three statements are potentially misleading because they refer only to significance without describing the size of the difference. For the first statement, we would want to know on what scale the outcome was measured and the values of the means (and standard deviations). For the second statement, we would want to know the value of the correlation coefficient. For the third statement, we would want to know the frequencies and percentages of cases in each group that reported relief from symptoms. In short, we cannot determine whether the differences are large without examining the descriptive statistics on which the inferential significance tests were performed. Because of this, it is traditional to report descriptive statistics first and then to report inferential statistics in the results sections of research reports.

The next section of this book describes measures of the size of differences.

Terms to Review Before Attempting Worksheet 63

reliable, *t* **test** (see Section 43), **variance** (see Sections 14 and 15)

Worksheet 63 Limitations of Inferential Statistics: II

> *Riddle*: What is the newest modern law of physics?

DIRECTIONS: To find the answer to the riddle, write the answer to each question in the space immediately below it. In the solution section, the word in parentheses next to the answer to the first question is the first word in the answer to the riddle, the word beside the answer to the second question is the second word, and so on.

1. "The only purpose of inferential statistics is to indicate how large a difference is." Is this statement true *or* false?

   false

2. When we say we have identified a reliable difference, what we are referring to?

   consistency

3. Is the difference in Example 1 described as large *or* small?

   small

4. Is it possible for significance tests to identify reliable differences even if they are very small?

   yes

5. How many basic factors underlie the *t* test?

   3

6. Are large *or* small samples more likely to result in statistical significance?

   large

Worksheet 63 (continued)

7. "The smaller the variance, the more likely that the difference will be found statistically significant." Is this statement true *or* false?

   true

8. Are studies with larger samples more likely to have significant differences than studies with smaller samples?

   yes

9. Is the limitation discussed in this section a flaw?

   NO

10. For the second numbered statement near the end of this section (Statement 2), we would want to know the value of the correlation _____.

    coefficient

11. In short, we cannot determine whether differences are large without examining what type of statistics (other than inferential statistics)?

    differential

Solution section:

```
two (physical)  large (at)  one (measures)  no (speed)  significant (sound)

three (mail)  hypothesis (being)  false (bills)  significance (gravity)

coefficient (of)  five (assuming)  yes (the)  research (stamps)  sample (of)

small (through)  percentages (sometimes)  true (twice)  yes (the)

descriptive (checks)  sampling (generalize)  variation (though)

deviation (possibility)  consistency (travel)  correlational (people)
```

Worksheet 63 (continued)

Write the answer to the riddle here, putting one word on each line: _Bills_ _travel_ _through_ _the_ _mail_ _at_ _twice_ _the_ _speed_ _of_ _checks_

Section 64   Statistical Versus Practical Significance

As indicated in the previous section, statistically significant differences are not necessarily large differences. Likewise, a statistically significant correlation coefficient is not necessarily large.[1] Because of this, it is important to carefully consider the descriptive statistics (including measures of effect size [see Section 65]) before drawing conclusions and considering the implications of statistically significant results. This is illustrated in the next two examples.

Example 1

A college admissions officer developed an experimental admissions test and administered it to a random sample of the incoming freshmen in September. At the end of their freshman year, he correlated the admissions test scores with freshman-year GPA and obtained a ***Pearson r*** of 0.20 (see Sections 33 and 34). For the sample size used, the value of 0.20 was found statistically significant at the .05 probability level. To interpret the results further, the researcher calculated the ***coefficient of determination*** (a descriptive statistic described in Section 36), which equals 0.04 in this case. Multiplying 0.04 by 100%, the researcher learned that the amount of variation in GPA accounted for by the experimental test was only 4.0%. The researcher subjectively concluded that the experimental test was not an important predictor of freshman GPA, even though the underlying correlation coefficient was statistically significant.[2]

Note that the decision on the importance of the result in Example 1 can also be made in light of what is already known about the effectiveness of other predictors of college grades. For instance, high school grades often account for about 25% of the variance in college freshman grades. In this context, the 4% discussed in Example 1 does not seem especially important.

---

[1]When a test of statistical significance is conducted on a correlation coefficient, the *difference* between the value obtained with a random sample of subjects is compared with a hypothetical *null value* of 0.00. If the value observed by the researcher is determined to be statistically significant, we know that the difference between the observed value and a value of 0.00 is reliable (i.e., unlikely to be due to sampling error).

[2]The researcher could have assessed the contribution of the experimental test in combination with other predictors by using ***multiple correlation*** (see Section 37).

Example 2

An educational researcher administered a standardized math test to a random sample of third graders in a large urban school district. The researcher also administered the test to a random sample of students in the suburban school districts that surrounded the urban school district. The difference between the two means was found statistically significant at the .01 probability level. Before reaching conclusions, the researcher reexamined the means, which were 45.75 for the urban sample and 55.75 for the suburban sample. Because the standardized test yields *T* **scores** (see Section 19) that can range from 20.00 to 80.00, the researcher reported that the 10-point difference between the two means was educationally important because it was 1/6 of the total possible difference that could be obtained (i.e., the 10-point difference was 1/6 of the maximum possible difference of 60 points between 20.00 and 80.00), *and* it was a reliable difference (i.e., statistically significant). This decision on educational importance was made subjectively. However, it had a statistical basis (i.e., the researcher had considered both the magnitude of the difference indicated by the descriptive statistics and the result of the significance test).

In Example 2, the data were obtained with a standardized test that yielded easily interpreted *T* scores. In much research, nonstandardized tests that have been custom-made for particular research objectives are used. When this is the case, comparing the possible maximum range of the difference with the obtained difference between means is helpful in reaching conclusions. For instance, if overall attitudes toward the homeless are measured with a statement that respondents rate on a scale from 1 to 10, you know that the maximum possible range is 9 (i.e., $10 - 1 = 9$). If two groups are compared and a statistically significant difference between their means is 3 points on such a scale, then we know that this is 1/3 of the maximum possible difference. While 3 points might not be considered important when using a test with a maximum possible difference of 600 points, such as *CEEB scores* (see Section 19), which range from 200 to 800, when using a measure with a possible range of only 9 points, the 3-point difference might be regarded as very important.

In applied research, the question of the importance of a given statistical result is often discussed in terms of ***practical significance***. A statistical result is of practical significance when it has direct implications for professionals in applied fields, such as clinical psychology, social work, and education.

It is important to note that statistical significance is *not* necessary for a result to be of practical significance. For instance, suppose the administrators of a social work department were considering using a new computerized system for tracking certain types of clients. If an experiment revealed that the difference between the outcomes obtained through use of the new system (which would have considerable new costs associated with it) and the tracking system already in use were not statistically significant, the following conclusion, which is of considerable practical importance, might be reached: Do *not* purchase and implement the new system.

Determining practical significance requires consideration of three issues in addition to direct statistical considerations. The first issue is ***cost in relation to benefit***. This is often thought of in terms of the *cost for each unit of benefit*. For instance, if an experiment showed that a new computerized math program was superior to the current program on average by 6 points, and that the difference was statistically significant, a researcher could ask how much it would cost for each of the 6 points of difference. (In this case, the cost per unit can be determined by calculating how much more the new program would cost than the old program and dividing the difference by 6.) If the cost per unit is subjectively judged to be excessive, the researcher would conclude that the new program is not of practical significance.

The second major issue in determining practical significance is whether there are ***side effects***. Researchers who study the effects of prescription and over-the-counter drugs almost always design their studies so that they will detect undesirable side effects. Likewise, researchers in other fields often formally study side effects. For instance, research on mathematics achievement often includes measures of attitudes toward math because a program that produces superior math achievement but causes a deterioration of attitudes toward math might be of limited practical value.

The third issue is ***acceptability*** to clients, students, parents, and other stakeholders. For instance, if statistics indicate that there are benefits in requiring public school students to wear uniforms but the parents in a particular school district are strongly opposed to uniform requirements, a policy requiring them might not be politically acceptable to the school board.

Practical significance is also influenced by *legal and ethical issues*. Programs, treatments, and other procedures that are found to be statistically superior but are illegal or unethical obviously should be avoided.

In short, descriptive statistics summarize and organize the results of a study so that they can be understood more fully and communicated concisely. Inferential statistics tell us whether any differences are reliable in light of the possibility that the differences were created by random error. Determining practical significance is the last step in the research process, and it is based on sound judgment that goes beyond mathematical reasoning.

Terms to Review Before Attempting Worksheet 64

Pearson *r* (see Sections 33 and 34), **coefficient of determination** (see Section 36), **multiple correlation** (see Section 37), ***T* scores** (see Section 19), **CEEB scores** (see Section 19), **practical significance, cost in relation to benefit, side effects, acceptability, legal and ethical issues**

Worksheet 64 Statistical Versus Practical Significance

> *Riddle:* **What is the new motto of the Internal Revenue Service?**

DIRECTIONS: To find the answer to the riddle, write the answer to each question in the space immediately below it. In the solution section, the word in parentheses next to the answer to the first question is the first word in the answer to the riddle, the word beside the answer to the second question is the second word, and so on.

1. Was the correlation coefficient in Example 1 statistically significant?

yes

2. Did the researcher in Example 1 decide that the correlation was important?

NO

3. In Example 2, was the decision on educational importance made subjectively *or* objectively?

subjectvay

4. "The decision on educational importance in Example 2 has a statistical basis." Is this statement true *or* false?

True

5. "Standardized tests are almost always used in research." Is this statement true *or* false?

false

6. A difference is of practical significance when it has what?

direct implications

Worksheet 64 (continued)

7. What is the second major issue in determining practical significance?

Side effects

8. What is the third issue in determining practical significance?

acceptibility

9. Practical significance is also influenced by legal and what other kinds of issues?

ethical

10. Determining practical significance is which step in the research process?

last

Solution section:

true (it)   test (owe)   subjectively (what)   *T* (if)   false (takes)   CEEB (almost)

size (only)   direct implications (to)   significant (taxes)   no (got)   benefit (check)

unit (refund)   yes (we've)   null (government)   ethical (you've)   research (money)

cost (dollars)   probability (audit)   hypothesis (welfare)   side effects (get)

hypothesis (exempt)   sampling (claim)   acceptability (what)   last (got)

objective (going)   error (strong)   practical (in)   practicality (dollars)

Write the answer to the riddle here, putting one word on each line: *we've   got   what   it   takes   to   get   what   you've   got*

Section 65   Introduction to Effect Size (*d*)

To understand the need to consider the *effect size* of a difference, consider a practical problem in interpreting research. Suppose that Experimenter A administered a new treatment for depression (Treatment X) to an experimental group, while the control group received a standard treatment. Furthermore, suppose that Experimenter A used a 20-item true-false depression scale (with possible raw scores from 0 to 20) and obtained the results on the posttest shown in Table 1.[1] Note that the difference between the two means is 5 raw-score points.

Table 1
Statistics Obtained in Experiment A (Treatment X)

Group	*m*	*sd*
Experimental group (*n* = 50)	12.00	4.00
Control group (*n* = 50)	7.00	4.00
Difference between two means	5.00	

Suppose that Experimenter B administered Treatment Y to an experimental group, while treating the control group with the standard treatment. Furthermore, suppose Experimenter B used a 30-item scale with choices from *strongly agree* to *strongly disagree*, with possible scores from 0 to 120, and obtained the results in Table 2. Note the difference of 10 raw-score points in favor of the experimental group.

Table 2
Statistics Obtained in Experiment B (Treatment Y)

Group	*m*	*sd*
Experimental group (*n* = 50)	80.00	14.00
Control group (*n* = 50)	70.00	14.00
Difference between two means	10.00	

Which treatment is superior? Treatment X, which resulted in a 5-point raw-score difference between the two means, *or* Treatment Y, which resulted in a 10-

---

[1] Note that in the experiments in this topic, the researchers used instruments that yield *higher* scores when there is *less* depression.

point raw-score difference between the two means? Of course, the answer is not clear because the two experimenters used different measurement scales (0 to 20 versus 0 to 120).

For the results of the two studies to be comparable, they need to be *standardized* so that both differences can be expressed on the same scale. The most straightforward way to do this is to express both differences in terms of their *standard-deviation units* (instead of their raw-score units).[2] In Experiment A, one standard-deviation unit equals 4.00 raw-score points. Dividing the difference between the means (5.00) by the size of the standard-deviation unit for Experiment A (4.00 points) produces an answer of 1.25. This value is known as d and is obtained with the following formula, in which m_e stands for the mean of the experimental group, and m_c stands for the mean of the control group:

$$d = \frac{m_e - m_c}{sd} = \frac{12.00 - 7.00}{4.00} = 1.25$$

The result indicates that the experimental group exceeded the control group by 1.25 (one-and-one-quarter) standard-deviation units.

For all practical purposes, there are only three standard-deviation units on each side of the mean. Thus, d is expressed in standard-deviation units and has an effective range from 0.00 (no difference between the means) to 3.00 (the maximum difference between the means).[3] Thus, for Experiment A, the experimental group is one-and-one-quarter standard-deviation units above no difference (0.00) on a standardized scale that ranges from 0.00 to 3.00. On such a limited scale, a value of d of 1.25 indicates that the difference is substantially above 0.00.

When the formula is applied to Experiment B, the difference between the means is divided by the standard deviation (10.00/14.00), yielding $d = 0.71$, which is almost three-quarters of a standard deviation above 0.00. The following is now known about the differences in the two experiments when both are expressed on a common (i.e., standardized) scale called d: Clearly, the difference in Experiment A (1.25) is greater than the difference in Experiment B (0.71).

---

[2] See Sections 15 through 17 to review the meaning of the standard deviation.
[3] While it seldom does, theoretically d can exceed 3.00. If a control group has a higher mean than the experimental group, the value of d will be negative, with an effective range from 0.00 to –3.00.

0.00 0.50 0.75 1.00 1.50 1.75 2.00 2.50 2.75 3.00
    ↑   ↑
   Exp. B Exp. A

Table 3 summarizes these differences. Remember that the two raw-score differences are not directly comparable because different measurement scales were used (0 to 20 points versus 0 to 120 points). Examining the standardized values of *d*, which range from 0.00 to 3.00, yields a meaningful comparison of the results of the two experiments.

Within each of the two examples in this section, the two standard deviations are equal. When they are unequal, a special averaging procedure that results in the *pooled standard deviation* should be used. See Appendix I near the end of this book for more information.

An important definition to remember is that *effect size* is a measure of the *magnitude* (i.e., size) of a difference expressed on a standardized scale. The statistic *d* is one of the most popular statistics for describing the effect size of the difference between two means. In the next section, the interpretation of *d* is discussed in more detail. In Section 67, an alternative statistic for expressing effect size is described.

Table 3
Differences Expressed in Raw Scores and in Values of d

Group	Raw-score difference	Standardized difference (*d*)
Experimenter A	5 points	1.25
Experimenter B	10 points	0.71

Term to Review Before Attempting Worksheet 65

effect size

Worksheet 65   Introduction to Effect Size (*d*)

> ***Riddle***: What should you do if you think nobody cares about you?

DIRECTIONS: To find the answer to the riddle, write the answer to each question in the space immediately below it. In the solution section, the word in parentheses next to the answer to the first question is the first word in the answer to the riddle, the word beside the answer to the second question is the second word, and so on.

1. For an experimental group, $m = 50.00$ and $sd = 3.00$. For the control group, $m = 47.00$ and $sd = 3.00$. For this experiment, what is the value of *d*?

2. For an experimental group, $m = 30.00$ and $sd = 5.00$. For the control group, $m = 20.00$ and $sd = 5.00$. For this experiment, what is the value of *d*?

3. "The effect size is larger for Question 1 than for Question 2." Is this statement true *or* false?

4. If an experiment yields an effect size of 2.55, the experimental group's mean exceeds the control group's mean by how many standard deviations?

5. When an experimental group has a higher mean than the control group, the effective range of *d* is from 0.00 to what higher value?

Worksheet 65 (continued)

6. Can the value of *d* ever be negative?

7. What is the symbol for one of the most popular statistics for describing variability?

8. Which appendix in this book should be consulted when the standard deviations of the experimental group and the control group are not equal?

Solution section:

yes (credit)	no (counseling)	true (cheerful)	3.00 (of)	4.00 (the)	*d* (card)
	sd (being)	Appendix I (payments)	false (a)	2.00 (missing)	
Appendix E (help)	2.55 (couple)	1.00 (try)	5.00 (jump)	10.00 (yesterday)	

Write the answer to the riddle here, putting one word on each line: _____ _____ _____ _____

_____ _____ _____ _____

Notes

Section 66   Interpretation of Effect Size (*d*)

In the previous section, **effect size,** expressed as *d,* was introduced. The two examples in that section had values of *d* of 0.71 and 1.25. Obviously, the experiment with a value of 1.25 had a larger effect than the one with a value of 0.71.

While there are no universally accepted standards for describing values of *d* in words, many researchers use Cohen's (1992)[1] suggestions: (1) A value of *d* of about 0.20 (one-fifth of a standard deviation) is *small*, (2) a value of 0.50 (one-half of a standard deviation) is *medium*, and (3) a value of 0.80 (eight-tenths of a standard deviation) is *large*. (Keep in mind that in terms of values of *d*, an experimental group can rarely exceed a control group by more than 3.00 because the effective range of standard-deviation units is only three on each side of the mean. Thus, for the most practical purposes, 3.00 [or –3.00] is the maximum value of *d*.)[2]

Extrapolating from Cohen's (1992) suggestions, a value of 1.10 might be called *very large*, and a value of 1.40 or more might be called *extremely large*. Values this large are rarely found in social and behavioral research.

Table 1 summarizes the new material covered so far in this section.

Table 1
Labels for Values of d

Value of *d*	Label
0.20	Small
0.50	Medium
0.80	Large
1.10	Very large
1.40+	Extremely large

Using the labels in the table, the value of *d* of 0.71 in the previous section would be described as closer to large than to medium, while the value of 1.25 would be described as between very large and extremely large.

---

[1] Cohen, J. (1992). A power primer. *Psychological Bulletin, 112,* 155–159.
[2] A negative is obtained when the control group's mean is higher than the experimental group's mean. Note that less than one-half of 1% of a normal distribution lies above +3.00 and below –3.00, which means that it is technically possible—but highly unlikely—to obtain values larger than +3.00 and –3.00.

The labels being discussed should not be used arbitrarily without consideration of the full context in which the values of *d* were obtained and the possible implications of the results. This leads to two principles: (1) A small effect size might represent an important result, and (2) a large effect size might represent an unimportant result.

Consider the first principle. Suppose that researchers have been frustrated by consistently finding values of *d* well below 0.20 when trying various treatments for solving an important problem (such as treatments for a new and deadly disease). If a subsequent researcher finds a treatment that results in a value of about 0.20, this might be considered a very important finding. At this low level (0.20), the effect of the treatment is small, but it might be of immense importance to ill individuals helped by the treatment—however small the effect size. In addition, the results might point the scientific community in a fruitful direction for additional research on treatments for the problem in question.

The second principle is that a large value of *d*—even one above 1.40—might be of limited importance. This is most likely when the results lack practical significance in terms of cost, public and political acceptability, and ethical and legal concerns. (See Section 64 for considerations in determining the practical significance of research results.)

Here are three steps for interpreting the difference between two means. First, determine whether the difference is statistically significant at an acceptable probability level, such as $p < .05$. If it is not, the difference usually should be regarded as unreliable and should be interpreted as such. Second, for a statistically significant difference, consider the value of *d* and the labels in Table 1 on the previous page for describing the magnitude of the difference. Third, consider the implications of the difference for validating any relevant theories as well as the practical significance of the results.

Of course, before following the three steps outlined in the previous paragraph, the researcher should consider the adequacy of the methodology employed. Woefully inadequate sampling (such as a very biased sample), clearly invalid instrumentation (such as a test that measures a variable other than the one the researcher wanted to study), or a very poor research design (such as a design that will not answer the research question) would lead to very serious questions regarding the validity of the results. In such cases, consideration of values of *d* might be meaningless.

Terms to Review Before Attempting Worksheet 66

effect size, *d*

Worksheet 66   Interpretation of Effect Size (*d*)

> *Riddle*: The early bird may get the worm, but...

DIRECTIONS: To find the answer to the riddle, write the answer to each question in the space immediately below it. In the solution section, the word in parentheses next to the answer to the first question is the first word in the answer to the riddle, the word beside the answer to the second question is the second word, and so on.

1. If an experimental group exceeds a control group by one-fifth of a standard deviation unit, what label should be used?

2. What label is associated with $d = 0.50$?

3. A label of *large* is associated with what value of *d*?

4. What label is associated with a value of *d* of 1.40?

5. "A small effect size might represent an important result." Is this statement true *or* false?

6. "Large effect sizes necessarily represent important results." Is this statement true *or* false?

Worksheet 66 (continued)

7. Should d be calculated and interpreted before a significance test is conducted?

8. Does a negative value of d indicate that the control group has a higher mean than the experimental group?

9. It is highly unlikely to obtain a positive value of d that exceeds what value?

Solution section:

---

false (cheese)   3.00 (trap)   0.50 (robin)   no (in)

small (the)   1.00 (morning)   yes (the)   extremely large (gets)

2.00 (fly)   0.80 (mouse)   large (seeds)   medium (second)

very large (feed)   true (the)   large (wing)

Write the answer to the riddle here, putting one word on each line: _____ _____ _____ _____

_____ _____ _____ _____ _____

Notes

Section 67   Effect Size and Correlation (*r*)

Cohen's *d* is so widely used as a measure of **effect size** that some researchers use the term *effect size* and **d** interchangeably—as though they are synonyms. However, *effect size* refers to any statistic that *describes the size of a difference on a standardized metric*. For instance, *d* describes the size of the difference between two means.[1] Furthermore, *d* is standardized because, regardless of what variables are being studied and regardless of what raw-score scale is being used to express the difference, the value of *d* is always expressed on a standard-deviation scale that almost always ranges only from –3.00 to 3.00.[2] (See the two previous sections to review *d*.)

In addition to *d*, a number of other measures of effect size have been proposed. One that is very widely reported is **effect-size r**, which is simply the Pearson correlation coefficient (*r*) described in Sections 33 through 36. As stated in those sections, *r* indicates the direction and strength of a relationship between two variables expressed on a scale that ranges from –1.00 to 1.00, where 0.00 indicates no relationship. Values of *r* are interpreted by first squaring them (r^2). For instance, when $r = 0.50$, $r^2 = .25$ (i.e., $0.50 \times 0.50 = 0.25$). Then, the value of r^2 should be multiplied by 100. Thus, $0.25 \times 100 = 25\%$, which indicates that the value of *r* of 0.50 is 25% greater than 0.00 on a scale that extends to a maximum possible value of 1.00.

In simple, straightforward studies, the choice between reporting means and the associated values of *d* (which can range from –3.00 to 3.00) and reporting correlation coefficients and the associated values of r^2 (which can range from 0.00 to 1.00)[3] is usually quite straightforward. If a researcher wants to determine which of two groups is superior *on average*, a comparison of means using *d* is usually the preferred method of analysis. On the other hand, if there is one group of participants with two scores per participant, and if the goal is to determine the *degree of relationship between the two sets of scores*, then *r* and r^2 should be used.

---

[1] If the means of two groups are identical, $d = 0.00$.

[2] Note that it is mathematically possible for *d* to exceed 3.00 because a very small percentage of the cases lie three standard deviations above the mean. Such values are seldom seen in the social and behavioral sciences.

[3] Note that all values of r^2 are positive because squaring a negative correlation coefficient results in a positive product. Thus, the bottom of the range for values of r^2 is 0.00, not –1.00.

For instance, if a group of students was administered a vocabulary knowledge test and a reading comprehension test, it would not be surprising to obtain a correlation coefficient as high as 0.70, which would indicate a substantial degree of relationship between the two variables (i.e., a strong tendency for students who score high in vocabulary knowledge to score high in reading comprehension). As indicated in Section 36, for interpretive purposes, 0.70 squared equals 0.49, which is equivalent to 49%. Knowing this allows a researcher to say that the relationship between the two variables is 49% higher than a relationship of 0.00.

When reviewing a body of literature on a given topic, some studies present means and values of d, while other studies on the same topic present values of r, depending on the specific research purposes and research designs. When interpreting such a set of studies, it can be useful to think in terms of the equivalence of d and r. Table 1 shows the equivalents for selected values.

Table 1
Equivalent Values of d, r, and r^2

d	r	r^2	% for r^2
0.20	0.100	0.010	1.0%
0.50	0.243	0.059	5.9%
0.80	0.371	0.138	13.8%
1.20	0.514	0.264	26.4%
1.50	0.600	0.360	36.0%
2.00	0.707	0.500	50.0%

Consider an example that illustrates the usefulness of Table 1. Suppose a researcher was examining the literature on anxiety and depression and found a study in which one group was administered scales that measured the two variables, and r = 0.37 was obtained. Suppose that in another study, an experimental group was administered a treatment designed to induce anxiety while the control group received a neutral control treatment. Then, all participants were administered a depression scale (to see whether anxiety induces depression). Further, suppose that the experimenter reported that d = 0.80 for the difference between the posttest means for the two groups. From Table 1, it can be seen that the effect sizes (i.e., the magnitude of the differences) in the two studies are the same (i.e., for a value of d

of 0.80 in the first column, the corresponding value of r in the second column is 0.371).

For values not shown in Table 1, it is often sufficient to locate the closest values and make mental approximations. To obtain more precise equivalent values of d and r, use the formulas provided near the end of Appendix I near the end of this book.

Terms to Review Before Attempting Worksheet 67

effect size, *d*, effect-size *r*

Worksheet 67   Effect Size and Correlation (*r*)

> **Riddle**: In life, change is inevitable except...

DIRECTIONS: To find the answer to the riddle, write the answer to each question in the space immediately below it. In the solution section, the word in parentheses next to the answer to the first question is the first word in the answer to the riddle, the word beside the answer to the second question is the second word, and so on.

1. Does the term *effect size* always refer to *d*?

2. "The Pearson correlation coefficient can be used as a measure of effect size." Is this statement true *or* false?

3. "If a researcher wants to examine the relationship between two sets of scores, the most appropriate statistic is *d*." Is this statement true *or* false?

4. If *r* equals 0.600, what is the corresponding percentage?

5. If *r* equals 0.100, what is the corresponding value of r^2?

6. For a value of *d* of 0.80, what is the corresponding value of *r*?

Worksheet 67 (continued)

7. For a value of d of 2.00, what is the corresponding value of r?

8. For a value of d of 2.00, what is the corresponding value of r^2?

Solution section:

0.707 (vending)   0.360 (death)   0.371 (a)   yes (health)

no (when)   0.80 (money)   0.500 (machine)   2.00 (living)

36.0% (purchase)   1.0% (failure)   true (making)

0.243 (failure)   0.010 (from)   0.737 (dark)   false (a)

Write the answer to the riddle here, putting one word on each line: _____   _____   _____   _____

_____   _____   _____   _____

Notes

Supplement Basic Math Review

The sections in this supplement show you how to perform basic arithmetic operations that are required in statistics. Even if you will be using a calculator or a computer, you need to understand them so you can check the reasonableness of your answers and catch errors. The answers to many of the exercise problems at the end of each section are given at the end of this supplement.

Section A: Order of Operations

In statistics, you will be using the four basic operations: addition, subtraction, multiplication, and division. Keep the following in mind:

>(3)(7) means *multiply 3 by 7.*
>6/2 means *6 divided by 2.*
>The result of addition is known as the *sum.*
>The result of multiplication is known as the *product.*
>The result of subtraction is known as the *difference.*
>The result of division is known as the *quotient.*

✔ **Rule 1:** When there are parentheses, perform the operations inside the parentheses first. Here are three examples:

>$(4)(2 + 1) = ?$
>Thus, $(4)(3) = 12$
>
>$(4 - 3)/(5 - 4) = ?$
>Thus, $1/1 = 1$
>
>$(9)(7 + 3 - 2) = ?$
>Thus, $(9)(10 - 2) = ?$
>and $(9)(8) = 72$

✔ **Rule 2:** Unless parentheses indicate otherwise, multiply and divide before adding and subtracting.

In these examples, you must multiply before adding:

$5 + (3)(2) = ?$

Thus, $5 + 6 = 11$

$8 + (5)(10) + 1 = ?$

Thus, $8 + 50 + 1 = 59$

In these examples, you must divide before subtracting:

$6 - 2/2 = ?$

Thus, $6 - 1 = 5$

$20 - 36/6 - 5 = ?$

Thus, $20 - 6 - 5 = 9$

In these examples, you must multiply and divide before adding and subtracting:

$(5)(2) - 1 + 4/2 = ?$

Thus, $10 - 1 + 2 = 11$

$11 + (10)(3) - 4/2 = ?$

Thus, $11 + 30 - 2 = 39$

✓ **Rule 3:** If there are both parentheses and brackets, solve first within the parentheses, then within the brackets, and then perform any remaining operations.

Study the following examples.

$[(2)(2) - (5 - 3)][7 - 1] = ?$

Thus, $[4 - 2][6] = ?$

and $[2][6] = 12$

$[(25)(10 - 5)]/5 = ?$

Thus, $[(25)(5)]/5 = ?$

and $125/5 = 25$

Exercise for Section A

(*Note*: The answers to items 1–12 are provided at the end of this supplement.)

1. $(10)(3 + 5) = ?$
2. $(5 + 4)/(2 + 1) = ?$
3. $(6 - 5 + 2)(5) = ?$
4. $8 + (5)(4) = ?$
5. $(10)(11) - 1 = ?$
6. $5 + 12/4 = ?$
7. $10 + (2)(5) - 5 = ?$
8. $25 - (9)(2) + 3 = ?$
9. $[(4 + 7)(3 - 1)][8 - 3] = ?$
10. $[(3 + 5) + (1)(2)]/2 = ?$
11. The result of multiplication is known as the
    A. Product. B. Quotient. C. Sum. D. Difference.
12. The result of addition is known as the
    A. Product. B. Quotient. C. Sum. D. Difference.
13. $(4 + 6)(11) = ?$
14. $(7 - 1 + 2)(4) = ?$
15. $20/(5 + 5) = ?$
16. $9 + 8/2 = ?$
17. $(12)(12) - 3 = ?$
18. $9 + (4)(8) = ?$
19. $15/3 + 5 - 6/2 = ?$
20. $19 + (2)(6) - 4 = ?$
21. $[(5 - 3) + (2)(3)]/8 = ?$
22. $[(9 + 3) - (1)(3)][6 - 2] = ?$
23. The result of division is known as the
    A. Product. B. Quotient. C. Sum. D. Difference.
24. The result of subtraction is known as the
    A. Product. B. Quotient. C. Sum. D. Difference.

Section B: Squares and Square Roots

In statistics, you will be squaring many numbers. To square a number, multiply it by itself, as in this example:

$$4^2 = 4 \times 4 = 16$$

Note that in the example, 4 is the *base* and 2 is the *exponent*.

CALCULATOR HINT: To square a number using a calculator, you only have to enter the number once. For instance, on your calculator:

1. Press 4.
2. Press the multiplication sign ($\times$).
3. Press the equals sign ($=$).
4. You should see 16, which is the square, displayed.

Calculating a square root is the opposite of squaring. Thus, the square root of 16 is 4. To calculate a square root on a calculator, enter the number and then press the square root sign ($\sqrt{}$). The formal name of the square root sign is the *radical sign*.

Notice that

$\sqrt{16}$ is read *the square root of 16*, which is 4.

When a square root sign (i.e., a radical sign) appears in a formula, it has the same effect as parentheses in the order of operations. That is, everything under a radical sign must be solved and the square root calculated before any operations on its value are performed. For instance, the following tells us to multiply 4 by the square root of the sum under the radical sign.

$$4\sqrt{20 + 5} = ?$$

Because of the radical sign, you must sum 20 and 5 and take the square root of the sum before multiplying by 4:

Thus, $4\sqrt{25} = ?$

and $(4)(5) = 20$

Notice that 4^2 is read *four squared*, while $\sqrt{4}$ is read *the square root of 4*.

Exercise for Section B

(*Note*: The answers to items 1–10 are provided at the end of this supplement.)

1. 14^2 is read

   A. 14 squared.   B. The square root of 14.   C. Double 14.

2. The 14 in Question 1 is known as the

   A. Base.   B. Exponent.   C. Radical sign.

3. $\sqrt{9}$ is read as

   A. 9 squared.   B. The square root of 9.   C. Half of 9.

4. The $\sqrt{}$ sign is known as the

   A. Base.   B. Exponent.   C. Radical sign.

5. What is the square root of 144?

6. What is the square of 100?

7. $\sqrt{225} = ?$

8. $18^2 = ?$

9. $6\sqrt{100-19} = ?$

10. $\sqrt{324} + 2(11-2) = ?$

11. $\sqrt{49}$ is read

   A. 49 squared.   B. The square root of 49.   C. Double 49.

12. In 9^2, the 2 is known as the

   A. Base.   B. Exponent.   C. Radical sign.

13. 67^2 is read as

   A. 67 squared.   B. Half of 67.   C. The square root of 67.

14. The 2 in Question 13 is known as the

   A. Base.   B. Exponent.   C. Radical sign.

15. What is the square root of 81?

16. What is the square of 60?

17. $\sqrt{169} = ?$

18. $51^2 = ?$

19. $4\sqrt{55 - 6} = ?$

20. $\sqrt{250 + 6}/(3 + 5) = ?$

Section C: Negatives

We frequently use negative numbers in statistics. Because we mainly use positive numbers in everyday situations, your knowledge of negative numbers and how to work with them may be rusty, so we will start with the basics. First, you may recall that a number line looks like this:

−5	−4	−3	−2	−1	0	+1	+2	+3	+4	+5

Negative numbers are to the left of zero.

When a number is shown without a sign, it is understood to be positive. Thus, 3 is understood to be +3. When a number is negative, its sign is always shown.

When working with negatives, follow these rules:

✓ **Rule 1:** When you multiply or divide numbers with different signs, the answer is always negative. Here are two examples:

Specifically, when you multiply a positive number by a negative number, the result (product) is negative.

$$(5)(-2) = -10 \quad \text{and} \quad (-5)(2) = -10$$

When you divide using a positive and a negative number, the result (quotient) is negative.

$$10/-2 = -5 \quad \text{and} \quad -10/2 = -5$$

✓ **Rule 2:** When you multiply or divide numbers with the same sign, the result is positive, as in these examples:

$$-50/-5 = 10 \quad \text{and} \quad 50/10 = 5$$
$$(-3)(-9) = 27 \quad \text{and} \quad (3)(9) = 27$$

✓ **Rule 3:** When you add a set of numbers, all of which are negative, the result (sum) is negative, as in these examples:

$$-1 + (-4) + -3 = -8$$
$$-10 + (-11) = -21$$

✓ **Rule 4:** When you add a positive number and a negative number, temporarily ignore the signs and *subtract* the smaller from the larger. Then assign to the sum the sign of the larger number. Study this example:

$$3 + (-7) = ?$$

First, ignoring signs, $7 - 3 = 4$. Because 7 is larger than 3 and because the 7 was originally negative, the sum is negative. Thus, the answer is −4. It helps to understand this example if you refer to the number line at the beginning of this section. If you start at +3 and add to that 7 points in the negative direction (moving left from +3 seven points), you come to −4, which is the answer.

Here is another example:

$$15 + (-3) = ?$$

Subtract the smaller from the larger: $15 - 3 = 12$. The answer is a positive 12 because the larger number is positive.

✓ **Rule 5:** If there are some positive and some negative numbers, all of which are to be summed, first add all the positive numbers to get their sum. Then add all the negative numbers using Rule 3 to get their sum. Then add the two sums using Rule 4.

$$4 + -2 + 5 + 6 + 6 + -1 + 7 + -3 = ?$$

First, sum the positive numbers:

$4 + 5 + 6 + 6 + 7 = 28$

Then sum the negative numbers using Rule 3:

$-2 + (-1) + (-3) = -6$

Then sum the two sums using Rule 4:

$28 - 6 = 22$

The answer is +22 because the larger number is positive.

✔ **Rule 6:** When you subtract a negative from a negative, temporarily ignore the signs and *subtract*. The result is negative.

$-10 - (-2) = ?$

Thus, $10 - 2 = 8$

When a negative sign is assigned, the answer is –8.

Note that when we ignore the sign of a number, we are using its *absolute value*—its value without regard to sign. For instance, +8 and –8 have the same absolute value. If you take away their signs, they are the same.

✔ **Rule 7:** When you subtract a negative from a positive, the negative number becomes a positive. *Add* the two numbers to get the difference.

$5 - (-4) = ?$

Thus, $5 + 4 = 9$.

At first, this rule may be confusing. It helps to think about it as though it were a double negative (for instance, – –4) in English. If someone says, "We are not (negative) sure that we are not (negative) going," that person is making the positive statement that he/she, in fact, might be going.

Another way to look at Rule 7 is to consider the following number line. It illustrates that the difference between +5 and –4 is 9. (Remember that when you subtract, you are getting a difference.)

–4 –3 –2 –1 0 +1 +2 +3 +4 +5

✓ **Rule 8:** When you subtract a positive from a negative, temporarily ignore the signs and *add*. The result is negative. For instance:

> −8 − 7 = ?
>
> Then 8 + 7 = 15
>
> The answer is −15.

CALCULATOR HINT: Most calculators have a ± button. Use it when you enter negative numbers. Here is an example:

To solve (5)(−2) = ?

1. Press 5.
2. Press the multiplication sign (×).
3. Press 2 (enter it as positive).
4. Press the ± button (which will make the 2 negative).
5. Press = (the equals sign).
6. The display should show −10, the answer.

Pressing the ± button informs the calculator that the most recently entered number is a negative number.

Exercise for Section C

(*Note*: The answers to items 1–17 are provided at the end of this supplement.) Suggestion: Before you solve these problems with a calculator, mentally estimate whether the answer to each will be positive or negative.

1. (−8)(7) = ?
2. (4)(−50) = ?
3. 49/−7 = ?
4. −121/11 = ?
5. −36/−6 = ?
6. (−12)(−10) = ?
7. −5 + (−9) + (−6) = ?
8. 5 + (−9) = ?

9. $-12 + 8 = ?$

10. $-9 + 8 + (-3) + 1 = ?$

11. $3 + (-5) + 12 + (-2) = ?$

12. $-29 - (-14) = ?$

13. $-47 - (-17) = ?$

14. $10 - (-9) = ?$

15. $12 - (-21) = ?$

16. $-20 - 18 = ?$

17. The *absolute value* of a number is its value

    A. When it is negative.   B. Without regard to its sign.   C. With its sign.

18. $(-9)(12) = ?$

19. $(15)(-7) = ?$

20. $-66/11 = ?$

21. $169/-13 = ?$

22. $-12/-3 = ?$

23. $(-15)(-14) = ?$

24. $-8 + (-7) + (-9) = ?$

25. $10 + (-13) = ?$

26. $-17 + 9 = ?$

27. $5 + (-7) + (-6) + 4 = ?$

28. $8 + (-2) + 9 + (-1) = ?$

29. $-30 - (-29) = ?$

30. $-17 - (-18) = ?$

31. $20 - (-11) = ?$

32. $14 - (-18) = ?$

33. $-40 - 11 = ?$

34. How does "$-18 - 14 = ?$" read?

    A. Minus 18 minus negative 14 = ?

    B. Negative 18 minus negative 14 = ?

    C. Negative 18 minus positive 14 = ?

Section D: Decimals and Rounding

As you probably recall,

3.2 is *three and two-tenths*.

3.02 is *three and two-hundredths*.

3.002 is *three and two-thousandths*.

It is customary in statistics to report answers to the hundredths' or thousandths' place. In *informal discussions*, we sometimes refer to 3.02 as *three point zero two* and to 3.002 as *three point zero zero two*.

Sometimes a number is less than one, such as

0.56, which is *zero and 56 hundredths*; and

.56 is also *zero and 56 hundredths* (the zero is implied).

It is a good idea to show the zero, however, because it helps to call your readers' attention to the decimal point and to the fact that the value is less than one.

Modern calculating devices have eliminated the need to keep track of decimal places when computing. However, these devices have not eliminated errors in entering the data, which lead to incorrect answers. Hence, the following calculator hint:

CALCULATOR HINT: Make mental estimates by first rounding to whole numbers before using your calculator. For instance, to divide 9.362 by 3.190, mentally round 9.362 to 9 and 3.190 to 3. Because $9/3 = 3$, the answer your calculator gives you should be close to 3. In fact, the answer is 2.935. If your calculator does not show an answer close to 3, you will know that you entered one or more wrong numbers or entered one or more decimal places at the wrong points.

Frequently, when you divide using a calculator, you will obtain a long string of decimal places, such as

$$7.7/3 = 2.566666666666$$

You will want to round this. To the nearest hundredth, it rounds to 2.57. To the nearest thousandth, it rounds to 2.567.

Review this terminology:

10.366 = 10.37 is an example of *rounding up*.

10.361 = 10.36 is an example of *rounding down*.

A special rule for rounding off 5 that is often used in statistics is

✓Round all numbers ending in 5 to the nearest even number.

Another way to state the same rule is

✓ When rounding off the 5 in a number ending in 5, round down if the preceding number is even, and round up if the preceding number is odd.

Here are two examples of the application of the special rule for 5:

10.335 = 10.34 (round up).

10.345 = 10.34 (round down).

By using this special rule, we will, in the long run, round up about half the time and down about half the time when a number ends in 5. This is a compromise because there is no mathematical solution regarding how to round off a 5. Remember that 5 is exactly halfway between 0 and 9.

If you are not comfortable with this special rule, study these examples:

113.485 = 113.48 (round down because the 8 is even).

27.65 = 27.6 (round down because the 6 is even).

9.1135 = 9.114 (round up because the 3 is odd).

896.875 = 896.88 (round up because the 7 is odd).

Notice that in all cases, after we round off the 5 in a number that ends with 5, the rounded numbers always end in an even number.

It is very important to notice that the special rule described above is *only for numbers that end in 5*. If a number ends in more than 5, round up.

2.1659 = 2.17 when rounded to the nearest hundredth.

9.248 = 9.25 when rounded to the nearest hundredth.

If a number ends in less than 5, round down.

> 1.454 = 1.45 when rounded to the nearest hundredth.
> 2.332 = 2.33 when rounded to the nearest hundredth.

A rule for reporting answers is: If you have zeros in the tenths' and hundredths' place, keep them if you are asked to report an answer to the nearest hundredth. For instance, 35.004 should be rounded to 35.00 and reported as 35.00 and *not* as 35. By keeping the two zeros, you are showing that your answer is accurate to the nearest hundredth. A simple 35 may be a rounded result of some other value, such as 35.23.

There are many multistep problems in statistics. That is, there are many problems in which, after you perform one computation, you will use the answer you obtained in the next computation, the second answer will be used in the third computation, and so on. At the end of each step, to how many places should you round your answer? Here are two general rules to guide you:

> ✓ The more decimal places you retain at the end of each step, the more accurate your answer will be.

> ✓ At the end of each step in a problem, retain at least one more decimal place than you will be reporting in the answer to the final step. For instance, if you plan to report the answer to the final step in a problem to two decimal places, keep at least three in all steps leading up to that answer. Then round the final answer to two decimal places.

If you, your instructor, and your classmates keep a different number of decimal places at the end of each step in a problem, you may obtain slightly different answers. Slight differences in the hundredths' place are usually not of concern for all practical purposes—as long as they are attributable to rounding and not to an error.

Exercise for Section D

(*Note*: The answers to items 1–12 are provided at the end of this supplement.)

1. "5.24 is read as *five and twenty-four tenths*." True *or* false?
2. "16.1 is read as *sixteen and one-tenth*." True *or* false?
3. "It is customary in statistics to report an answer to the nearest whole number." True *or* false?
4. "When rounded to a whole number, 5.189 becomes 5." True *or* false?
5. "The answer to 100.0812/9.8746 should be close to 10." True *or* false?
6. "The answer to (19.953)(5.162) should be close to 20." True *or* false?
7. "When rounded to the nearest hundredth, 6.4734 becomes 6.473." True *or* false?
8. "When rounded to the nearest thousandth, 7.5766 becomes 7.577." True *or* false?
9. "When rounded to the nearest tenth, 15.657 becomes 15.7." True *or* false?
10. "If the special rule is applied, 10.25 becomes 10.3 when rounded to the nearest tenth." True *or* false?
11. "If the special rule is applied, 111.665 becomes 111.66 when rounded to the nearest hundredth." True *or* false?
12. "If the special rule is applied, 15.5555 becomes 15.556 when rounded to the nearest thousandth." True *or* false?
13. "6.12 is read as *six and twelve-hundredths*." True *or* false?
14. "7.101 is read as *seven and one hundred and one thousandths*." True *or* false?
15. "It is customary in statistics to report answers to the nearest hundredth or thousandth." True *or* false?
16. "When rounded to a whole number, 3.119 becomes 4." True *or* false?
17. "The answer to 10.2 plus 40.18129 should be close to 50." True *or* false?
18. "The answer to 24.98762/4.823423 should be close to 5." True *or* false?
19. "When rounded to the nearest tenth, 8.129 becomes 8.2." True *or* false?
20. "When rounded to the nearest hundredth, 121.564 becomes 121." True *or* false?
21. "When rounded to the nearest thousandth, 14.47451 becomes 14.475." True *or* false?

22. "If the special rule is applied, 5.545 becomes 5.54 when rounded to the nearest hundredth." True *or* false?

23. "If the special rule is applied, 19.445 becomes 19.45 when rounded to the nearest hundredth." True *or* false?

24. "If the special rule is applied, 12.2535 becomes 12.253 when rounded to the nearest thousandth." True *or* false?

Section E: Fractions

Many formulas in statistics contain fractions. In order to understand these formulas, it is essential that you know the basics about fractions, which are illustrated here by example:

In 1/6, 1 is the *numerator* and 6 is the *denominator*.

1/6 may be represented as follows. The whole consists of six equal parts, and one of them (1/6) is shaded:

As the numerator increases, the value of the fraction increases. For instance, 2/6 is greater than 1/6. Here, 2/6 of the area is shaded:

As the denominator increases, the value of the fraction decreases. For instance, 1/12 is less than 1/6, which represents 1/12:

Notice that 1/12 is half the size of 1/6.

When performing calculations involving fractions, follow these rules:

✓ **Rule 1:** Use your calculator to convert fractions to their decimal equivalents, and solve problems using the decimal equivalents. Suppose you have to multiply 29 by 1/4:

To solve $(29)(1/4) = ?$

First, convert 1/4 to its decimal equivalent by dividing 1 by 4, which equals 0.25.

Then multiply on your calculator: $(29)(0.25) = 7.25$.

✓ **Rule 2:** If a formula specifies operations in the numerator and/or denominator, perform those operations before converting to a decimal equivalent.

To solve $\dfrac{1+5}{(6)(2)}$

First, perform the addition in the numerator and the multiplication in the denominator to get

$$\frac{6}{12}$$

Then divide 6 by 12 to get 0.50.

Note that in statistics, you should report decimal equivalents and *not* fractions as answers. Thus, you should report 0.50 and *not* 6/12 or 1/2.

If a number consists of a whole number and a fraction, it is known as a *mixed number*.

5 1/7 is a mixed number that consists of 5 and 1/7.

Before working with mixed numbers, convert the fractional part to its decimal equivalent. For instance, to convert 5 1/7 to its decimal equivalent:

Divide 1 by 7 = 0.14.

Add it to the whole number: $5 + 0.14 = 5.14$.

Thus, 5 1/7 equals 5.14.

Exercise for Section E

(*Note*: The answers to items 1–8 are provided at the end of this supplement.)

1. "In 3/4, 3 is the denominator." True *or* false?
2. "In 3/4, 3 is the numerator." True *or* false?
3. "In 5/6, 6 is the denominator." True *or* false?
4. "Other things being equal, as the numerator increases, the value of the fraction decreases." True *or* false?
5. "Other things being equal, as the denominator increases, the value of the fraction decreases." True *or* false?
6. What is the decimal equivalent of 2/5?
7. What is the decimal equivalent of 1/12?
8. What is the decimal equivalent of 3/4?
9. "In 7/8, 7 is the numerator." True *or* false?
10. "In 7/8, 7 is the denominator." True *or* false?
11. "In 1/4, 4 is the numerator." True *or* false?
12. Other things being equal, as the denominator increases, what happens to the value of the fraction?
13. Other things being equal, as the numerator increases, what happens to the value of the fraction?
14. What is the decimal equivalent of 10/100?
15. What is the decimal equivalent of 1/3?
16. What is the decimal equivalent of 1/2?

Section F: Percentages

We often use percentages to describe data. A percentage represents a part of 100.

25% stands for 25 out of 100.
50% stands for 50 out of 100.

By using percentages, we are using 100 as the base regardless of how many subjects we are describing. For instance, if 10 out of 20 subjects are male, we would report that 50% are male. If, for another group, 15 out of 30 subjects are male, we would also report that 50% are male. By employing a common base, percentages facilitate the comparison of groups of unequal size.

To convert a fraction to a percentage, divide the numerator by the denominator and multiply by 100, as in these examples:

$$1/3 = 0.333 \times 100 = 33.3\%$$
$$2/9 = 0.222 \times 100 = 22.2\%$$

In scientific writing, authors usually report percentages to one or two decimal places. Notice that in the answer to the following problem, the value in the tenths' place is zero:

$$3/4 = 0.750 \times 100 = 75.0\%$$

We show the zero in the tenths' place in order to be consistent in our reporting (e.g., if other percentages, such as 33.3%, have been reported) and to show that the answer is accurate to the tenths' place.

Note that when computing a percentage, you may simply move the decimal point two places to the right, which has the same effect as multiplying by 100. For instance, for 1/3, divide 1 by 3 to get 0.333. Then move the decimal point two places to the right to get 33.3%.

Suppose that we are studying 79 voters, and 35 of them classified themselves as Liberals. We could report that 35/79 are Liberals. In scientific writing, however, authors usually would compute the corresponding percentage:

$$35 \text{ divided by } 79 = 0.443 \times 100 = 44.3\%$$

and report that

$$44.3\% \ (N = 35) \text{ are Liberals.}$$

N stands for *number of subjects* or *cases*. It is desirable when reporting percentages to also report the number of cases underlying each percentage. The number of cases is an important piece of information for your reader, as these examples illustrate:

Study A: 80% (N = 5) of the dentists recommend Brand X.

Study B: 80% (N = 103) of the dentists recommend Brand X.

Even though the percentages are the same in the two studies, the larger N in Study B indicates that the results of Study B are more reliable than the results of Study A.

The percentages for a group may not always sum to exactly 100%, as illustrated by Table 1. There were no computational errors. Instead, the total of 100.1% is slightly greater than 100% because of rounding. For instance, for Method A, the precise percentage is 18.75%. Because this was rounded to 18.8%, a slight amount of error was introduced. For most practical purposes, this error is of little consequence. Note that in the last column, the uppercase P is used, which is a symbol for *percentage*.

Table 1

Number and Percentage of Teachers Who Prefer Each Method

Method	N	P
Method A	9	18.8%
Method B	18	37.5%
Method C	21	43.8%
Total	48	100.1%

If you still do not feel comfortable computing percentages, consider the example of the teachers more carefully:

For Method A, first divide 9 by 48 = 0.1875.

Then multiply by 100: 0.1875 × 100 = 18.75%, which rounds to 18.8%.

For Method B, first divide 18 by 48 = 0.3750.

Then multiply by 100: 0.3750 × 100 = 37.50%, which rounds to 37.5%.

For Method C, first divide 21 by 48 = 0.4375.

Then multiply by 100: 0.4375 × 100 = 43.75, which rounds to 43.8%.

Exercise for Section F

(*Note*: The answers to items 1–8 are provided at the end of this supplement.)

1. "25% stands for 25 out of 50." True *or* false?

2. "The base for percentages is 100." True *or* false?

3. What percentage corresponds to 1/5?

4. What percentage corresponds to 3/10?

5. If 95 subjects were studied and 71 of them expressed Opinion A, what percentage of them expressed Opinion A?

6. If 200 subjects were studied and 120 of them expressed a preference for Brand X, what percentage expressed a preference for Brand X?

7. "It is recommended that when you report a percentage, you should also report the corresponding value of N." True *or* false?

8. "In statistics, the lowercase p stands for *percentage*." True *or* false?

9. "11% stands for 11 out of 100." True *or* false?

10. "By employing a common base of 100, percentages facilitate the comparison of groups of unequal size." True *or* false?

11. What percentage corresponds to 2/5?

12. What percentage corresponds to 1/100?

13. If 66 subjects were studied and 21 of them expressed Opinion X, what percentage of them expressed Opinion X?

14. If 462 subjects were studied and 99 of them expressed a preference for Brand Y, what percentage expressed a preference for Brand Y?

15. "When writing a scientific report, there is no need to report Ns if percentages are being reported." True *or* false?

16. "In statistics, the uppercase P stands for *percentage*." True *or* false?

Answers to Selected Questions

Section A:

1. 80 **2.** 3 **3.** 15 **4.** 28 **5.** 109 **6.** 8 **7.** 15 **8.** 10 **9.** 110 **10.** 5 **11.** A
12. C

Section B:

1. A **2.** A **3.** B **4.** C **5.** 12 **6.** 10,000 **7.** 15 **8.** 324 **9.** 54 **10.** 36

Section C:

1. –56 **2.** –200 **3.** –7 **4.** –11 **5.** 6 **6.** 120 **7.** –20 **8.** –4 **9.** –4 **10.** –3
11. 8 **12.** –15 **13.** –30 **14.** 19 **15.** 33 **16.** –38 **17.** B

Section D:

1. F **2.** T **3.** F **4.** T **5.** T **6.** F **7.** F **8.** T **9.** T **10.** F **11.** T **12.** T

Section E:

1. F **2.** T **3.** T **4.** F **5.** T **6.** 0.40 **7.** 0.08 **8.** 0.75

Section F:

1. F **2.** T **3.** 20.0% **4.** 30.0% **5.** 74.7% **6.** 60.0% **7.** T **8.** F

"I think you need a heart transplant, my associate thinks
you need a bypass, and our statistician thinks
you just need to be rebooted."

Appendix A
Computational Formulas for the Standard Deviation

For the standard deviation of a population (i.e., all members of the population tested), use the following formula.

$$S = \frac{1}{N}\sqrt{N\sum X^2 - (\sum X)^2}$$

Where

    N = number of cases,
    $\sum X^2$ = sum of the squared scores (sum after squaring each score), and
    $(\sum X)^2$ = square of the sum of the scores (sum and then square).

Example

	X		X^2
	3		9
	5		25
	7		49
	8		64
$\sum X =$	23	$\sum X^2 =$	147

$$S = \frac{1}{4}\sqrt{(4)(147) - (23)^2}$$
$$= .25\sqrt{588 - 529}$$
$$= .25\sqrt{59}$$
$$= (.25)(7.681) = 1.920 = 1.92$$

For the standard deviation of a population estimated from a sample (i.e., only a sample of the population tested), use the following formula, which is applied here to the scores shown earlier.[1]

$$s = \sqrt{\frac{N \sum X^2 - (\sum X)^2}{N(N-1)}} = \sqrt{\frac{(4)(147) - (23)^2}{4(4-1)}} = \sqrt{\frac{588 - 529}{12}}$$

$$= \sqrt{\frac{59}{12}} = \sqrt{4.917} = 2.217 = 2.22$$

---

[1]The two formulas are applied to the same set of scores here for instructional purposes only. As you can see, the second formula gives a higher value for the standard deviation. This is because of an adjustment made by the second formula that takes into account the fact that extreme scores tend to be underestimated when small samples are used. With a large N, the two formulas yield almost identical results. Of course, in practice, only one formula should be applied to a given set of scores. If you are analyzing scores for an entire population, use the first formula. If you are analyzing those of a sample, use the second formula.

Appendix B
Notes on Interpreting the Pearson *r*

The value of a Pearson *r* can be misleadingly low for two reasons. First, its value is diminished if the variability in a group is artificially low. For the sake of illustration, let us assume that we wanted to study the relationship between height and weight in the adult population but, foolishly, selected only subjects who were exactly six feet tall. When weighing them, we found some variation in their weights. What is the correlation between height and weight among such a group? Even though there is a positive relationship between the two variables in the general adult population, the correlation in this odd sample is zero. This must be the result because those who weigh more and those who weigh less are all of the same height. (This sample cannot show that those who are taller tend to weigh more because all subjects are of the same height. Thus, the value of the Pearson *r* will equal 0.00.) A more realistic example is the relationship between scores on a college admissions test and grades earned in college. Although the test is given to all applicants in order for admissions decisions to be made about all of them, grades are available only for those who were admitted, and the correlation between scores and grades can be computed only for those subjects on whom we have complete data. Those for whom we have complete data are those with higher but less variable scores. Thus, the value of the Pearson *r* will be lower than would be obtained if we correlated using scores and grades for *all* applicants.

Second, an *r* can be misleadingly low if the underlying relationship is curvilinear. For instance, the relationship between test-taking anxiety and performance on standardized tests might be curvilinear. That is, small amounts of anxiety might be beneficial in motivating subjects to do well on a test, but larger amounts might be detrimental. Thus, as anxiety increases, up to a point there is a positive relationship with anxiety. Beyond a critical point, however, as anxiety increases, there is a negative relationship. If the Pearson *r* is computed for such data, the negative part of the relationship will cancel out the positive part, yielding an *r* near zero. Pearson recognized this problem and warned against using his statistic for describing curvilinear relationships. Other techniques, such as the *correlation ratio*, which are beyond the scope of this book, are available for describing curvilinear relationships. Fortunately, such relationships are relatively rare in the social and behavioral sciences.

Appendix C
Definition Formula for the Pearson *r*

After studying Sections 33 and 34, you may wonder how it is possible to correlate variables that have scales as diverse as GPAs (0.00 to 4.00) and SAT scores (200 to 800) and, regardless of the scale, obtain a value of *r* that always ranges from –1.00 to 1.00. At first, it may seem like we are comparing apples to oranges. However, the answer is rather straightforward if you recall the characteristics of standard scores (i.e., *z*-scores).[1] For instance, a person who has a GPA that is average for the group has a *z*-score of 0.00 on GPA. If the same person has an SAT score that is also average for the group, her *z*-score is also 0.00 for the SAT. In other words, *z*-scores make it possible to compare scores that were *not* directly comparable in their original form. Taking advantage of this property, Pearson defined a perfect, direct correlation as one in which each person had the same *z*-score on both variables. A perfect, inverse correlation is defined as one in which each person has the exact opposite *z*-score on each variable (e.g., a person with a *z*-score of 1.50 on one variable has a –1.50 on the other). The definition formula for the Pearson *r* expressed in terms of *z*-scores is

$$r = \frac{\Sigma(z_x z_y)}{N}$$

Thus, in order to use this formula, first compute the *z*-score for each subject on Variable *X* and then on Variable *Y*. Multiply the corresponding *z*-scores, and sum their products. Finally, divide by *N*.

The computational formula for *r* presented in Section 34 is algebraically equivalent to the one shown above. However, the one in Section 34 eliminates the need to calculate the *z*-scores for each subject, which would be a major task if there were a large number of subjects.

---

[1]See Section 18 for a thorough review.

Notes

Appendix D
Spearman's *rho*

A statistician named Spearman developed a formula for calculating a product-moment correlation coefficient that is easier to compute than the Pearson r when subjects are ranked on both variables. Usually, a rank of 1 is given to the subject with the best performance, a rank of 2 to the subject with the next-best performance, and so on.

When the following formula is used, the result is usually referred to as *rho*, or r_s.

$$rho = 1 - \frac{6 \sum D^2}{N(N^2 - 1)}$$

Where

D is the difference between the two ranks for each subject,

N is the number of subjects, and

both 1 and 6 are constants.

Application of the formula is illustrated for the ranks in columns 2 and 3.

Col. 1	Col. 2	Col. 3	Col. 4 Difference	Col. 5 Squared difference
Subject	Rank on X	Rank on Y	D	D^2
Alexis	1	3	2	4
Allen	5	4	1	1
Bob	2	1	1	1
Mary	3	5	2	4
Joe	4	2	2	4
				$\sum D^2 = 14$

$$rho = 1 - \frac{(6)(14)}{(5)(5^2 - 1)} = 1 - \frac{84}{(5)(25 - 1)} = 1 - \frac{84}{120} = 1 - .70 = .30$$

Application of the formula becomes more difficult if there are ties (e.g., two subjects tied at number 1 on the same variable). Dealing with ties is not covered here. However, you may obtain the correct answer when there are ties by applying the formula for the Pearson *r*, which is illustrated in Section 34. In other words, simply treat the ranks as though they were scores, and apply the formula for the Pearson *r*.

Spearman's *rho* was developed as a shortcut computational procedure for a specialized situation (when there are ranks) before there were handheld calculators or computers. In the presence of computers, *rho* is not as important as it once was.

Because *rho* is a product-moment correlation, for all practical purposes it is interpreted in the same way as a Pearson *r*.

Appendix E
Standard Error of Estimate

When the correlation between a predictor variable (called X) and the variable being predicted (called Y or *the criterion variable*) is less than perfect, as it usually is, we will make errors when we predict from X to Y. Thus, we should allow for a margin of error when making predictions. To do this, first compute the ***standard error of estimate*** (S_{yx}) using the following formula. Its application is represented with the data from Table 1 in Section 36, for which there is a correlation of $-.77$ between X and Y.

$$S_{yx} = \sqrt{\frac{\left[\sum Y^2 - \frac{(\sum Y)^2}{N}\right] - \left[\sum XY - \frac{(\sum X)(\sum Y)}{N}\right]^2 \div \left[\sum X^2 - \frac{(\sum X)^2}{N}\right]}{N-2}}$$

$$= \sqrt{\frac{\left[207 - \frac{31^2}{6}\right] - \left[67 - \frac{(19)(31)}{6}\right]^2 \div \left[95 - \frac{19^2}{6}\right]}{6-2}}$$

$$= \sqrt{\frac{46.833 - (971.382 \div 34.833)}{4}} = \sqrt{\frac{18.946}{4}} = \sqrt{4.7365} = 2.176 = 2.18$$

The result, 2.18, is an estimate of the standard deviation of the scatter around the prediction line. Within one standard deviation, we expect to find about 68% of the cases in a normal distribution. Thus, for the data we are considering, we can say that we have 68% confidence that the true score a person will earn will be within 2.18 points of the predicted score. For instance, in Section 39 we saw that, for the above data, a person with a score of 6 on X has a predicted score on Y of 2.66. To apply the rule for using the standard error of estimate, do the following: Subtract the standard error of estimate from the predicted score (2.66 − 2.18 = 0.48), and add it to the predicted score (2.66 + 2.18 = 4.84). The result is a confidence interval. We can now say that we have 68% confidence that the true score a person will earn will be between 0.48 and 4.84.

455

It is beyond the scope of this book to explore the theory underlying the standard error of estimate. However, the theoretical underpinnings are analogous to those underlying the standard error of the mean, which is explored in detail in Section 28.

Appendix F
Standard Error of a Median
and a Percentage

The *standard error of a median* is greater than the standard error of the mean, as indicated by this formula:

$$se\ (median) = \frac{1.253s}{\sqrt{n}}$$

The formula is easy to use. Just multiply the standard deviation (s) by 1.253 and divide by the square root of n.

The *standard error of a percentage* is defined by this formula:

$$se\ (percentage) = \sqrt{\frac{PQ}{N}}$$

Where

> P is the percentage in question,
>
> $Q = 100 - P$, and
>
> N is the number of cases.

Notes

Appendix G

Confidence Interval for the Mean: Small Samples

When using small sample sizes, such as 60 or less, the sampling distribution of the mean is not normal, and the constants of 1.96 (for 95% confidence) and 2.58 (for 99% confidence) will lead to inaccurate results. A statistician named W.S. Gossett developed the t table (see Table 3 near the end of this book), which can be used to obtain the appropriate constants. To use the table, first compute a statistic known as degrees of freedom (df), using this formula:

$$df = n - 1$$

Thus, if $n = 11$, then $df = 10$. Look up the df of 10 in the first column of Table 3. To get the constant for the 95% confidence interval, go to the second column, labeled *95% C.I.* There, you will find a constant of 2.228. (Note that this is larger than the constant of 1.96 that you learned about in Section 29.)

Multiply the standard error of the mean by the constant that you find in Table 3. Thus, if $SE_m = 2.00$, then $2.00 \times 2.228 = 4.456$. Add 4.456 to the mean and subtract 4.456 from the mean in order to obtain the 95% confidence interval. Thus, if $M = 100.00$, the limits of the 95% confidence interval equal 95.544 and 104.456.

For a 99% confidence interval with a df of 10, use the constant 3.169 found in the third column of Table 3, labeled *99% C.I.*

"Your résumé is bloated with half-truths, false praise, exaggeration, and unsubstantiated accomplishments. I'd like to hire you to prepare the statistical charts for our annual report."

Appendix H
Computation of the Precise Median

In Section 13, you learned how to compute the median. When there are ties in the middle of the distribution, you can obtain the precise median by first putting the scores in a frequency distribution and then applying the formula shown below.[1]

Score	Frequency (f)	Cumulative frequency (cf)
20	2	22
19	0	20
18	4	20
17	6	16
16	5	10
15	3	5
14	2	2
	$N = 22$	

The formula is

$$\text{Median} = L + \frac{N(.5) - cfb}{f}$$

Where

L is the exact lower limit of the interval that contains the median. This is the *interval of interest*. To find this interval, divide N by 2 (in this case, 22/2 = 11), and go *up* the *cf* column looking for Subject 11. The *cf* column indicates that up to a score of 16, there are 10 subjects. The next score interval (17) contains subjects 11 through 16. Because we are looking for Subject 11, the score interval of interest is 17. Subtract .5 from

---

[1]Notice that for all scores, except 19, there are ties, as indicated by frequencies (f) of more than one. Section 13 shows how to compute the precise median when there are no ties near the median. The above method will yield the precise median whether or not there are ties.

the score of interest to obtain the exact lower limit (i.e., $17 - .5 = 16.5$),

N is the total number of cases. In this example, it is 22,

cfb is the cumulative frequency (cf) for the score immediately *below* the *interval of interest* (in this case, $cfb = 10$ for the score of 16, which is the score below 16.5), and

f is the frequency of the interval of interest (in this case, 6 for the interval associated with a score of 17).

Substituting into the formula, we obtain the following:

$$\text{Median} = 16.5 + \frac{(22)(.5) - 10}{6} = 16.5 + \frac{1}{6} = 16.5 + .167 = 16.667$$

**"Yes, we have *Chicken Soup for the Statistics Professor's Soul*.
The price is $(4)(SD) + M - r^2/t + (F)(df)(12)/100 - z + T - p$."**

Appendix I
A Closer Look at Effect Size[1]

Reporting effect sizes in research reports has become common only in recent years, and they still are not universally reported. Hence, consumers of research (who typically do not need to compute statistics) may find it beneficial to be able to calculate some simple statistics that will allow them to more accurately interpret results in which effect sizes have been omitted in research reports.

In Section 65, the calculation of d was illustrated in the examples in which the two standard deviations were equal. When they are not equal, most researchers divide the difference between means by the *pooled standard deviation*, which is a special type of average standard deviation that can be obtained by using the formula that follows. Its use is illustrated for an experiment in which the experimental group's standard deviation is 10.00 (with 15 participants, $n = 15$), and the control group's standard deviation is 14.00 (with 12 participants, $n = 12$). Note that for an experiment, the subscript 1 designates the experimental group, and the subscript 2 designates the control group.

$$sd_{pooled} = \sqrt{\frac{(n_1 - 1)sd_1^2 + (n_2 - 1)sd_2^2}{n_1 + n_2 - 2}} = \sqrt{\frac{(15-1)10.00^2 + (12-1)14.00^2}{15 + 12 - 2}} = 11.93$$

Note that the pooled standard deviation of 11.93 is very close to the simple average of the standard deviations (10.00 + 14.00 = 24.00/2 = 12.00). The larger the difference between the numbers of participants in the two groups, and the larger the difference between the two standard deviations, the greater the difference between the pooled standard deviation and the simple average of the standard deviations.

---

[1] Reprinted with permission from Patten, M. L. (2014). *Understanding research methods: An overview of the essentials* (9th ed.).

The usual formula for Cohen's *d* is the difference between the means divided by the pooled standard deviation, which is shown here in symbols:[2]

$$d = \frac{m_1 - m_2}{sd_{pooled}}$$

As a practical solution for consumers of research who do not want to engage in extensive calculations, a good *estimate* of *d* can usually be obtained by dividing the difference between the means by the *simple average* of the standard deviations. As indicated in the preceding example, the simple average of the standard deviations is $10.00 + 14.00 = 24.00/2 = 12.00$. Divide the difference between the two means by 12.00 for an estimate. Another practical solution when one is conducting meta-analyses on experiments is to use only the standard deviation of the control group (and hence avoid averaging standard deviations altogether), as is discussed in the next paragraph.

When analyzing the difference between an experimental group and a control group, some researchers prefer to divide the difference between the means by the standard deviation of the control group only (as opposed to the pooled standard deviation for both groups). The resulting statistic is widely known as Glass's delta (Δ), although it is sometimes also referred to as *d* in research literature. This is understandable because the value of *d* and the value of Δ are very similar when the two standard deviations are very similar. For instance, in a perfect case in which the two standard deviations are identical, the standard deviation of the control group will equal the pooled standard deviation of the two groups, so *d* and Δ will have exactly the same value.

In Section 65, the examples were *experiments* (with experimental and control groups). Cohen's *d* is also appropriate for describing the difference between two means in *nonexperimental studies*. For instance, a researcher could survey a random

---

[2] Students who have taken statistics should note that the population value of the standard deviation (computed without the minus one [−1] in the denominator of the computational formula) should be used to obtain Cohen's *d*. If the sample standard deviation is used, the result is Hedge's *g*, which, for small samples, can differ noticeably from Cohen's *d*. Values of *g* can be converted to values of *d* with the following formula:

$$d = g\sqrt{N/df}$$

sample of girls and a random sample of boys (without any physical treatments), compute a mean and standard deviation for each group, and compare the two groups using *d*. In such a study, it is usually best to subtract the smaller mean from the larger mean (so that the difference is a positive number) and then divide by either the pooled standard deviation (for an exact value of *d*) or by the simple average of the two standard deviations (for an estimate of the value of *d*).

As indicated in Section 67, when one is examining a body of literature, it is sometimes helpful to be able to directly compare the effect sizes represented by values of *d* with effect sizes represented by values of *r*. The following formula yields a good approximation of the value of *d* corresponding to a value of *r*:

$$d = \frac{2r}{\sqrt{1-r^2}}$$

The following formula is recommended for calculating the effect size *r* from a value of *d*. The subscript *es* for *effect size* is used in the formula to distinguish the result from a value of *r* that is computed directly from raw scores (as opposed to being computed from a value of *d*).

$$r_{es} = \frac{d}{\sqrt{d^2 + 4}}$$

Notes

Appendix J
Summary of Statistical Equations

Statistical Problem Flowchart

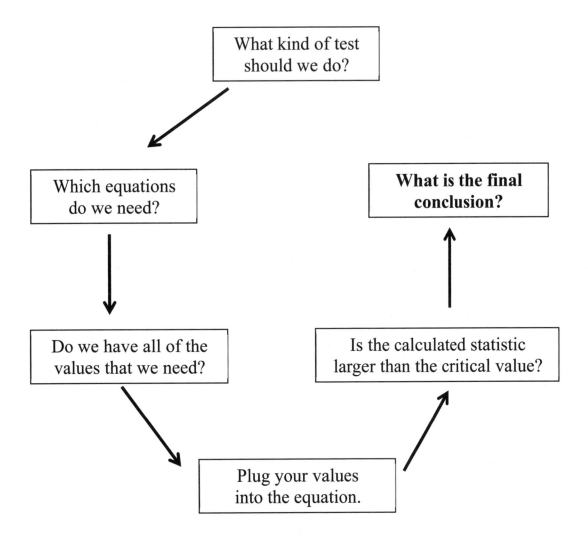

Continued →

Statistical test	Purpose	Values necessary	Formulas necessary	df
z-test	For calculating how a sample mean deviates from the population when you know the population *SD*	sample mean (*m*), population mean (*μ*), population standard deviation (σ), sample size (*n*)	$SE_M = \dfrac{\sigma}{\sqrt{n}}$ $z = \dfrac{m-\mu}{SE_M}$	—
Independent samples *t*-test	For calculating how 2 sample means differ from each other in a between-groups design	sample mean for each group (*m₁* and *m₂*), sample standard deviation for each group (*s₁* and *s₂*), sample size for each group (*n₁* and *n₂*)	$s_{Dm} = \sqrt{\dfrac{s_1^2}{n_1} + \dfrac{s_2^2}{n_2}}$ $t = \dfrac{m_1 - m_2}{S_{DM}}$	$n_1 + n_2 - 2$
Dependent samples *t*-test (also known as paired samples *t*-test)	For calculating how 2 sample means differ from each other in a within-groups design	Difference score for each participant (*D*), mean of the difference scores (*m_d*), sample size (*n*)	$s_D = \sqrt{\dfrac{\Sigma(D - m_D)^2}{n-1}}$ $s_{mD} = \dfrac{s_D}{\sqrt{n}}$ $t = \dfrac{m_1 - m_2}{s_{mD}}$	$n - 1$
F-test for randomized ANOVA	For calculating how 3 or more sample means differ from each other in a between-groups design	Each individual's observed scores (*X*), mean for each group (*m_g*), grand mean across all participants (*m_G*), sample size for each group (*n*), total sample size (*N*), number of comparisons (*k*)	$SS_b = \Sigma(m_g - m_G)^2 n$ $SS_w = \Sigma(X - m_G)^2$ ***OR*** $SS_T = \sqrt{\Sigma X^2 - \dfrac{(\Sigma X_T)^2}{N}}$ $SS_b = \Sigma\dfrac{(\Sigma X)^2}{n} - \dfrac{(\Sigma X_T)^2}{N}$ $SS_w = SS_T - SS_b$ ***AND*** $MS_b = \dfrac{SS_b}{df_b}$ $MS_w = \dfrac{SS_w}{df_w}$ $F = \dfrac{MS_b}{MS_w}$	$df_b = k - 1$ $df_w = N - k$

Statistical test	Purpose	Values necessary	Formulas necessary	df
Tukey's *HSD* test	Post-hoc test for comparing only 2 means at a time after an ANOVA was performed if sample sizes are equal	Studentized range statistic (q), mean square within (MS_w), group sample size (n)	$HSD_{.05} = q\sqrt{\dfrac{MS_w}{n}}$	—
Scheffès test	Post-hoc test for comparing only 2 means at a time after an ANOVA was performed	Critical *F*-value from the ANOVA (CV_{ANOVA}), number of comparisons (k), mean for each group (m_1 and m_2), mean square within (MS_w), sample size for each group (n_1 and n_2)	$CV_s = \left(CV_{ANOVA}\right)\left(k-1\right)$ $F_S = \dfrac{\left(m_1 - m_1\right)^2}{MS_w\left(n_1 + n_1\right)/\left(n_1\right)\left(n_2\right)}$	—
Pearson's correlation	For identifying the relationship between 2 variables	The z-scores of the *X*-values (z_X), the z-scores of the *Y*-values (z_Y), the number of paired cases (n)	$r = \dfrac{\Sigma z_x z_y}{n-1}$ **OR** $r = \dfrac{N\Sigma XY - \left(\Sigma X\right)\left(\Sigma Y\right)}{\sqrt{\left[N\Sigma X^2 - \left(\Sigma X\right)^2\right]\left[N\Sigma Y^2 - \left(\Sigma Y\right)^2\right]}}$	$n-2$
Multiple correlation	For identifying how well 2 variables in combination predict a 3rd variable	The correlation between Variables 1 and 2 (r_{12}), between Variables 1 and 3 (r_{13}), and between Variables 2 and 3 (r_{23})	$R = \sqrt{\dfrac{r_{12}^2 + r_{13}^2 - 2r_{12}r_{13}r_{23}}{1 - r_{23}^2}}$	$n-2$
Regression	For predicting scores, based on a correlation	The value of the Pearson correlation (r), the standard deviation of the *X*-values (s_X), the standard deviation of the *Y*-values (s_Y), the mean of the *X*-values (m_X), and the mean of the *Y*-values (m_Y)	$b = r\left(\dfrac{s_Y}{s_X}\right)$ **OR** $b = \dfrac{\Sigma XY - \left[\left(\Sigma X\right)\left(\Sigma Y\right)/N\right]}{\Sigma X^2 - \left[\left(\Sigma X\right)^2/N\right]}$ **AND** $a = m_y - b\left(m_x\right)$ $Y' = a + bX$	—

Continued →

Statistical test	Purpose	Values necessary	Formulas necessary	df
One-way chi-square	For comparing observed frequencies to expected frequencies when 1 category is used	Observed frequencies (O) and expected frequencies (E)	$\chi^2 = \frac{\Sigma(O-E)^2}{E}$	Number of levels of a category – 1
Two-way chi-square	For comparing observed frequencies to expected frequencies when 2 categories are used	Column total (CT), row total (RT), grand total (GT), observed frequencies (O), expected frequencies (E)	$E = \frac{(CT)(RT)}{GT}$ $\chi^2 = \frac{\Sigma(O-E)^2}{E}$	(Number of rows –1) × (Number of columns – 1)
Cramer's Phi	Describes the strength of the relationship between 2 variables in the 2-way chi-square	The value of chi-square (χ^2), the total number of cases (N), the smaller number of categories (k)	$\phi = \sqrt{\frac{\chi^2}{N(k-1)}}$	—
Mann-Whitney U test	For calculating how 2 distributions of scores differ	Number of cases in each group (n_1 and n_2), the sum of the ranks in each group (ΣR_1 and ΣR_2)	$U_1 = (n_1)(n_2) + \frac{n_1(n_1+1)}{2} - \Sigma R_1$ $U_2 = (n_1)(n_2) + \frac{n_2(n_2+1)}{2} - \Sigma R_2$	—

Table 1

Table of the Normal Curve

z Table: Negative Values

Body of table gives area under *z* curve to the left of *z*.

z	.00	.01	.02	.03	.04	.05	.06	.07	.08	.09
−3.80	.0001	.0001	.0001	.0001	.0001	.0001	.0001	.0001	.0001	.0001
−3.70	.0001	.0001	.0001	.0001	.0001	.0001	.0001	.0001	.0001	.0001
−3.60	.0002	.0002	.0001	.0001	.0001	.0001	.0001	.0001	.0001	.0001
−3.50	.0002	.0002	.0002	.0002	.0002	.0002	.0002	.0002	.0002	.0002
−3.40	.0003	.0003	.0003	.0003	.0003	.0003	.0003	.0003	.0003	.0002
−3.30	.0005	.0005	.0005	.0004	.0004	.0004	.0004	.0004	.0004	.0003
−3.20	.0007	.0007	.0006	.0006	.0006	.0006	.0006	.0005	.0005	.0005
−3.10	.0010	.0009	.0009	.0009	.0008	.0008	.0008	.0008	.0007	.0007
−3.00	.0013	.0013	.0013	.0012	.0012	.0011	.0011	.0011	.0010	.0010
−2.90	.0019	.0018	.0018	.0017	.0016	.0016	.0015	.0015	.0014	.0014
−2.80	.0026	.0025	.0024	.0023	.0023	.0022	.0021	.0021	.0020	.0019
−2.70	.0035	.0034	.0033	.0032	.0031	.0030	.0029	.0028	.0027	.0026
−2.60	.0047	.0045	.0044	.0043	.0041	.0040	.0039	.0038	.0037	.0036
−2.50	.0062	.0060	.0059	.0057	.0055	.0054	.0052	.0051	.0049	.0048
−2.40	.0082	.0080	.0078	.0075	.0073	.0071	.0069	.0068	.0066	.0064
−2.30	.0107	.0104	.0102	.0099	.0096	.0094	.0091	.0089	.0087	.0084
−2.20	.0139	.0136	.0132	.0129	.0125	.0122	.0119	.0116	.0113	.0110
−2.10	.0179	.0174	.0170	.0166	.0162	.0158	.0154	.0150	.0146	.0143
−2.00	.0228	.0222	.0217	.0212	.0207	.0202	.0197	.0192	.0188	.0183
−1.90	.0287	.0281	.0274	.0268	.0262	.0256	.0250	.0244	.0239	.0233
−1.80	.0359	.0351	.0344	.0336	.0329	.0322	.0314	.0307	.0301	.0294
−1.70	.0446	.0436	.0427	.0418	.0409	.0401	.0392	.0384	.0375	.0367
−1.60	.0548	.0537	.0526	.0516	.0505	.0495	.0485	.0475	.0465	.0455
−1.50	.0668	.0655	.0643	.0630	.0618	.0606	.0594	.0582	.0571	.0559
−1.40	.0808	.0793	.0778	.0764	.0749	.0735	.0721	.0708	.0694	.0681
−1.30	.0968	.0951	.0934	.0918	.0901	.0885	.0869	.0853	.0838	.0823
−1.20	.1151	.1131	.1112	.1093	.1075	.1056	.1038	.1020	.1003	.0985
−1.10	.1357	.1335	.1314	.1292	.1271	.1251	.1230	.1210	.1190	.1170
−1.00	.1587	.1562	.1539	.1515	.1492	.1469	.1446	.1423	.1401	.1379
−0.90	.1841	.1814	.1788	.1762	.1769	.1711	.1685	.1660	.1635	.1611
−0.80	.2119	.2090	.2061	.2033	.2005	.1977	.1949	.1922	.1894	.1867
−0.70	.2420	.2389	.2358	.2327	.2296	.2266	.2236	.2206	.2177	.2148
−0.60	.2743	.2709	.2676	.2643	.2611	.2578	.2546	.2514	.2483	.2451
−0.50	.3085	.3050	.3015	.2981	.2946	.2912	.2877	.2843	.2810	.2776
−0.40	.3446	.3409	.3372	.3336	.3300	.3264	.3228	.3192	.3156	.3121
−0.30	.3821	.3783	.3745	.3707	.3669	.3632	.3594	.3557	.3520	.3483
−0.20	.4207	.4168	.4129	.4090	.4052	.4013	.3974	.3936	.3897	.3859
−0.10	.4602	.4562	.4522	.4483	.4443	.4404	.4634	.4325	.4286	.4247
0.00	.5000	.4960	.4920	.4880	.4840	.4801	.4761	.4721	.4681	.4641

Continued →

Table 1 (continued)

z Table: Positive Values

Body of table gives area under z curve to the left of z.

z	.00	.01	.02	.03	.04	.05	.06	.07	.08	.09
0.00	.5000	.5040	.5080	.5120	.5160	.5199	.5239	.5279	.5319	.5359
0.10	.5398	.5438	.5478	.5517	.5557	.5596	.5636	.5675	.5714	.5753
0.20	.5793	.5832	.5871	.5910	.5948	.5987	.6026	.6064	.6103	.6141
0.30	.6179	.6217	.6255	.6293	.6331	.6368	.6406	.6443	.6480	.6517
0.40	.6554	.6591	.6628	.6664	.6700	.6736	.6772	.6808	.6844	.6879
0.50	.6915	.6950	.6985	.7019	.7054	.7088	.7123	.7157	.7190	.7224
0.60	.7257	.7291	.7324	.7357	.7389	.7422	.7454	.7486	.7517	.7549
0.70	.7580	.7611	.7642	.7673	.7704	.7734	.7764	.7794	.7823	.7852
0.80	.7881	.7910	.7939	.7967	.7995	.8023	.8051	.8078	.8106	.8133
0.90	.8159	.8186	.8212	.8238	.8264	.8289	.8315	.8340	.8365	.8389
1.00	.8413	.8438	.8461	.8485	.8508	.8531	.8554	.8577	.8599	.8621
1.10	.8643	.8665	.8686	.8708	.8729	.8749	.8770	.8790	.8810	.8830
1.20	.8849	.8869	.8888	.8907	.8925	.8944	.8962	.8980	.8997	.9015
1.30	.9032	.9049	.9066	.9082	.9099	.9115	.9131	.9147	.9162	.9177
1.40	.9132	.9207	.9222	.9236	.9251	.9265	.9279	.9292	.9306	.9319
1.50	.9332	.9345	.9357	.9370	.9382	.9394	.9406	.9418	.9429	.9441
1.60	.9452	.9463	.9474	.9484	.9495	.9505	.9515	.9525	.9535	.9545
1.70	.9554	.9564	.9573	.9582	.9591	.9599	.9608	.9616	.9625	.9633
1.80	.9641	.9649	.9656	.9664	.9671	.9678	.9686	.9693	.9699	.9706
1.90	.9713	.9719	.9726	.9732	.9738	.9744	.9750	.9756	.9761	.9767
2.00	.9772	.9778	.9783	.9788	.9793	.9798	.9803	.9808	.9812	.9817
2.10	.9821	.9826	.9830	.9834	.9838	.9842	.9846	.9850	.9854	.9857
2.20	.9861	.9864	.9868	.9871	.9875	.9878	.9881	.9884	.9887	.9890
2.30	.9893	.9896	.9898	.9901	.9904	.9906	.9909	.9911	.9913	.9916
2.40	.9918	.9920	.9922	.9925	.9927	.9929	.9931	.9932	.9934	.9936
2.50	.9938	.9940	.9941	.9943	.9945	.9946	.9948	.9949	.9951	.9952
2.60	.9953	.9955	.9956	.9957	.9959	.9960	.9961	.9962	.9963	.9964
2.70	.9965	.9966	.9967	.9968	.9969	.9970	.9971	.9972	.9973	.9974
2.80	.9974	.9975	.9976	.9977	.9977	.9978	.9979	.9979	.9980	.9981
2.90	.9981	.9982	.9982	.9983	.9984	.9984	.9985	.9985	.9986	.9986
3.00	.9987	.9987	.9987	.9988	.9988	.9989	.9989	.9989	.9990	.9990
3.10	.9990	.9991	.9991	.9991	.9992	.9992	.9992	.9992	.9993	.9993
3.20	.9993	.9993	.9994	.9994	.9994	.9994	.9994	.9995	.9995	.9995
3.30	.9995	.9995	.9995	.9996	.9996	.9996	.9996	.9996	.9996	.9997
3.40	.9997	.9997	.9997	.9997	.9997	.9997	.9997	.9997	.9997	.9998
3.50	.9998	.9998	.9998	.9998	.9998	.9998	.9998	.9998	.9998	.9998
3.60	.9998	.9998	.9999	.9999	.9999	.9999	.9999	.9999	.9999	.9999
3.70	.9999	.9999	.9999	.9999	.9999	.9999	.9999	.9999	.9999	.9999
3.80	.9999	.9999	.9999	.9999	.9999	.9999	.9999	.9999	.9999	.9999

Table 2
Table of Random Numbers

Row #																	
1	2	1	0	4	9	8	0	8	8	8	0	6	9	2	4	8	2	6
2	0	7	3	0	2	9	4	8	2	7	8	9	8	9	2	9	7	1
3	4	4	9	0	0	2	8	6	2	6	7	7	7	3	1	2	5	1
4	7	3	2	1	1	2	0	7	7	6	0	3	8	3	4	7	8	1
5	3	3	2	5	8	3	1	7	0	1	4	0	7	8	9	3	7	7
6	6	1	2	0	5	7	2	4	4	0	0	6	3	0	2	8	0	7
7	7	0	9	3	3	3	7	4	0	4	8	8	9	3	5	8	0	5
8	7	5	1	9	0	9	1	5	2	6	5	0	9	0	3	5	8	8
9	3	5	6	9	6	5	0	1	9	4	6	6	7	5	6	8	3	1
10	8	5	0	3	9	4	3	4	0	6	5	1	7	4	4	6	2	7
11	0	5	9	6	8	7	4	8	1	5	5	0	5	1	7	1	5	8
12	7	6	2	2	6	9	6	1	9	7	1	1	4	7	1	6	2	0
13	3	8	4	7	8	9	8	2	2	1	6	3	8	7	0	4	6	1
14	1	9	1	8	4	5	6	1	8	1	2	4	4	4	2	7	3	4
15	1	5	3	6	7	6	1	8	4	3	1	8	8	7	7	6	0	4
16	0	5	5	3	6	0	7	1	3	8	1	4	6	7	0	4	3	5
17	2	2	3	8	6	0	9	1	9	0	4	4	7	6	8	1	5	1
18	2	3	3	2	5	5	7	6	9	4	9	7	1	3	7	9	3	8
19	8	5	5	0	5	3	7	8	5	4	5	1	6	0	4	8	9	1
20	0	6	1	1	3	4	8	6	4	3	2	9	4	3	8	7	4	1
21	9	1	1	8	2	9	0	6	9	6	9	4	2	9	9	0	6	0
22	3	7	8	0	6	3	7	1	2	6	5	2	7	6	5	6	5	1
23	5	3	0	5	1	2	1	0	9	1	3	7	5	6	1	2	5	0
24	7	2	4	8	6	7	9	3	8	7	6	0	9	1	6	5	7	8
25	0	9	1	6	7	0	3	8	0	9	1	5	4	2	3	2	4	5
26	3	8	1	4	3	7	9	2	4	5	1	2	8	7	7	4	1	3

Table 3

Constants Based on *t* for Computing Confidence Intervals for the Mean Based on Small Samples[1]

df	95% *C.I.*	99% *C.I.*		*df*	95% *C.I.*	99% *C.I.*
1	12.706	63.657		24	2.064	2.797
2	4.303	9.925		25	2.060	2.787
3	3.182	5.841		26	2.056	2.779
4	2.776	4.604		27	2.052	2.771
5	2.571	4.032		28	2.048	2.763
6	2.447	3.707		29	2.045	2.756
7	2.365	3.499		30	2.042	2.750
8	2.306	3.355		40	2.021	2.704
9	2.262	3.250		60	2.000	2.660
10	2.228	3.169		120	1.980	2.617
11	2.201	3.106		Infinity	1.960	2.576
12	2.179	3.055				
13	2.160	3.012				
14	2.145	2.977				
15	2.131	2.947				
16	2.120	2.921				
17	2.110	2.898				
18	2.101	2.878				
19	2.093	2.861				
20	2.086	2.845				
21	2.080	2.831				
22	2.074	2.819				
23	2.069	2.807				

[1]Abridged from Fisher, R. A., & Yates, F. (1963). *Statistical tables for biological, agricultural, and medical research*. Edinburgh, Scotland: Oliver & Boyd Ltd.

Table 4

Critical Values of *t* for Two-Tailed *t* Test[1]

df	.05 level	.01 level	.001 level
1	12.706	63.657	636.619
2	4.303	9.925	31.598
3	3.182	5.841	12.941
4	2.776	4.604	8.610
5	2.571	4.032	6.859
6	2.447	3.707	5.959
7	2.365	3.499	5.405
8	2.306	3.355	5.041
9	2.262	3.250	4.781
10	2.228	3.169	4.587
11	2.201	3.106	4.437
12	2.179	3.055	4.318
13	2.160	3.012	4.221
14	2.145	2.977	4.140
15	2.131	2.947	4.073
16	2.120	2.921	4.015
17	2.110	2.898	3.965
18	2.101	2.878	3.922
19	2.093	2.861	3.883
20	2.086	2.845	3.850
21	2.080	2.831	3.819
22	2.074	2.819	3.792
23	2.069	2.807	3.767

df	.05 level	.01 level	.001 level
24	2.064	2.797	3.745
25	2.060	2.787	3.725
26	2.056	2.779	3.707
27	2.052	2.771	3.690
28	2.048	2.763	3.674
29	2.045	2.756	3.659
30	2.042	2.750	3.646
40	2.021	2.704	3.551
60	2.000	2.660	3.460
120	1.980	2.617	3.373
Infinity	1.960	2.576	3.291

[1]Abridged from Fisher, R. A., & Yates, F. (1963). *Statistical tables for biological, agricultural, and medical research*. Edinburgh, Scotland: Oliver & Boyd Ltd.

Table 5

Critical Values of *t* for One-Tailed *t* Test[1]

df	.05 level	.01 level	.001 level		*df*	.05 level	.01 level	.001 level
1	6.314	31.821	318.310		24	1.711	2.492	3.467
2	2.920	6.965	22.326		25	1.708	2.485	3.450
3	2.353	4.541	10.213		26	1.706	2.479	3.435
4	2.132	3.747	7.173		27	1.703	2.473	3.421
5	2.015	3.365	5.893		28	1.701	2.467	3.408
6	1.943	3.143	5.208		29	1.699	2.462	3.396
7	1.895	2.998	4.785		30	1.697	2.457	3.385
8	1.860	2.896	4.501		40	1.684	2.423	3.307
9	1.833	2.821	4.297		60	1.671	2.390	3.232
10	1.812	2.764	4.144		120	1.658	2.358	3.160
11	1.796	2.718	4.025		Infinity	1.645	2.326	3.090
12	1.782	2.681	3.930					
13	1.771	2.650	3.852					
14	1.761	2.624	3.787					
15	1.753	2.602	3.733					
16	1.746	2.583	3.686					
17	1.740	2.567	3.646					
18	1.734	2.552	3.610					
19	1.729	2.539	3.579					
20	1.725	2.528	3.552					
21	1.721	2.518	3.527					
22	1.717	2.508	3.505					
23	1.714	2.500	3.485					

[1]Abridged from Fisher, R. A., & Yates, F. (1963). *Statistical tables for biological, agricultural, and medical research*. Edinburgh, Scotland: Oliver & Boyd Ltd.

Table 6

Critical Values of *F* for the .05 Level

Within-Groups Degrees of Freedom	Between-Groups Degrees of Freedom (Numerator)												
	1	2	3	4	5	6	7	8	9	10	11	12	14
1	161	200	216	225	230	234	237	239	241	242	243	244	245
2	18.51	19.00	19.16	19.25	19.30	19.33	19.36	19.37	19.38	19.39	19.40	19.41	19.42
3	10.13	9.55	9.28	9.12	9.01	8.94	8.88	8.84	8.81	8.78	8.76	8.74	8.71
4	7.71	6.94	6.59	6.39	6.26	6.16	6.09	6.04	6.00	5.96	5.93	5.91	5.87
5	6.61	5.79	5.41	5.19	5.05	4.95	4.88	4.82	4.78	4.74	4.70	4.68	4.64
6	5.99	5.14	4.76	4.53	4.39	4.28	4.21	4.15	4.10	4.06	4.03	4.00	3.96
7	5.59	4.74	4.35	4.12	3.97	3.87	3.79	3.73	3.68	3.63	3.60	3.57	3.52
8	5.32	4.46	4.07	3.84	3.69	3.58	3.50	3.44	3.39	3.34	3.31	3.28	3.23
9	5.12	4.26	3.86	3.63	3.48	3.37	3.29	3.23	3.18	3.13	3.10	3.07	3.02
10	4.96	4.10	3.71	3.48	3.33	3.22	3.14	3.07	3.02	2.97	2.94	2.91	2.86
11	4.84	3.98	3.59	3.36	3.20	3.09	3.01	2.95	2.90	2.86	2.82	2.79	2.74
12	4.75	3.88	3.49	3.26	3.11	3.00	2.92	2.85	2.80	2.76	2.72	2.69	2.64
13	4.67	3.80	3.41	3.18	3.02	2.92	2.84	2.72	2.77	2.63	2.63	2.60	2.55
14	4.60	3.74	3.34	3.11	2.96	2.85	2.77	2.70	2.65	2.60	2.56	2.53	2.48
15	4.54	3.68	3.29	3.06	2.90	2.79	2.70	2.64	2.59	2.55	2.51	2.48	2.43
16	4.49	3.63	3.24	3.01	2.85	2.74	2.66	2.59	2.54	2.49	2.45	2.42	2.37
17	4.45	3.59	3.20	2.96	2.81	2.70	2.62	2.55	2.50	2.45	2.41	2.38	2.33
18	4.41	3.55	3.16	2.93	2.77	2.66	2.58	2.51	2.46	2.41	2.37	2.34	2.29
19	4.38	3.52	3.13	2.90	2.74	2.63	2.55	2.48	2.43	2.38	2.34	2.31	2.26
20	4.35	3.49	3.10	2.87	2.71	2.60	2.52	2.45	2.40	2.35	2.31	2.28	2.23
21	4.32	3.47	3.07	2.84	2.68	2.57	2.49	2.42	2.37	2.32	2.28	2.25	2.20
22	4.30	3.44	3.05	2.82	2.66	2.55	2.47	2.40	2.35	2.30	2.26	2.23	2.18
23	4.28	3.42	3.03	2.80	2.64	2.53	2.45	2.38	2.32	2.28	2.24	2.20	2.14
24	4.26	3.40	3.01	2.78	2.62	2.51	2.43	2.36	2.30	2.26	2.22	2.18	2.13
25	4.24	3.38	2.99	2.76	2.60	2.49	2.41	2.34	2.28	2.24	2.20	2.16	2.11
26	4.22	3.37	2.98	2.74	2.59	2.47	2.39	2.32	2.27	2.22	2.18	2.15	2.10
27	4.21	3.35	2.96	2.73	2.57	2.46	2.37	2.30	2.25	2.20	2.16	2.13	2.08
28	4.20	3.34	2.95	2.71	2.56	2.44	2.36	2.29	2.24	2.19	2.15	2.12	2.06
29	4.18	3.33	2.93	2.70	2.54	2.43	2.35	2.28	2.22	2.18	2.14	2.10	2.05

Continued →

Table 6 (continued)

			Between-Groups Degrees of Freedom (Numerator)								Within-Groups Degrees of Freedom
16	20	24	30	40	50	75	100	200	500	Infinity	
246	248	249	250	251	252	253	253	254	254	254	1
19.43	19.44	19.45	19.46	19.47	19.47	19.48	19.49	19.49	19.50	19.50	2
8.69	8.66	8.64	8.62	8.60	8.58	8.57	8.56	8.54	8.54	8.53	3
5.84	5.80	5.77	5.74	5.71	5.70	5.68	5.66	5.65	5.64	5.63	4
4.60	4.56	4.53	4.50	4.46	4.44	4.42	4.40	4.38	4.37	4.36	5
3.92	3.87	3.84	3.81	3.77	3.75	3.72	3.71	3.69	3.68	3.67	6
3.49	3.44	3.41	3.38	3.34	3.32	3.29	3.28	3.25	3.24	3.23	7
3.20	3.15	3.12	3.08	3.05	3.03	3.00	2.98	2.96	2.94	2.93	8
2.98	2.93	2.90	2.86	2.82	2.80	2.77	2.76	2.73	2.72	2.71	9
2.82	2.77	2.74	2.70	2.67	2.64	2.61	2.59	2.56	2.55	2.54	10
2.70	2.65	2.61	2.57	2.53	2.50	2.47	2.45	2.42	2.41	2.40	11
2.60	2.54	2.50	2.46	2.42	2.40	2.36	2.35	2.32	2.31	2.30	12
2.51	2.46	2.42	2.38	2.34	2.32	2.28	2.26	2.24	2.22	2.21	13
2.44	2.39	2.35	2.31	2.27	2.24	2.21	2.19	2.16	2.14	2.13	14
2.39	2.33	2.29	2.25	2.21	2.18	2.15	2.12	2.10	2.08	2.07	15
2.33	2.28	2.24	2.20	2.16	2.13	2.09	2.07	2.04	2.02	2.01	16
2.29	2.23	2.19	2.15	2.11	2.08	2.04	2.02	1.99	1.97	1.96	17
2.25	2.19	2.15	2.11	2.07	2.04	2.00	1.98	1.95	1.93	1.92	18
2.21	2.15	2.11	2.07	2.02	2.00	1.96	1.94	1.91	1.90	1.88	19
2.18	2.12	2.08	2.04	1.99	1.96	1.92	1.90	1.87	1.85	1.84	20
2.15	2.09	2.05	2.00	1.96	1.93	1.89	1.87	1.84	1.82	1.81	21
2.13	2.07	2.03	1.98	1.93	1.91	1.87	1.84	1.81	1.80	1.78	22
2.10	2.04	2.00	1.96	1.91	1.88	1.84	1.82	1.79	1.77	1.76	23
2.09	2.02	1.98	1.94	1.89	1.86	1.82	1.80	1.76	1.74	1.73	24
2.06	2.00	1.96	1.92	1.87	1.84	1.80	1.77	1.74	1.72	1.71	25
2.05	1.99	1.95	1.90	1.85	1.82	1.78	1.76	1.72	1.70	1.69	26
2.03	1.97	1.93	1.88	1.84	1.80	1.76	1.74	1.71	1.68	1.67	27
2.02	1.96	1.91	1.87	1.81	1.78	1.75	1.72	1.69	1.67	1.65	28
2.00	1.94	1.90	1.85	1.80	1.77	1.73	1.71	1.68	1.65	1.64	29

Table 6 (continued)

Within-Groups Degrees of Freedom	Between-Groups Degrees of Freedom (Numerator)												
	1	2	3	4	5	6	7	8	9	10	11	12	14
30	4.17	3.32	2.92	2.69	2.53	2.42	2.34	2.27	2.21	2.16	2.12	2.09	2.04
32	4.15	3.30	2.90	2.67	2.51	2.40	2.32	2.25	2.19	2.14	2.10	2.07	2.02
34	4.13	3.28	2.88	2.65	2.49	2.38	2.30	2.23	2.17	2.12	2.08	2.05	2.00
36	4.11	3.26	2.86	2.63	2.48	2.36	2.28	2.21	2.15	2.10	2.06	2.03	1.98
38	4.10	3.25	2.85	2.62	2.46	2.35	2.26	2.19	2.14	2.09	2.05	2.02	1.96
40	4.08	3.23	2.84	2.61	2.45	2.34	2.25	2.18	2.12	2.07	2.04	2.00	1.95
42	4.07	3.22	2.83	2.59	2.44	2.32	2.24	2.17	2.11	2.06	2.02	1.99	1.94
44	4.06	3.21	2.82	2.58	2.43	2.31	2.23	2.16	2.10	2.05	2.01	1.98	1.92
46	4.05	3.20	2.81	2.57	2.42	2.30	2.22	2.14	2.09	2.04	2.00	1.97	1.91
48	4.04	3.19	2.80	2.56	2.41	2.30	2.21	2.14	2.08	2.03	1.99	1.96	1.90
50	4.03	3.18	2.79	2.56	2.40	2.29	2.20	2.13	2.07	2.02	1.98	1.95	1.90
55	4.02	3.17	2.78	2.54	2.38	2.27	2.18	2.11	2.05	2.00	1.97	1.93	1.88
60	4.00	3.15	2.76	2.52	2.37	2.25	2.17	2.10	2.04	1.99	1.95	1.92	1.86
65	3.99	3.14	2.75	2.51	2.36	2.24	2.15	2.08	2.02	1.98	1.94	1.90	1.85
70	3.98	3.13	2.74	2.50	2.35	2.23	2.14	2.07	2.01	1.97	1.93	1.89	1.84
80	3.96	3.11	2.72	2.48	2.33	2.21	2.12	2.05	1.99	1.95	1.91	1.88	1.82
100	3.94	3.09	2.70	2.46	2.30	2.19	2.10	2.03	1.97	1.92	1.88	1.85	1.79
125	3.92	3.07	2.68	2.44	2.29	2.17	2.08	2.01	1.95	1.90	1.86	1.83	1.77
150	3.91	3.06	2.67	2.43	2.27	2.16	2.07	2.00	1.94	1.89	1.85	1.82	1.76
200	3.89	3.04	2.65	2.41	2.26	2.14	2.05	1.98	1.92	1.87	1.83	1.80	1.74
400	3.86	3.02	2.62	2.39	2.23	2.12	2.03	1.96	1.90	1.85	1.81	1.78	1.72
1000	3.85	3.00	2.61	2.38	2.22	2.10	2.02	1.95	1.89	1.84	1.80	1.76	1.70
Infinity	3.84	2.99	2.60	2.37	2.21	2.09	2.01	1.94	1.88	1.83	1.79	1.75	1.69

Continued →

Table 6 (continued)

Between-Groups Degrees of Freedom (Numerator)											Within-Groups Degrees of Freedom
16	20	24	30	40	50	75	100	200	500	Infinity	
1.99	1.93	1.89	1.84	1.79	1.76	1.72	1.69	1.66	1.64	1.62	30
1.97	1.91	1.86	1.82	1.76	1.74	1.69	1.67	1.64	1.61	1.59	32
1.95	1.89	1.84	1.80	1.74	1.71	1.67	1.64	1.61	1.59	1.57	34
1.93	1.87	1.82	1.78	1.72	1.69	1.65	1.62	1.59	1.56	1.55	36
1.92	1.85	1.80	1.76	1.71	1.67	1.63	1.60	1.57	1.54	1.53	38
1.90	1.84	1.79	1.74	1.69	1.66	1.61	1.59	1.55	1.53	1.51	40
1.89	1.82	1.78	1.73	1.68	1.64	1.60	1.57	1.54	1.51	1.49	42
1.88	1.81	1.76	1.72	1.66	1.63	1.58	1.56	1.52	1.50	1.48	44
1.87	1.80	1.75	1.71	1.65	1.62	1.57	1.54	1.51	1.48	1.46	46
1.86	1.79	1.74	1.70	1.64	1.61	1.56	1.53	1.50	1.47	1.45	48
1.85	1.78	1.74	1.69	1.63	1.60	1.55	1.52	1.48	1.46	1.44	50
1.83	1.76	1.72	1.67	1.61	1.58	1.52	1.50	1.46	1.43	1.41	55
1.81	1.75	1.70	1.65	1.59	1.56	1.50	1.48	1.44	1.41	1.39	60
1.80	1.73	1.68	1.63	1.57	1.54	1.49	1.46	1.42	1.39	1.37	65
1.79	1.72	1.67	1.62	1.56	1.53	1.47	1.45	1.40	1.37	1.35	70
1.77	1.70	1.65	1.60	1.54	1.51	1.45	1.42	1.38	1.35	1.32	80
1.75	1.68	1.63	1.57	1.51	1.48	1.42	1.39	1.34	1.30	1.28	100
1.72	1.65	1.60	1.55	1.49	1.45	1.39	1.36	1.31	1.27	1.25	125
1.71	1.64	1.59	1.54	1.47	1.44	1.37	1.34	1.29	1.25	1.22	150
1.69	1.62	1.57	1.52	1.45	1.42	1.35	1.32	1.26	1.22	1.19	200
1.67	1.60	1.54	1.49	1.42	1.38	1.32	1.28	1.22	1.16	1.13	400
1.65	1.58	1.53	1.47	1.41	1.36	1.30	1.26	1.19	1.13	1.08	1000
1.64	1.57	1.52	1.46	1.40	1.35	1.28	1.24	1.17	1.11	1.00	Infinity

Table 7

Critical Values of *F* for the .01 Level

Within-Groups Degrees of Freedom	Between-Groups Degrees of Freedom (Numerator)												
	1	2	3	4	5	6	7	8	9	10	11	12	14
1	4,052	4,999	5,403	5,625	5,764	5,859	5,928	5,981	6,022	6,056	6,082	6,106	6,142
2	98.49	99.00	99.17	99.25	99.30	99.33	99.34	99.36	99.38	99.40	99.41	99.42	99.43
3	34.12	30.82	29.46	28.71	28.24	27.91	29.67	27.49	27.34	27.23	27.13	27.05	26.92
4	21.20	18.00	16.69	15.98	15.52	15.21	14.98	14.80	14.66	14.54	14.45	14.37	14.24
5	16.26	13.27	12.06	11.39	10.97	10.67	10.45	10.27	10.15	10.05	9.96	9.89	9.77
6	13.74	10.92	9.78	9.15	8.75	8.47	8.26	8.10	7.98	7.87	7.79	7.72	7.60
7	12.25	9.55	8.45	7.85	7.46	7.19	7.00	6.84	6.71	6.62	6.54	6.47	6.35
8	11.26	8.65	7.59	7.01	6.63	6.37	6.19	6.03	5.91	5.82	5.74	5.67	5.56
9	10.56	8.02	6.99	6.42	6.06	5.80	5.62	5.47	5.35	5.26	5.18	5.11	5.00
10	10.04	7.56	6.55	5.99	5.64	5.39	5.21	5.06	4.95	4.85	4.78	4.71	4.60
11	9.65	7.20	6.22	5.67	5.32	5.07	4.88	4.74	4.63	4.54	4.46	4.40	4.29
12	9.33	6.93	5.95	5.41	5.06	4.82	4.65	4.50	4.39	4.30	4.22	4.16	4.05
13	9.07	6.70	5.74	5.20	4.86	4.62	4.44	4.30	4.19	4.10	4.02	3.96	3.85
14	8.86	6.51	5.56	5.03	4.69	4.46	4.28	4.14	4.03	3.94	3.86	3.80	3.70
15	8.68	6.36	5.42	4.89	4.56	4.32	4.14	4.00	3.89	3.80	3.73	3.67	3.56
16	8.53	6.23	5.29	4.77	4.44	4.20	4.03	3.89	3.78	3.69	3.61	3.55	3.45
17	8.40	6.11	5.18	4.67	4.34	4.10	3.93	3.79	3.68	3.59	3.52	3.45	3.35
18	8.28	6.01	5.09	4.58	4.25	4.01	3.85	3.71	3.60	3.51	3.44	3.37	3.27
19	8.18	5.93	5.01	4.50	4.17	3.94	3.77	3.63	3.52	3.43	3.36	3.30	3.19
20	8.10	5.85	4.94	4.43	4.10	3.87	3.71	3.56	3.45	3.37	3.30	3.23	3.13
21	8.02	5.78	4.87	4.37	4.04	3.81	3.65	3.51	3.40	3.31	3.24	3.17	3.07
22	7.94	5.72	4.82	4.31	3.99	3.76	3.59	3.45	3.35	3.26	3.18	3.12	3.02
23	7.88	5.66	4.76	4.26	3.94	3.71	3.54	3.41	3.30	3.21	3.14	3.07	2.97
24	7.82	5.61	4.72	4.22	3.90	3.67	3.50	3.36	3.25	3.17	3.09	3.03	2.93
25	7.77	5.57	4.68	4.18	3.86	3.63	3.46	3.32	3.21	3.13	3.05	2.99	2.89
26	7.72	5.53	4.64	4.14	3.82	3.59	3.42	3.29	3.17	3.09	3.02	2.96	2.86
27	7.68	5.49	4.60	4.11	3.79	3.56	3.39	3.26	3.14	3.06	2.98	2.93	2.83
28	7.64	5.45	4.57	4.07	3.76	3.53	3.36	3.23	3.11	3.03	2.95	2.90	2.80
29	7.60	5.42	4.54	4.04	3.73	3.50	3.33	3.20	3.08	3.00	2.92	2.87	2.77

Continued →

Table 7 (continued)

			Between-Groups Degrees of Freedom (Numerator)								Within-Groups Degrees of Freedom
16	20	24	30	40	50	75	100	200	500	Infinity	
6,169	6,208	6,234	6,258	6,286	6,302	6,323	6,334	6,352	6,361	6,366	1
99.44	99.45	99.46	99.47	99.48	99.48	99.49	99.49	99.49	99.50	99.50	2
26.83	26.69	26.60	26.50	26.41	26.35	26.27	26.23	26.18	26.14	26.12	3
14.15	14.02	13.93	13.83	13.74	13.69	13.61	13.57	13.52	13.48	13.46	4
9.68	9.55	9.47	9.38	9.29	9.24	9.17	9.13	9.07	9.04	9.02	5
7.52	7.39	7.31	7.23	7.14	7.09	7.02	6.99	6.94	6.90	6.88	6
6.27	6.15	6.07	5.98	5.90	5.85	5.78	5.75	5.70	5.67	5.65	7
5.48	5.36	5.28	5.20	5.11	5.06	5.00	4.96	4.91	4.88	4.86	8
4.92	4.80	4.73	4.64	4.56	4.51	4.45	4.41	4.36	4.33	4.31	9
4.52	4.41	4.33	4.25	4.17	4.12	4.05	4.01	3.96	3.93	3.91	10
4.21	4.10	4.02	3.94	3.86	3.80	3.74	3.70	3.66	3.62	3.60	11
3.98	3.86	3.78	3.70	3.61	3.56	3.49	3.46	3.41	3.38	3.36	12
3.78	3.67	3.59	3.51	3.42	3.37	3.30	3.27	3.21	3.18	3.16	13
3.62	3.51	3.43	3.34	3.26	3.21	3.14	3.11	3.06	3.02	3.00	14
3.48	3.36	3.29	3.20	3.12	3.07	3.00	2.97	2.92	2.89	2.87	15
3.37	3.25	3.18	3.10	3.01	2.96	2.89	2.86	2.80	2.77	2.75	16
3.27	3.16	3.08	3.00	2.92	2.86	2.79	2.76	2.70	2.67	2.65	17
3.19	3.07	3.00	2.91	2.83	2.78	2.71	2.68	2.62	2.59	2.57	18
3.12	3.00	2.92	2.84	2.76	2.70	2.63	2.60	2.54	2.51	2.49	19
3.05	2.94	2.86	2.77	2.69	2.63	2.56	2.53	2.47	2.44	2.42	20
2.99	2.88	2.80	2.72	2.63	2.58	2.51	2.47	2.42	2.38	2.36	21
2.94	2.83	2.75	2.67	2.58	2.53	2.46	2.42	2.37	2.33	2.31	22
2.89	2.78	2.70	2.62	2.53	2.48	2.41	2.37	2.32	2.28	2.26	23
2.85	2.74	2.66	2.58	2.49	2.44	2.36	2.33	2.27	2.23	2.21	24
2.81	2.70	2.62	2.54	2.45	2.40	2.32	2.29	2.23	2.19	2.17	25
2.77	2.66	2.58	2.50	2.41	2.36	2.28	2.25	2.19	2.15	2.13	26
2.74	2.63	2.55	2.47	2.38	2.33	2.25	2.21	2.16	2.12	2.10	27
2.71	2.60	2.52	2.44	2.35	2.30	2.22	2.18	2.13	2.09	2.06	28
2.68	2.57	2.49	2.41	2.32	2.27	2.19	2.15	2.10	2.06	2.03	29

Table 7 (continued)

Within-Groups Degrees of Freedom	Between-Groups Degrees of Freedom (Numerator)												
	1	2	3	4	5	6	7	8	9	10	11	12	14
30	7.56	5.39	4.51	4.02	3.70	3.47	3.30	3.17	3.06	2.98	2.90	2.84	2.74
32	7.50	5.34	4.46	3.97	3.66	3.42	3.25	3.12	3.01	2.94	2.86	2.80	2.70
34	7.44	5.29	4.42	3.93	3.61	3.38	3.21	3.08	2.97	2.89	2.82	2.76	2.66
36	7.39	5.25	4.38	3.89	3.58	3.35	3.18	3.04	2.94	2.86	2.78	2.72	2.62
38	7.35	5.21	4.34	3.86	3.54	3.32	3.15	3.02	2.91	2.82	2.75	2.69	2.59
40	7.31	5.18	4.31	3.83	3.51	3.29	3.12	2.99	2.88	2.80	2.73	2.66	2.56
42	7.27	5.15	4.29	3.80	3.49	3.26	3.10	2.96	2.86	2.77	2.70	2.64	2.54
44	7.24	5.12	4.26	3.78	3.46	3.24	3.07	2.94	2.84	2.75	2.68	2.62	2.52
46	7.21	5.10	4.24	3.76	3.44	3.22	3.05	2.92	2.82	2.73	2.66	2.60	2.50
48	7.19	5.08	4.22	3.74	3.42	3.20	3.04	2.90	2.80	2.71	2.64	2.58	2.48
50	7.17	5.06	4.20	3.72	3.41	3.18	3.02	2.88	2.78	2.70	2.62	2.56	2.46
55	7.12	5.01	4.16	3.68	3.37	3.15	2.98	2.85	2.75	2.66	2.59	2.53	2.43
60	7.08	4.98	4.13	3.65	3.34	3.12	2.95	2.82	2.72	2.63	2.56	2.50	2.40
65	7.04	4.95	4.10	3.62	3.31	3.09	2.93	2.79	2.70	2.61	2.54	2.47	2.37
70	7.01	4.92	4.08	3.60	3.29	3.07	2.91	2.77	2.67	2.59	2.51	2.45	2.35
80	6.96	4.88	4.04	3.56	3.25	3.04	2.87	2.74	2.64	2.55	2.48	2.41	2.32
100	6.90	4.82	3.98	3.51	3.20	2.99	2.82	2.69	2.59	2.51	2.43	2.36	2.26
125	6.84	4.78	3.94	3.47	3.17	2.95	2.79	2.65	2.56	2.47	2.40	2.33	2.23
150	6.81	4.75	3.91	3.44	3.14	2.92	2.76	2.62	2.53	2.44	2.37	2.30	2.20
200	6.76	4.71	3.88	3.41	3.11	2.90	2.73	2.60	2.50	2.41	2.34	2.28	2.17
400	6.70	4.66	3.83	3.36	3.06	2.85	2.69	2.55	2.46	2.37	2.29	2.23	2.12
1000	6.66	4.62	3.80	3.34	3.04	2.82	2.66	2.53	2.43	2.34	2.26	2.20	2.09
Infinity	6.64	4.60	3.78	3.32	3.02	2.80	2.64	2.51	2.41	2.32	2.24	2.18	2.07

Continued →

Table 7 (continued)

Between-Groups Degrees of Freedom (Numerator)											Within-Groups Degrees of Freedom
16	20	24	30	40	50	75	100	200	500	Infinity	
2.66	2.55	2.47	2.38	2.29	2.24	2.16	2.13	2.07	2.03	2.01	30
2.62	2.51	2.42	2.34	2.25	2.20	2.12	2.08	2.02	1.98	1.96	32
2.58	2.47	2.38	2.30	2.21	2.15	2.08	2.04	1.98	1.94	1.91	34
2.54	2.43	2.35	2.26	2.17	2.12	2.04	2.00	1.94	1.90	1.87	36
2.51	2.40	2.32	2.22	2.14	2.08	2.00	1.97	1.90	1.86	1.84	38
2.49	2.37	2.29	2.20	2.11	2.05	1.97	1.94	1.88	1.84	1.81	40
2.46	2.35	2.26	2.17	2.08	2.02	1.94	1.91	1.85	1.80	1.78	42
2.44	2.32	2.24	2.15	2.06	2.00	1.92	1.88	1.82	1.78	1.75	44
2.42	2.30	2.22	2.13	2.04	1.98	1.90	1.86	1.80	1.76	1.72	46
2.40	2.28	2.20	2.11	2.02	1.96	1.88	1.84	1.78	1.73	1.70	48
2.39	2.26	2.18	2.10	2.00	1.94	1.86	1.82	1.76	1.71	1.68	50
2.35	2.23	2.15	2.06	1.96	1.90	1.82	1.78	1.71	1.66	1.64	55
2.32	2.20	2.12	2.03	1.93	1.87	1.79	1.74	1.68	1.63	1.60	60
2.30	2.18	2.09	2.00	1.90	1.84	1.76	1.71	1.64	1.60	1.56	65
2.28	2.15	2.07	1.98	1.88	1.82	1.74	1.69	1.62	1.56	1.53	70
2.24	2.11	2.03	1.94	1.84	1.78	1.70	1.65	1.57	1.52	1.49	80
2.19	2.06	1.98	1.89	1.79	1.73	1.64	1.59	1.51	1.46	1.43	100
2.15	2.03	1.94	1.85	1.75	1.68	1.59	1.54	1.46	1.40	1.37	125
2.12	2.00	1.91	1.83	1.72	1.66	1.56	1.51	1.43	1.37	1.33	150
2.09	1.97	1.88	1.79	1.69	1.62	1.53	1.48	1.39	1.33	1.28	200
2.04	1.92	1.84	1.74	1.64	1.57	1.47	1.42	1.32	1.24	1.19	400
2.01	1.89	1.81	1.71	1.61	1.54	1.44	1.38	1.28	1.19	1.11	1000
1.99	1.87	1.79	1.69	1.59	1.52	1.41	1.36	1.25	1.15	1.00	Infinity

Table 8
Studentized Range Statistic (q)
for the .05 Level

Degrees of Freedom (denominator)	Number of Treatments										
	2	3	4	5	6	7	8	9	10	11	12
5	3.64	4.60	5.22	5.67	6.03	6.33	6.58	6.80	6.99	7.17	7.32
6	3.46	4.34	4.90	5.30	5.63	5.90	6.12	6.32	6.49	6.65	6.79
7	3.34	4.16	4.68	5.06	5.36	5.61	5.82	6.00	6.16	6.30	6.43
8	3.26	4.04	4.53	4.89	5.17	5.40	5.60	5.77	5.92	6.05	6.18
9	3.20	3.95	4.41	4.76	5.02	5.24	5.43	5.59	5.74	5.87	5.98
10	3.15	3.88	4.33	4.65	4.91	5.12	5.30	5.46	5.60	5.72	5.83
11	3.11	3.82	4.26	4.57	4.82	5.03	5.20	5.35	5.49	5.61	5.71
12	3.08	3.77	4.20	4.51	4.75	4.95	5.12	5.27	5.39	5.51	5.61
13	3.06	3.73	4.15	4.45	4.69	4.88	5.05	5.19	5.32	5.43	5.53
14	3.03	3.70	4.11	4.41	4.64	4.83	4.99	5.13	5.25	5.36	5.46
15	3.01	3.67	4.08	4.37	4.59	4.78	4.94	5.08	5.20	5.31	5.40
16	3.00	3.65	4.05	4.33	4.56	4.74	4.90	5.03	5.15	5.26	5.35
17	2.98	3.63	4.02	4.30	4.52	4.70	4.86	4.99	5.11	5.21	5.31
18	2.97	3.61	4.00	4.28	4.49	4.67	4.82	4.96	5.07	5.17	5.27
19	2.96	3.59	3.98	4.25	4.47	4.65	4.79	4.92	5.04	5.14	5.23
20	2.95	3.58	3.96	4.23	4.45	4.62	4.77	4.90	5.01	5.11	5.20
24	2.92	3.53	3.90	4.17	4.37	4.54	4.68	4.81	4.92	5.01	5.10
30	2.89	3.49	3.85	4.10	4.30	4.46	4.60	4.72	4.82	4.92	5.00
40	2.86	3.44	3.79	4.04	4.23	4.39	4.52	4.63	4.73	4.82	4.90
60	2.83	3.40	3.74	3.98	4.16	4.31	4.44	4.55	4.65	4.73	4.81
120	2.80	3.36	3.68	3.92	4.10	4.24	4.36	4.47	4.56	4.64	4.71
Infinity	2.77	3.31	3.63	3.86	4.03	4.17	4.29	4.39	4.47	4.55	4.62

Table 9

Studentized Range Statistic (*q*) for the .01 Level

Degrees of Freedom	Number of Treatments										
	2	3	4	5	6	7	8	9	10	11	12
5	5.70	6.98	7.80	8.42	8.91	9.32	9.67	9.97	10.24	10.48	10.70
6	5.24	6.33	7.03	7.56	7.97	8.32	8.61	8.87	9.10	9.30	9.48
7	4.95	5.92	6.54	7.01	7.37	7.68	7.94	8.17	8.37	8.55	8.71
8	4.75	5.64	6.20	6.62	6.96	7.24	7.47	7.68	7.86	8.03	8.18
9	4.60	5.43	5.96	6.35	6.66	6.91	7.13	7.33	7.49	7.65	7.78
10	4.48	5.27	5.77	6.14	6.43	6.67	6.87	7.05	7.21	7.36	7.49
11	4.39	5.15	5.62	5.97	6.25	6.48	6.67	6.84	6.99	7.13	7.25
12	4.32	5.05	5.50	5.84	6.10	6.32	6.51	6.67	6.81	6.94	7.06
13	4.26	4.96	5.40	5.73	5.98	6.19	6.37	6.53	6.67	6.79	6.90
14	4.21	4.89	5.32	5.63	5.88	6.08	6.26	6.41	6.54	6.66	6.77
15	4.17	4.84	5.25	5.56	5.80	5.99	6.16	6.31	6.44	6.55	6.66
16	4.13	4.79	5.19	5.49	5.72	5.92	6.08	6.22	6.35	6.46	6.56
17	4.10	4.74	5.14	5.43	5.66	5.85	6.01	6.15	6.27	6.38	6.48
18	4.07	4.70	5.09	5.38	5.60	5.79	5.94	6.08	6.20	6.31	6.41
19	4.05	4.67	5.05	5.33	5.55	5.73	5.89	6.02	6.14	6.25	6.34
20	4.02	4.64	5.02	5.29	5.51	5.69	5.84	5.97	6.09	6.19	6.28
24	3.96	4.55	4.91	5.17	5.37	5.54	5.69	5.81	5.92	6.02	6.11
30	3.89	4.45	4.80	5.05	5.24	5.40	5.54	5.65	5.76	5.85	5.93
40	3.82	4.37	4.70	4.93	5.11	5.26	5.39	5.50	5.60	5.69	5.76
60	3.76	4.28	4.59	4.82	4.99	5.13	5.25	5.36	5.45	5.53	5.60
120	3.70	4.20	4.50	4.71	4.87	5.01	5.12	5.21	5.30	5.37	5.44
Infinity	3.64	4.12	4.40	4.60	4.76	4.88	4.99	5.08	5.16	5.23	5.29

Table 10

Minimum Values for Significance
of a Pearson r[1]

df	.05 level	.01 level	.001 level		df	.05 level	.01 level	.001 level
1	.996	.999	.999		40	.304	.393	.490
2	.950	.990	.999		45	.288	.372	.465
3	.878	.959	.991		50	.273	.354	.443
4	.811	.917	.974		60	.250	.325	.408
5	.754	.874	.951		70	.232	.302	.380
6	.707	.834	.925		80	.217	.283	.357
7	.666	.798	.898		90	.205	.267	.338
8	.632	.765	.872		100	.195	.254	.321
9	.602	.735	.847					
10	.576	.708	.823					
11	.553	.684	.801					
12	.532	.661	.780					
13	.514	.641	.760					
14	.497	.623	.742					
15	.482	.606	.725					
16	.468	.590	.708					
17	.456	.575	.693					
18	.444	.561	.679					
19	.433	.549	.665					
20	.423	.537	.652					
25	.381	.487	.597					
30	.349	.449	.554					
35	.325	.418	.519					

[1]Abridged from Fisher, R. A., & Yates, F. (1963). *Statistical tables for biological, agricultural, and medical research.* Edinburgh, Scotland: Oliver & Boyd Ltd.

Table 11
Critical Values of Chi-Square[1]

df	.05 level	.01 level	.001 level	df	.05 level	.01 level	.001 level
1	3.841	6.635	10.827	24	36.415	42.980	51.179
2	5.991	9.210	13.815	25	37.652	44.314	52.620
3	7.815	11.345	16.268	26	38.885	45.642	54.052
4	9.488	13.277	18.465	27	40.113	46.963	55.476
5	11.070	15.086	20.517	28	41.337	48.278	56.893
6	12.592	16.812	22.457	29	42.557	49.588	58.302
7	14.067	18.475	24.322	30	43.773	50.892	59.703
8	15.507	20.090	26.125				
9	16.919	21.666	27.877				
10	18.307	23.209	29.588				
11	19.675	24.725	31.264				
12	21.026	26.217	32.909				
13	22.362	27.688	34.528				
14	23.685	29.141	36.123				
15	24.996	30.578	37.697				
16	26.296	32.000	39.252				
17	27.587	33.409	40.790				
18	28.869	34.805	42.312				
19	30.144	36.191	43.820				
20	31.410	37.566	45.315				
21	32.671	38.932	46.797				
22	33.924	40.289	48.268				
23	35.172	41.638	49.728				

[1]Abridged from Fisher, R. A., & Yates, F. (1963). *Statistical tables for biological, agricultural, and medical research*. Edinburgh, Scotland: Oliver & Boyd Ltd.

Table 12

Critical Values of U for the .05 Level[1]

	N_2											
N_1	9	10	11	12	13	14	15	16	17	18	19	20
1												
2	0	0	0	1	1	1	1	1	2	2	2	2
3	2	3	3	4	4	5	5	6	6	7	7	8
4	4	5	6	7	8	9	10	11	11	12	13	13
5	7	8	9	11	12	13	14	15	17	18	19	20
6	10	11	13	14	16	17	19	21	22	24	25	27
7	12	14	16	18	20	22	24	26	28	30	32	34
8	15	17	19	22	24	26	29	31	34	36	38	41
9	17	20	23	26	28	31	34	37	39	42	45	48
10	20	23	26	29	33	36	39	42	45	48	52	55
11	23	26	30	33	37	40	44	47	51	55	58	62
12	26	29	33	37	41	45	49	53	57	61	65	69
13	28	33	37	41	45	50	54	59	63	67	72	76
14	31	36	40	45	50	55	59	64	67	74	78	83
15	34	39	44	49	54	59	64	70	75	80	85	90
16	37	42	47	53	59	64	70	75	81	86	92	98
17	39	45	51	57	63	67	75	81	87	93	99	105
18	42	48	55	61	67	74	80	86	93	99	106	112
19	45	52	58	65	72	78	85	92	99	106	113	119
20	48	55	62	69	76	83	90	98	105	112	119	127

[1]Abridged from Wilcoxon, F. (1949). *Some rapid approximate statistical procedures.* New York, NY: American Cyanamid Co.

Table 13
Critical Values of *U* for the .01 Level[1]

N_1	N_2											
	9	10	11	12	13	14	15	16	17	18	19	20
1												
2											0	0
3	0	0	0	1	1	1	2	2	2	2	3	3
4	1	2	2	3	3	4	5	5	6	6	7	8
5	3	4	5	6	7	7	8	9	10	11	12	13
6	5	6	7	9	10	11	12	13	15	16	17	18
7	7	9	10	12	13	15	16	18	19	21	22	24
8	9	11	13	15	17	18	20	22	24	26	28	30
9	11	13	16	18	20	22	24	27	29	31	33	36
10	13	16	18	21	24	26	29	31	34	37	39	42
11	16	18	21	24	27	30	33	36	39	42	45	48
12	18	21	24	27	31	34	37	41	44	47	51	54
13	20	24	27	31	34	38	42	45	49	53	56	60
14	22	26	30	34	38	42	46	50	54	58	63	67
15	24	29	33	37	42	46	51	55	60	64	69	73
16	27	31	36	41	45	50	55	60	65	70	74	79
17	29	34	39	44	49	54	60	65	70	75	81	86
18	31	37	42	47	53	58	64	70	75	81	87	92
19	33	39	45	51	56	63	69	74	81	87	93	99
20	36	42	48	54	60	67	73	79	86	92	99	105

[1]Abridged from Wilcoxon, F. (1949). *Some rapid approximate statistical procedures*. New York, NY: American Cyanamid Co.

Table 14

Critical Values of *T* for Wilcoxon's Matched-Pairs Test[1]

df	.05 level	.01 level
6	0	—
7	2	—
8	4	0
9	6	2
10	8	3
11	11	5
12	14	7
13	17	10
14	21	13
15	25	16
16	30	20
17	35	23
18	40	28
19	46	32
20	52	38
21	59	43
22	66	49
23	73	55
24	81	61
25	89	68

[1]From Wilcoxon, F. (1949). *Some rapid approximate statistical procedures*. New York, NY: American Cyanamid Co.

Notes

Index

Notes

Notes

Notes

Notes

Notes

Notes